The "Backwards" Research Guide for Writers

Frameworks for Writing
Series Editor: Martha C. Pennington, Georgia Southern University

The *Frameworks for Writing* series offers books focused on writing and the teaching and learning of writing in educational and real-life contexts. The hallmark of the series is the application of approaches and techniques to writing and the teaching of writing that go beyond those of English literature to draw on and integrate writing with other disciplines, areas of knowledge, and contexts of everyday life. The series entertains proposals for textbooks as well as books for teachers, teacher educators, parents, and the general public. The list includes teacher reference books and student textbooks focused on innovative pedagogy aiming to prepare teachers and students for the challenges of the twenty-first century.

Forthcoming

The College Writing Toolkit: Tried and Tested Ideas for Teaching College Writing
Edited by Martha C. Pennington and Pauline Burton

Writing Poetry through the Eyes of Science: A Teacher's Guide to Scientific Literacy and Poetic Response
Nancy Gorrell with Erin Colfax

Exploring College Writing: Reading, Writing, and Researching across the Curriculum
Dan Melzer

Tend your Garden: Nurturing Motivation in Young Adolescent Writers
Mary Anna Kruch

Becoming a Teacher who Writes: Let Teaching be your Writing Muse
Nancy Gorrell

Writing from the Inside: The Power of Reflective Writing in the Classroom
Olivia Archibald and Maureen Hall

Arting, Writing, and Culture: Teaching to the 4th Power
Anna Sumida, Meleanna Meyer, and Miki Maeshiro

Seriously Creative Writing: Stylistic Strategies in Non-Fictional Writing
Sky Marsen

Reflective Writing for English Language Teachers
Thomas S. C. Farrell

The "Backwards" Research Guide for Writers

Using Your Life for Reflection, Connection, and Inspiration

Sonya Huber

equinox

SHEFFIELD OAKVILLE

Published by Equinox Publishing Ltd.

UK: Unit S3, Kelham House, 3, Lancaster Street, Sheffield S3 8AF
USA: DBBC, 28 Main Street, Oakville, CT 06779

www.equinoxpub.com

First published 2011

British Library Cataloguing-in-Publication Data

A catalogue record for this book is available from the British Library.

ISBN   978-1-84553-441-7   (hardback)
        978-1-84553-442-4   (paperback)

Library of Congress Cataloging-in-Publication Data

Huber, Sonya, 1971-
The "backwards" research guide for writers: using your life for reflection, connection, and inspiration / by Sonya Huber.
    p. cm. – (Frameworks for writing)
  Include bibliographical references and index.
    ISBN 978-1-84553-441-7 – ISBN 978-1-84553-442-4 (pbk.) 1. English language—Rhetoric–Study and teaching (Higher) 2. Research–Methodology–Study and teaching (Higher) 3. Academic writing–Study and teaching (Higher) 4. Report writing—study and teaching (Higher) 5. College teaching–Handbooks, manuals, etc. I. Title
  PE1404.H83 2010
  808'.0420711-dc22
                        2009054037

Typeset by S.J.I. Services, New Delhi
Printed and bound in the UK by the MPG Books Group

Contents

Editor's Preface   xv

Acknowledgments   xvii

Introduction for Instructors: The Context for
Seeking as Research   1
   What is Research?   1
   Process and Contemplative Approaches to Research   3
   Technologies of Knowing   6
   Relax   7
   Reflect   8
   Book Sections and Features   10
   Conversations   12
   Gray Matter   12
   Experiments   13
   Using This Book in Class   14
   Research Schedules and Projects   15
   Process and Outcomes in the Classroom   16

Section I. Research: An Inside Job

1. Write About Anything   21
   Introduction to Chapter 1: Research Trouble   21
   Torturing Students with Research   23
   Research Starts with You   24

Experiment 1.1: Your Research Stories   25

Research as Self-Discovery and World-Discovery   26

The Question of Objectivity   27

Beginning the Search   30

The Mind as Research Tool   31

Thinking about Thinking   33

Noticing: The First Research Skill   34

Experiment 1.2: Just Sit   35

Conclusion to Chapter 1   36

2. Meet the Author: You   39

Introduction to Chapter 2   39

How Not to Write a Research Paper   40

What Thinking Feels Like   41

Experiment 2.1: Sit with a Word   42

Freedom of Association   43

Hunters and Gatherers   44

What Type of Hunter/Gatherer Are You?   44

Experiment 2.2: Hunter/Gatherer Profile   45

Watching the Brain During a Brainstorm   47

Obsessions: Fuel for the Fire   48

Brain Chatter and Brain Grooves   50

Experiment 2.3: Interview Your Friends   51

The Interest in the Obvious   55

Excavating the Obvious   55

Experiment 2.4: Five Objects   56

Making the Familiar Strange   56

The Gray Matter: What We Don't Want to See   57

Experiment 2.5: Room for Improvement   58

Conclusion to Chapter 2   59

Conversation 1 with Ben Vogt: Wandering Research   62

3. Areas of Expertise: Using What You Already
   Know   69
     Introduction to Chapter 3   69
     Experiment 3.1: Activities and Questions   71
     No Such Thing as a Stupid Question   72
     Nothing to Brag About   75
     Experiment 3.2: Catalogue the Unseen Skills   77
     The Gray Matter: Decisions as Experience   78
     Tough Choices as Research Questions   79
     Experiment 3.3: Choices, Choices, Choices   80
     Choices and Outcomes   82
     Conclusion to Chapter 3   82

4. Living and Loving the Questions   85
     Introduction to Chapter 4   85
     Experiment 4.1: Questions and Questioners   86
     Questions in a Culture of Answers   87
     Using Questions to Generate Research Ideas   88
     Experiment 4.2: Questions without Answers   89
     What Makes a Good Question?   90
     A Healthy Dose of Skepticism   91
     Adding Fuel to the Fire   92
     Experiment 4.3: Two Hundred Questions   92
     Conclusion to Chapter 4   104

Section II. The Inside Meets the Outside: Paying Attention as Research

5. Learning to See   107
     Introduction to Chapter 5   107
     Experiment 5.1: You Are Here   108

Contemplative Research   109
Experiment 5.2: Take Three   110
Student-Driven Research   111
Brain-Watching and Field Notes   111
Obsession Notebook   112
Experiment 5.3: Obsession Notebook   113
Shared Obsessions and Public Issues   114
Experiment 5.4: The National Association of
Yo-Yo Aficionados   116
Group Think   117
The Gray Matter: No Right Answer   118
Experiment 5.5: Real-World Research   119
Open Questions   120
Experiment 5.6: Real-World Research, Part II   121
Conclusion to Chapter 5   122

Conversation 2 with Bill Roorbach: Immersion Research   124

6. Responding to Reality   127
Introduction to Chapter 6   127
Experiment 6.1: Reading the Newspaper with
Scissors   128
Boring Topics   129
Experiment 6.2: Don't Know Much About History   131
Connections   132
The Portable Researcher   133
Experiment 6.3: Research in Motion   133
Post-Walk Field Notes   135
The Gray Matter: Beyond the Edges of the
Newspaper Page   136
Experiment 6.4: Reading Between the Lines   137
Experiment 6.5: Comparing Two Frames   138
Conclusion to Chapter 6   139

7. Uncharted Obsessions   141
    Introduction to Chapter 7   141
    Nerddom and the Kingdom of the Geeks   142
    Experiment 7.1: Geek, Nerd, Freak   143
    Intuition as Research   144
    Bubble Charts   146
    Experiment 7.2: Outward Bubbles   147
    Beyond Bubbles   147
    Experiment 7.3: Six Degrees   149
    The Gray Matter: Why We Love What We Love   150
    Experiment 7.4: Double-Bubble Chart   151
    Conclusion to Chapter 7   153

Conversation 3 with Steve Almond: Freakdom   154

8. Beginner's Mind   159
    Introduction to Chapter 8   159
    The Discomfort of Not-Knowing   161
    Experiment 8.1: I Don't Know   162
    Know-It-Alls and Beginner's Mind   163
    Experiment 8.2: The Power of Not-Knowing   165
    The Work of Not-Knowing   166
    Open vs. Closed Questions   167
    The Gray Matter, Part I: Ethical Questions   168
    Experiment 8.3: Questions to Consider   170
    Bias and Conflict of Interest   171
    Experiment 8.4: Question Launch Pads   172
    Beginner's Mind into Researcher's Mind   172
    Experiment 8.5: Research Sampler   173
    The Gray Matter, Part II: Don't Patch Over the Gaps   174
    Questions for Thought or Discussion   175
    Conclusion to Chapter 8   176

Section III. Big Bang: Form and Structured Chaos in Research

9. Take Note   179
      Introduction to Chapter 9   179
      Cut-and-Paste or Mix-and-Cook   180
      Space for Your Research   181
      Experiment 9.1: Taking Notes   182
      Net of Questions   183
      Experiment 9.2: Fishing Net   183
      Nets to Catch Facts   184
      Double-Column Notebook   184
      Questions to Focus   186
      Cheat Sheets and Spreadsheets   187
      The Gray Matter: What is a Fact out of Context?   188
      Experiment 9.3: The Author in the Story   190
      Conclusion to Chapter 9   190

10. Noodling as a Research Method   193
      Introduction to Chapter 10   193
      A Wet Suit for Deep-Sea Diving   194
      Noodling Online   195
      Experiment 10.1: Online and Aimless   195
      Free Databases to Noodle   197
      Search Terms   197
      Wikis   198
      Databases of Published Works   199
      Government and Organizational Databases   200
      Restricted Databases to Noodle   201
      Experiment 10.2: Database Wandering   202
      Associative Reading   203
      Blogs: How Low Can You Go?   204

Experiment 10.3: Bunches of Blogs   206
Old-Fashioned Search Engines   207
Experiment 10.4: Rubber to the Road   207
Using Real-World Research Material   208
The Gray Matter: Giving Credit Where Credit is Due 209
Sorting the Information   210
Crediting Your Sources   211
Experiment 10.5: Infor-mess-ion   211
Conclusion to Chapter 10   212

Conversation 4 with Joe Mackall: Places, People, and
Paper   214

11. Conversations   219
Introduction to Chapter 11   219
Interview Anxiety   220
Active Listening   221
Experiment 11.1: Listen and Hear   221
Listening Behavior   222
Asking for a Formal Conversation   223
Experiment 11.2: Who Knows?   224
Seeking Sources   225
Invitation to an Interview   226
Brainstorming the List of Questions   227
Authentic Conversation   229
Experiment 11.3: Twenty Questions   230
Interview Process and Technology   232
Beyond the Quotes   233
Experiment 11.4: Practice Interview   234
The Gray Matter: Being Trustworthy with the
Stories of Others   234
Questions for Thought or Discussion   236
Conclusion to Chapter 11   237

Conversation 5 with Robin Hemley: Interviewing   238

Section IV. Open Minds Invite Surprises

12. Twists and Turns in the Research Story   245
    Introduction to Chapter 12   245
    Filter and Focus   246
    Experiment 12.1: Take Notes on the Rest of
    Your Life   247
    Rough Roads and Smooth Sailing   248
    Experiment 12.2: Know Your Equipment   249
    The Changeable Brain   250
    Seeing Chromosomes   251
    Experiment 12.3: More than a Feeling   254
    Feeling, Physics, and the Playground   255
    The Gray Matter: Nothing to Know?   257
    Questions for Thought or Discussion   257
    Conclusion to Chapter 12   258

Conversation 6 with Jill Christman: The Research Journey   260

13. The Research Road Map   267
    Introduction to Chapter 13   267
    Research Road Blocks   268
    Experiment 13.1: Choose Your Own Misadventure   269
    Roadblocks as Stepping Stones   269
    Confusion   270
    Huge Questions   271
    Red-Hot Debates   272
    No Available Sources   273
    Not Enough Time   274
    Experiment 13.2: The Adventure of Finding Your
    Material   275

Research Drama   275
Experiment 13.3: Research Flow Chart   277
The Gray Matter: Navigating Research with the
Moral Compass   278
Questions for Thought or Discussion   278
Conclusion to Chapter 13   278

14. Finding Your Way   281
Introduction to Chapter 14   281
Containers, Walls, and Buckets   282
The Simplicity of Scaffolding   284
Experiment 14.1: Winnowing   285
Experiment 14.2: Interest Ranking   286
Rocking Climbing   286
Experiment 14.3: Distance from the Center   287
Behind the Scenes   288
Experiment 14.4: Plunging into the Unknown   289
Focus and Cut   289
The Gray Matter: The Challenge of Giving Credit   290
Background Paragraphs   290
Footnotes and Endnotes for Your Comments   291
The Disagreeing Source   292
Questions for Thought or Discussion   292
Conclusion to Chapter 14   292

15. Writing the Story's Journey   295
Introduction to Chapter 15   295
Senses and Experiences as Research Hooks   296
Experiment 15.1: The Five Senses   297
Experiment 15.2: Characters in Your Story   298
What's a Scene?   299
Experiment 15.3: Scene and Heard   300
Plotting the Framework   300

Experiment 15.4: Refocusing on the Heart of the Story   302
The Last Step: The Introduction   302
Experiment 15.5: Letter to a Beekeeper   303
The Gray Matter: Known and Unknown   304
Questions for Thought or Discussion   305
Try This   305
Conclusion to Chapter 15   305

16. Revision: Seeing Again   307
Introduction to Chapter 16   307
Experiment 16.1: A Refreshing Pause   308
From a Word to a Conversation   309
Experiment 16.2: Re-seeing Your Revision Process   310
Clearly Unclear   311
Tone and Voice   311
Experiment 16.3: Letter to a Beekeeper, Part II   312
Experiment 16.4: Questions to Observations   313
Seeking Uncertainty   314
The Gray Matter: Integrity Check   314
Integrity Checklist   315
Questions for Thought or Discussion   315
Conclusion to the "Backwards" Research Guide   316

Appendices
Appendix A. Experiments in this Book: Short   319
Appendix B. Experiments in this Book: Long   321
Appendix C. Experiments in this Book: Take-Home   323
Appendix D. Recommended Reading   325
Appendix E. Source Citations Using MLA Style   329

References   331
Subject Index   336
Author Index   342

Editor's Preface

The practices of academic writing specialists are increasingly being questioned by other educators and by those outside of education concerned that the students of today and the citizens of tomorrow will be provided with the writing skills they are going to need in their lives. Challenges are being raised both inside and outside the academy about such practices as the grounding of writing pedagogy in literature and the teaching of academic writing as a general skill, under the assumption that either of these approaches develops abilities that can be transferred to other types and contexts of composing. Approaches to writing that are tied to specific disciplines or that make use of electronic technologies and online resources offer alternatives to traditional approaches and are in a period of rapid development.

The "Backwards" Research Guide for Writers: Using Your Life for Reflection, Connection, and Inspiration was born of a felt need by a writing specialist for a different way to approach the writing process in her classes. The approach modeled in this book, which has been developed over a period of years in the classroom, represents a unique synthesis of knowledge combining journalism, academic writing, fiction, creative nonfiction, poetry, and teaching in each of genres. The author, Sonya Huber, a gifted writer and teacher with a background and history of publication in all of these areas, has merged elements of each of them into a novel approach for learning to write on the basis of research. The program of the *Guide* seeks to engage first-year college students, aspiring journalists, and other would-be writers in the process of research in a way that inspires them to good writing by making writing and the research behind it relevant and exciting to them as individuals. The goal is to help students love the research process and the writing process that goes along with it as they explore themselves and the world outside themselves in an interactive way.

Following the program of *The "Backwards" Research Guide*, which draws on contemplative inquiry and on Ken Macrorie's "I-Search" process, aspiring writers are led through a series of steps that build a writing process through discovering and then researching areas of personal interest and relevance. The steps involve periods of silent reflection and freewriting "experiments" to raise students' awareness and to help them search their minds for questions that can lead them on journeys of discovery. They begin by first exploring their own sense of wonder and curiosity to identify topics, issues, and burning questions worth researching. They then experience different types of research in their world, using techniques such as research notebooks and interviewing, as they learn to build their research process and written product in stages. The pleasures and challenges of research and writing are considered through a series of conversations with working writers, and the issues and ethnical context of research are highlighted as a theme running through every chapter.

The "Backwards" Research Guide for Writers is the first writing text to conceptualize the research process in a personalized way that draws on journalistic and creative writing traditions and the first to intimately connect research so conceived with a writing process informed by contemplative practices. It is a highly original and promising approach for heightening students' engagement with writing as a means of seeking knowledge and gaining understanding of themselves and the world around them. In starting from the self and teaching novice writers research skills for progressing outward and making connections, this *"Backwards" Research Guide* offers a new direction for writing pedagogy and a way forward for students to develop the linguistic and cognitive skills they will need for a productive future.

– Martha C. Pennington
Series Editor, Frameworks for Writing

Acknowledgments

The author wishes to thank Dr. Martha Pennington for tireless support, encouragement, and vision in support of this manuscript.

Chapter 2: J632/F593 "The Brain is wider than the Sky" reprinted by permission of the publishers and the Trustees of Amherst College from THE POEMS OF EMILY DICKINSON, Thomas H. Johnson, ed., Cambridge, Mass.: The Belknap Press of Harvard University Press, Copyright © 1951, 1955, 1979, 1983 by the President and Fellows of Harvard College.

Conversation 2: Author photo of Bill Roorbach taken by John L. Buckingham, used with permission.

Conversation 5: Author photo of Robin Hemley taken by Peter Parson, used with permission of author.

Conversation 6: Author photo of Jill Christman taken by Tim Berg, used with permission of author.

Introduction for Instructors: The Context for Seeking as Research

What is Research?

When I ask students to react to the word *research*, they wrinkle their faces, cringe, and shake their heads. I ask what words or phrases come to mind, and they offer "boring," "quotes," and "bibliography." What do these reactions mean? One interpretation is that students reject and loathe the research process because it is difficult. Assuming this is true, the implied solution would be to teach easy and quick research methods to help students end the pain as quickly as possible.

This textbook began with the opposite perspective: based on my personal experience, I had a general understanding that research can be truly enjoyable, relevant, and beneficial – and that those three qualities are not necessarily mutually exclusive. In other words, I knew from personal experience that gathering information could be fun and could – nevertheless or as a result – produce a scholarly or academically sound text. Assuming the "no pain, no gain" motto in research, I believe, requires students to see the research process as inherently unpleasant and irrelevant to their lives.

This book takes a more nuanced view of the research process, breaking it down into several steps and connecting each step to the impulses and creative opportunities springing from the individual researcher. Concrete external research skills are addressed, but students will also develop a framework for understanding what the research process feels like. As students identify the phases in their research process, they begin to create a more complex view of opportunities and challenges within the broad area of research activity. My assumption is that students recoil from research not due to any inherent difficulty or intellectual challenge in the process itself. Instead, I believe students need a more detailed and flexible experience that links research to its heart: inspiration.

My students' reactions to research prompted me to review my research experiences as a journalist, academic, and creative writer. I began to see that the thrill of research itself – the creativity, excitement, and commitment inherent in any truly self-directed research project – was one of the reasons I loved to write. I wondered about the gap between my students' reactions and my own, and I also remembered that I had shared my students' reactions to research at one point. What happened, and how did I learn to love the research process?

I noted that as my writing career progressed, I devoted more and more time to choosing research ideas. In effect, I drew out and expanded the brainstorming stage as I gathered more experience in the world of research. This concrete fact seemed to contradict the general framework depicting research as a linear task with components to be learned and then employed in an ever more efficient fashion. Was I getting less efficient at the research task? With some reflection, I began to examine my own process of choosing research projects more closely and looked particularly at the stage of topic selection. I noticed that in my work as an essayist and journalist, my antennae or sense of topics that truly interested me had become well-honed over the years. I had learned to focus on a range of subjects for writing and research that I understood to be my core passions and interests. In effect, writing – creative writing, journalism, and any other form – had helped me to track the areas of my own interest. As I wrote and chose topics, I gathered more awareness about the subjects I enjoyed. This process-based approach led me to conclude that with attention and awareness, skill in topic selection can be built. Building from Ken Macrorie's I-Search framework, in which student investment is a key component to research, it is my experience that helping students to focus on their own subject-choosing skills can generate the self-awareness that is a missing component in the research process.

The personal roots of this research textbook are intertwined with my background in contemplative practices, especially the practice of meditation. Over the past 15 years, I wrote and taught while concurrently engaging in self-directed study and receiving formal training in meditation from a Buddhist perspective. At a certain point, the touchstones of one's life begin to speak to one another, and it would be impossible for me to identify whether writing practice fed my interest in meditation or vice versa. Instead, a symbiotic relationship began to develop as my brain nudged itself along a path with an unclear goal. As I attended to the process of meditation, I began to see certain themes emerging in contemplative practice that struck a chord for my writing life. As I learned to watch my thoughts in contemplation, my ability to untangle, record, and reflect on these thoughts began to improve. The contemplative tradition I practice emphasizes a focus on the moment at hand to avoid separating one's self from lived experience. The habit of mind promoted by this tradition – and shared by many other traditions and practices – is essential for inquiry. It was in this way that an external practice led me back to writing and allowed me to see the role of contemplative inquiry as a foundation for writing.

Process and Contemplative Approaches to Research

In the area of composition and writing, a *process approach* has been advocated for years by scholars such as Peter Elbow, who introduced such techniques as *freewriting* into the composition lexicon. Such brainstorming and pre-writing exercises help students build a foundation for writing by allowing them to discover topics and opinions for themselves in a low-stakes setting. Educator Tobin Hart writes: "Writing involves two main processes: vision – inspiration, flow of ideas, and so on – and revision – editing and crafting. These require two different and complementary cognitive operations" (Hart, 2004: 7). This book focuses on the "vision" component of Hart's description, with the understanding that investment in this first stage will result in a fundamental shift in students' relationship to their material and to the research process itself.

Hart (2004: 7) describes a process approach to writing as "a contemplative act." Used in this sense, *contemplative* merely means guided by or increasing self-awareness. Hart (2004:1) describes contemplative practice as part of the Western tradition as well as Eastern traditions, and references Plato's "radical questioning through dialogue" as a part of this mode of truth-seeking. The word *contemplative* carries a religious or spiritual connotation in some contexts, but in the realm of education, looking inward is not associated with doctrine or belief systems. Instead, the word refers to the skill of "cultivat[ing] an inner technology of knowing and thereby a technology of learning and pedagogy without any imposition of religious doctrine whatsoever" (Hart, 2004: 1).

The "inner technology of knowing" as described by Hart involves a series of simple practices that encourage students to notice the content of their own minds. The use of the word "technology" is important, as it emphasizes the workings of the brain as a system that can be analyzed and understood. Drawing links between inner and outer technology highlights for students the fact that using any tool – the brain or a computer – requires skill that can be built in increments. The word "technology" in reference to contemplative practice emphasizes the empirical nature of this practice; although the inner workings of a computer are as invisible as thought to most users, students may trust a computer more than their own thought processes due to an assumption that useful tools must be box-shaped and made out of metal or plastic. As with any technology, new or old, the classroom applications of the technology are as diverse as the instructors and students who use them. This is the first book I am aware of that uses this "inner technology of knowing" for the purposes of formal research.

While the process approach has been applied to composition and to creative writing, a focus on the contemplative elements of research choice and decision making has not, at least to my knowledge, been articulated. A process approach to research allows a researcher to become looser and more associative with ideas, resulting in brainstorms, connections, and inspiration. This full awareness of one's subject and one's connection to that subject then becomes an aid instead of a stumbling block in understanding bias and gaining perspective.

In this book, you will notice many writing exercises called EX-PERIMENTS in the text. Many of these include a first step of timed silence for reflection. Silent time gives students the opportunity to observe their own internal dialogue. Framing this observation skill as a research method is an important component of this text.

The practice of thought awareness builds on the process approach of a freewrite. Students who freewrite as an awareness and brain-storming practice often observe that their thoughts move faster than they are able to record on paper. In effect, students have to slow down their natural pace of free association in order to freewrite. By breaking up this practice into two phases – watching the thoughts and writing afterward – students are able to survey a wider range of reactions at a more rapid speed as they learn to pay attention internally and to analyze the contents of their thoughts for sparks of curiosity and new ideas. As students gain skill at watching their thought associations, they gain access to a wider range of their internal reactions and thus have a broader range of reactions from which to choose.

In an age in which *student-centered* has become a buzzword that overlaps and in some cases merges with the corporate lingo of *customer service*, a textbook that encourages students to dwell on their own thoughts and experiences might seem, to some, to pander to the self-centeredness of the consumer in the marketplace. This book is grounded in the opposite assumption: As students examine the content of their thoughts in a rigorous and focused fashion, they are encouraged and led to examine the ways in which their questions and reactions connect with the rest of the world.

According to Hart (2004: 3), the ability to monitor one's thoughts is an important cognitive skill and

> a developmental step beyond basic abstraction. Self-observation and reflection help to expose and deconstruct positions of role, belief, [and] culture ... to see more deeply or from multiple perspectives. This allows students the conceptual flexibility to see beyond the information given and beyond their own presuppositions.

The focus on contemplative technologies of mind is an effort to help students see themselves within context and to develop skills that will be of use in understanding the world.

Technologies of Knowing

A student's inability to formulate a specific research idea might, at first glance, appear to signal a worrisome lack of curiosity about the world. This book assumes that curiosity is a skill or a muscle, rather than an elusive substance that either exists or does not exist in one's mind. Giving students the technology to observe their own curiosity and to identify their own interests, and requiring students to exercise these skills, will increase students' comfort in exercising curiosity. All good research begins with a good question, and good questions are born of honest curiosity. Children who are four or five years old have no problem generating questions and exhibiting boundless curiosity about the world around them. But as young people progress through the school system, they are rewarded more often for mastering answers or appearing not to care about the outcome; it is no surprise that they absorb the rules of their context, a culture of expertise in which a question is often seen as an admission of ignorance.

Studies on creativity indicate that educational strategies emphasizing "surveillance, evaluation, rewards, competition, over-control, restricting choice, and pressure often inhibit students' ability to engage in imaginative and open-ended thought processes" (Goleman, Kaufman, and Ray, 1992: 62). As creativity skills atrophy through a lack of use and a focus on other cognitive areas, students lose the ability to access their innate question-asking ability and to use this ability to formulate concrete research proposals. Students are directed instead to focus on high-stakes educational tasks with outcomes and products designed to demonstrate the ability to follow narrowly prescribed formulas for research and writing. This focus on assignment-specific goals neglects self-observation in the research process. Adding self-observation will increase the likelihood that students transfer these skills from one research domain to another.

Many educators in the past four decades have observed a need for open spaces in which curiosity can thrive in the classroom. Exercises including brainstorming techniques and freewriting encourage students to follow their own thoughts and impulses. However, students often do not adopt these techniques as their own and will not usually employ them unless asked to. Techniques such as brainstorming and freewriting can be expanded beyond the moment of topic generation in order to allow students to build the skills necessary to reconnect with internal awareness, monitor thought processes, and become conscious of the experience of curiosity. To emphasize the framework of self-observation, I will refer repeatedly to a three-step reminder used throughout this book as a framework for building skills of curiosity and awareness: RELAX, REFLECT, RESEARCH.

Relax

The charged connotations of this word are in some ways at the heart of this book. *Relax* is the verb of choice for the weekend or vacation; putting in time on a job results in a longed-for chance to do nothing. At the same time, leisure pursuits have become professionalized and goal-based; hobbies require training, equipment, and investment. Even on the weekends, many people are haunted by the feeling that they are not doing enough with their leisure time. Relaxation becomes another impossible goal to attain, and perfectionism and a goal-oriented approach turn a weekend into an opportunity to fail at adequately "de-stressing" in order to arrive refreshed at work on Monday morning.

The word *relax* thus implies both an impossible goal for leisure and a state of thoughtlessness unsuitable for focused educational tasks. The word itself means simply "to render less firm or rigid," which is a necessary action for a muscle to perform as it prepares to do work. The skill of relaxing one's cognitive muscles does not, therefore, imply any weakness or anti-intellectualism. The RELAX steps in this book ask students to clear their minds and focus, to suspend judgment, and to openly survey reactions and thoughts without evaluation and without sorting immediately into categories such as *good/bad*, *useful/useless*, etc.

Reflect

The skills of reflection and contemplation address three main challenges I have observed in students' research process:

1. Difficulty identifying the feeling of curiosity
2. Research anxiety
3. Lack of continuity: Difficulty applying techniques to generate ideas for a new project

This book is designed to address the three challenges listed above, and students can expect to develop skills in these three areas to help them REFLECT. They should also complete the chapters with substantial improvement in these skill sets, which will directly help their ability to RESEARCH:

1. Ability to access and use their own innate sense of curiosity as stimulus for writing and research;
2. Ability to understand, address, and use research anxiety in productive ways to guide their writing and research;
3. A list of research ideas and a lasting sense of ownership of their research questions and areas of interest.

The feeling of *curiosity* is rarely discussed in an academic environment. Instead, a goal-oriented and managed set of assignments can turn curiosity into a handicap, and a student whose head buzzes with questions and ideas may even be labeled as lacking focus or easily distracted. While students definitely need to learn the skills to focus on a task, they also benefit from being able to see exactly what they are being distracted by and to analyze which of these thoughts might be relevant or helpful to the task at hand.

Students are often unable to see that an emotional reaction to a large task does not have to be either uniform or negative. Because educators often do not talk about their own or others' research processes, the universal feeling of *anxiety* accompanying any large project is taken by students to be an indication that they will fail at the task. If students repeat this process without learning skills for finding curiosity and without addressing research anxiety, they encounter repeated failure.

As research failures accrue, students experience research as a process guided by someone else focused on ends that have little to do with their lives. Allowing and encouraging students to brainstorm research questions outside the requirements of a specific assignment goal, in contrast, models for students the open-ended process of career researchers, who experience a continuity of research interests that connect one project to the next based on long-term questions and persistent themes.

Book Sections and Features

The sixteen chapters in this book are divided into four sections.

Section I. Research as an Inside Job focuses on the RELAX component in order to build skills in areas of self-observation and contemplation along with vocabulary for talking about the writing and research processes.

> **Chapter 1: Write About Anything** focuses on what research is in order to reframe the task and address cultural assumptions about what counts as research.
>
> **Chapter 2: Meet the Author: You** introduces contemplative techniques and begins an intensive interest inventory to begin a pool of research ideas.
>
> **Chapter 3: Areas of Expertise: Using What You Already Know** asks students to focus on the overlooked details and experiences in their own lives in order to look for research ideas.
>
> **Chapter 4: Living and Loving the Questions** prepares students for a more formalized contemplative research experience by focusing on the experience of generating questions rather than answers.

Section II. The Inside Meets the Outside: Paying Attention as Research expands on the first section and formalizes the REFLECT skill by asking students to use material generated in Section I to begin connecting personal questions to the world around them.

> **Chapter 5: Learning to See** asks students to revisit free association with an eye toward their environments and communities.
>
> **Chapter 6: Responding to Reality** prompts students to engage in several open-ended and curiosity-driven explorations of their surroundings.
>
> **Chapter 7: Uncharted Obsessions** asks students to focus on elements of their lives in which expertise is already high

in order to see how these obsessions connect to the larger world.

Chapter 8: Beginner's Mind reframes the research activity of question generating with a contemplative element in preparation for more focused research in Section III.

Section III. The Big Bang: Form and Structured Chaos in Research focuses on traditional research skills within a contemplative and self-awareness framework.

Chapter 9: Take Note focuses on basic techniques of note-taking to highlight the brainstorming and awareness practices required by in-depth research.

Chapter 10: Noodling as a Research Method outlines and encourages an associative research process in the pursuit of sources and evidence.

Chapter 11: Conversations details the technique of the interview as a research method and encourages students to engage in a self-aware version of this process.

Chapter 12: Twists and Turns in the Research Story explores the structure of the research process, focusing specifically on the author's changing relationship to the subject matter inherent in any research process.

Section IV. Open Minds Invite Surprises brings together the steps of RELAX, REFLECT, and RESEARCH in order to highlight the open-ended nature of a research project.

Chapter 13: The Research Road Map addresses several common roadblocks encountered by most researchers and describes the opportunities contained in each.

Chapter 14: Finding Your Way presents several pre-writing steps for structuring information and reflecting on it in order to develop a structure that reflects the writers' true interests and questions.

Chapter 15: Writing the Story's Journey invites students to share the research quest as a story in order to structure the research project, using material gathered in Experiments through previous Chapters.

Chapter 16: Revision: Seeing Again asks students to focus on their own revision process in order to use initial questions and research experiences to produce a project draft unified by these central questions and inspirations.

Each of these sections employs repeated components that can be used to build lesson plans, homework assignments, and in-class or out-of-class individual and group activities.

Conversations

Each section includes at least one Conversation, which is an informal interview excerpt with a professional researcher/writer who discusses his or her challenges in the research process, including the inevitable emotional, intellectual, and practical blocks and dead ends. The writers were selected for their ability to connect to students through humor, honesty about the writing process, and insight into the emotional and affective component of research itself.

Gray Matter

The moral dilemmas associated with research are usually addressed in cautionary tales about plagiarism, but the human interest at the core of good research is often intertwined with a series of ethical choices. In order to encourage student investment and involvement, these moral questions are highlighted as Gray Matter questions at the end of many chapters, along with questions for discussion and/or writing assignments.

One of the key moral questions for students and scholars alike is the challenge of objectivity. Current theoretical and practical research on the act of knowledge creation in fields such as anthropology and quantum physics have questioned the viewpoint of a sharp division between the scholar and his or her field of study. As educator Parker Palmer writes, "Knower and known are joined, and any claim about the nature of the known reflects the nature of the knower as well" (Palmer, 1998: 97). This complex issue does not imply that knowledge creation is meaningless because each piece of knowledge is tainted by an individual's bias. Rather, findings and research become more meaningful as we understand the perspectives from which they spring.

Since this book begins with the student's own experience as fodder for research questions, the student is thrown into an immediate and real-world dilemma about how to attain distance from one's subject matter. This book begins with the assumption that the researcher is always present as a guiding force in shaping the results of research. Prematurely imposing ideals of objectivity forces students to adopt a distance from subject matter before they have even explored their connection to it. As this guide will discuss, there are many other routes to acquiring this perspective and distance from one's subject. One of those routes is to first acknowledge one's own connections to the subject at hand.

Experiments

Each chapter of this book includes several EXPERIMENTS, which are exercises with written and contemplative components. The term *experiment* emphasizes the fact that these brainstorms and writing prompts are more than "practice" or "busy work." Students who engage in each of these experiences will produce results that they can examine as they build their own research agendas. Assumptions are often being tested, new modes of thought and analysis are being tried, and the outcomes should be examined in light of the process that produced them. Students can evaluate each experiment to see which ones worked best for them in their research process.

Many of these experiments begin with a period of silent reflection, often presented with a specific time requirement; in almost all cases the instructor may adjust the time frame based on classroom needs. Students should be encouraged to keep all of these together in a notebook or three-ring binder that can serve as the research notebook. This might also be considered as part of a final submission in a portfolio grading system.

Using This Book in Class

The components of this book can be used in any combination that is productive for specific students and curricular goals. Assessing the particular needs of a group of students may require a focus on chapters in which these skills are developed. The research process is twofold, with creativity and revision playing equal parts. In teaching research skills, therefore, it is important to also prioritize time for practice, mistakes, and exploration. In other words, the research process presented in this book focuses more time on the brainstorming phase – as much as a few weeks more – than on the specific packaging of this research into a final paper or project. Students using this text in class may therefore benefit from revised deadlines or revised expectations for the later stages of research projects in a classroom setting.

Individual instructors may want to use the lists of experiments categorized in the Appendices as "Short" and "Long" and "Take-Home" in order to choose activities based on course needs and student workload abilities. Instructors should also feel free to shorten or lengthen time requirements described in experiments as needed to fit their instructional circumstances.

Research Schedules and Projects

Adapting a syllabus to this mode of research will require a few adjustments in the calendar of assignments but will ultimately result in more fulfilling research projects for the student and for the instructor. Students will need to be evaluated and given credit for the brainstorming and contemplative skills highlighted in Sections I, II, and III of this book. There are various methods for accomplishing this and for evaluating the outcome of this work, but it is important that the instructor allow extra time for students whose curiosity and exploration does not immediately result in a usable and manageable research idea. Instructors might, for example, incorporate a research proposal as a component of the final grade or use the freewrite and research notebook as a major component of the final project.

If departmental or course goals require a finished research paper and/or peer review of drafted written projects, the instructor will need to examine whether all activities in Sections I or II should be included as the total time required for the Experiments may not fit with every course timeline. The key requirement is that students will need more time for research planning and topic selection, which may leave less time for the research itself, particularly if the course is structured in a limited time frame. Instructors should consider course goals, and, in particular, the length of final projects along with source requirements when deciding on realistic expectations for a research project in which more time is spent in the brainstorming phase.

As one option, instructors working on research skills might focus one section of a course or an entire course on the research idea notebook (which might be envisioned as a writer's version of the artist's sketchbook), and another section of a course or entire course on putting those ideas into practice in a research process. If a research course is part of a course sequence, instructors might consider using the brainstorming methods in Sections I-II of this book as raw material for a major research project in an upper-level writing course.

Process and Outcomes in the Classroom

The test of a research course is often seen to be a final project, but students may not be able to acquire and practice every research skill successfully in the creation of a final project, particularly when the skills learned are new or unfamiliar. Instructors might consider including other concrete outcomes and measures to indicate student success and to monitor observable evidence of these characteristics, as outlined below, in subject areas such as *curiosity*, *depth*, and *ethical engagement*. Rubrics used to evaluate research notebooks might track specific indicators of these subject areas by noting, for example, the number of topic ideas, the presence of brainstormed questions that are evaluated to be surprising or innovative, the number of topic ideas that link two or more unrelated subjects, or the quality of responses to the Gray Matter discussion questions. Students may also be asked to complete narrative self-assessments in response to these outcomes. In addition to outcomes that can be listed on a syllabus, instructors might be glad to know that contemplative-oriented courses often result in measurable differences for students in cognitive skills such as attention and focus as well as "emotional balance and pro-social behaviors" (Garrison Institute, 2005: 4).

Curiosity might seem too elusive to be measured and too intuitive to be learned. Yet all such cognitive processes can be broken down into components and even included along with measurable outcomes on a syllabus. The exercises in this book guide a student to follow a process of discovery, so instructors might adapt a syllabus to emphasize completion of this process rather than to specifically evaluate quality at each stage of that process. As one example, an instructor might consider grading based on completion of process tasks rather than on a qualitative evaluation at each stage.

An instructor might, for example, create one course goal in which students would generate 200 research questions (see Experiment 4.3: Two Hundred Questions) and evaluate students' progress at the end of the course based on the percentage completion of that goal. Completion of such a task is a measure of curiosity because the task itself asks students to complete an unfamiliar exercise, giving them the experience of brainstorming questions and allowing them to encounter the more mechanical side of curiosity: the work of generating unfamiliar questions and the methods for doing so. Going through this experience thus gives them a concrete feeling and experience to draw upon later, a referent to the "action" of curiosity that cannot be readily understood as an abstract concept.

Depth of thought is another outcome that can be measured by the number of connections a student makes within an area of inquiry. Projects emphasizing a contemplative approach beginning with issues in a student's life develop the cognitive ability to take basic concepts of research and apply them in a deep rather than superficial way. Hart (2004: 2) writes:

> Although some students can recall sophisticated theories and formulae, they remain unable to apply them outside of a limited classroom context. Depth implies higher order understanding and application, creativity, problem-solving, and self-reflection.

Depth can be concretely measured by counting the number of connections a student makes between one research issue and another and/or between a personal issue and a research topic. The right-hand column of the research notebook outlined in Chapter 9 can be an easy method for assessing depth in the research process.

Ethical engagement might be evaluated partially through students' responses to discussion questions in the Gray Matter sections of each chapter. A process approach to research may decrease students' impulses or felt needs to plagiarize as they are trained to focus on the moral choices made at each step of the research process. Many instructors have also noted that a process-oriented writing project with multiple drafts and freewrites also decreases plagiarism in that students are unable to present another student's finished project as their own. Ultimately, it is my hope that as students learn to become more engaged in the research process, the choice to engage with their subjects deeply also triggers a greater investment in the research and therefore a decreased temptation to engage in unethical research practices.

Section I
Research: An Inside Job

1   Write about Anything

You need a large field in writing.... Don't pull in the reins too quickly. Give yourself tremendous space to wander in, to be utterly lost with no name, and then come back and speak.
— Natalie Goldberg, *Writing Down the Bones:*
Freeing the Writer Within
(Goldberg, 2006: 217)

Introduction to Chapter 1: Research Trouble

My research trouble started with a light bulb hanging over my head. My high school sophomore English teacher, Mr. Provo, had announced an assignment: an oral presentation, with the dreaded open-ended topic. We could choose any subject in the world to research and to share with the class. My light bulb, however, was not an *a-ha!* cartoon of inspiration. Instead, it was a fluorescent tube humming in the fixture above my desk.

I was stumped. I looked up to think for about half a second. Baffled and panicked by the idea of researching *anything in the world*, of having to sort through the trillion-and-one topics offered up by the whole universe, I decided to end the agony as quickly as possible. I stared at the rectangular drop-ceiling tiles, which looked like Styrofoam with tiny holes. I stared at the fluorescent light covered in sheets of clear plastic. That's it: mission accomplished. I would write about the light bulb.

Here's what troubles me, decades later: I was, at the time, a card-carrying nerd. By definition, a nerd is passionately interested in many subjects. If I'd thought about my own obsessions for even two minutes, I could have picked a topic I actually wanted to talk about; I could have rambled endlessly about my favorite bands or about the things I worried about at night (nuclear war, the ozone hole, the Chicago White Sox) or about the things that mystified me (why the steel mills in nearby Joliet, Illinois, had all closed down, or why my German relatives settled in Arkansas). I read like a maniac on just about any topic any author had seen fit to write about: beaver dams, edible wild plants, Isaac Asimov's robot stories, anthropology, and primate behavior. I'm not saying I was unique; like most high-school kids, I just had definite opinions about what I liked.

But no. I picked the fluorescent light bulb. I'm not putting down the fluorescent lighting industry or its important contributions to saving electricity. I could have gotten very passionate about that, but I didn't even see those connections at the time.

Flooded with a sense of relief, I dutifully trekked to the local library and checked out books (this was way before Google) and filled out request forms to examine copies of *Popular Mechanics* detailing the latest advances in mid-1980s lighting technology. Despite my lack of passion for the topic, I got interested in Benjamin Franklin, and I made a multi-layered diagram of a light bulb with clear sheets that could be lifted to explain the various parts of the average incandescent bulb as a way to show the precursor to the fluorescent bulb. As I said before, I was a nerd and could get interested in just about anything (which isn't to imply that light bulbs aren't inherently fascinating).

Weeks later, as I stood up at the front of Mr. Provo's classroom to give my presentation, my friends sat in their seats and raised their eyebrows, looking at me strangely as if to ask, "Why did you pick this mind-numbing topic?" I soldiered on, explaining the function of the filament and the various attributes of the pear-shaped and tube-shaped bulbs. But that unasked question was a good one – Why, oh why had I chosen that topic?

After finishing that endless oral report on the light bulb, I graduated high school and college. I received training as a reporter and a creative writer. Both of these careers forced me to come up with research and story ideas just about every day of my life. I became pretty good at coming up with unique ones I actually wanted to write about, and it only took a little over a decade to figure out the tricks.

Torturing Students with Research

I did not expect to ever assign students a research paper, but sixteen years after the light bulb report, that's what I was doing. At first, I didn't remember the light bulb. I assigned those vague, anything-in-the-world topics and then watched as my students writhed in their seats in agony. I became baffled and frustrated when twelve of my twenty students each picked the same three topics, each of them impossible to write about in a five-page paper. I exhorted them to be creative, to choose something fun to learn and write about, something that would be of practical value to them. They almost invariably proposed topics they would freely admit they hated. It was almost as if they heard the word "research" and felt an instinctive obligation to choose a subject designed to make themselves suffer.

I searched back through my own experience of research and asked myself why I enjoyed it. I tried to trace back to my first research experiences, and there it was: the light bulb. But how was I supposed to steer my students away from a similar fate? Resisting the pull of the light bulb was more difficult than it seemed. I thought about it, and I reflected back on my career as a reporter and a writer. I realized that figuring out my true topics, the things

I couldn't stop writing about, was a much deeper challenge than it first appeared to be.

First, I had to think about my gutless moment in high school English class and understand it. As a sixteen-year-old, I knew what I liked. But if someone asked me what movie I wanted to see that weekend, I would have shrugged and said, "I dunno… whatever you want to see." Part of my challenge as a teenager was that I didn't really know how to <u>look</u> for what interested me. I surveyed the very narrow range of options (the four movie ads in the paper), and if none of them looked interesting, I assumed the problem was me: I was a boring person. Then I went to see the latest *Terminator* movie with my boyfriend and was bored out of my skull.

I didn't realize, back then, that sparking and firing up my curiosity was a practical skill, an ability as basic and real as making a sandwich. The real *a-ha* moment arrived gradually, over and over again while I worked as a reporter; I realized I had to search for what interested me. I had to develop and feed and exercise a general curiosity in life in order to open my own eyes to possibilities and also to get specifically and passionately interested in the things I was meant to do as a person. That didn't happen overnight. But I believe <u>that</u> is how you find what you really want to write about. First you have to take a few steps to discover yourself.

Research Starts with You

This book will help you start from yourself and move outward – a BACKWARDS research process referred to in the title of this guide. An inventory of your interests, quirks, experiences, personality, and obsessions will actually help you to see more clearly the world and your place in it. This book will help you discover the patterns of your thoughts, which are as unique as your fingerprints. You will learn how to monitor your own thought processes and then to see the ways in which your assumptions, patterns, and beliefs shape everything you see, which are in fact quite advanced research skills. A focus on you – student, writer, researcher – can help to illuminate your own limits: where you stop, the boundary zone or membrane where you meet the world, and all of the things you don't yet know but would like to understand. Ultimately, a focus on yourself can allow you to see the gray area between yourself and the world, which is the zone of engagement and the site for exciting research projects that connect you to the world.

As an example, consider the practical problem of a parking ticket. You might pull it off your windshield and feel a surge of strong emotion, maybe annoyance. Investigation and research starts almost immediately: you start to gather information by looking at the citation and the posted parking regulations. You notice that the posted regulations are unclear or maybe overly restrictive. Then the serious research begins. You look for contact information about parking tickets online, and you find a method for submitting an appeal regarding your ticket. In casual conversation over the following week, maybe you mention your ticket, and your friends and neighbors confirm a pattern of excessive ticketing on your street. Maybe you wonder how many other parking tickets are written for this neighborhood or whether students should be able to apply for parking permits. Before you know it, your curiosity has given you two gifts: you might find solutions or people to talk to about the problem, and your anger has given way to a desire to connect, a desire to help, a desire to understand. While those benefits aren't directly explored in this research guide, the practice of noticing, observing, and asking questions can lead to truly life-changing discoveries.

Experiment 1.1: Your Research Stories

Length: *Flexible (Short or Take-home)*

Timer: *4 minutes + 4 minutes= 8 minutes*

Discuss: *Recommended*

Step 1. Take four minutes to list as many experiences as you can think of in your life in which you conducted research in a focused way. For example, you might list times in which you gathered information to make a wise purchase, or even when you listened to two friends' versions of an incident to settle a dispute.

Step 2. Circle the three or four entries on your list in which the research process was most complex or time-consuming.

Step 3. Choose one of these more complex entries on your list. Write for four minutes about the steps you took, the skills required to conduct each of these steps, and the outcome of the research process.

Step 4. In class, discuss your findings. What kinds of research have you and your peers conducted? What skills might transfer to formal academic written research? What, if anything, was surprising about your reflections in Steps 1-3?

Research as Self-Discovery and World-Discovery

At first glance, an assignment to develop curiosity and discover yourself might sound both daunting and a little touchy-feely, as well as a very round-about method for coming up with a topic for an English paper, an article, or a personal essay. "This isn't about me," you might say. "This is about random bits of information put together in a way that will make my teacher happy." Even the word "research" sounds redundant and off-putting, as if one must search around for information, copy quotes onto index cards, and then spit them into paragraphs to prove a thesis. The prefix *re-*, which can mean "again," can also conjure up the feeling of having to do something monotonous and repetitive.

The word *research* actually comes from the Old French word *recerchier,* which just means "to seek." So that's all you need to do: seek. You can see research as a journey of discovery, a journey that should be, by its nature and original meaning, open-ended, variable, and spontaneous. You journey in a direction charted by your needs and desires, motivated by something that moves you deeply. You examine facts but don't assume they provide proof, and you study them to figure out what they really tell you, as well as observing and studying your own reaction to the facts.

This skill, once learned, can be applied to almost any project, in and beyond writing for a class. The underlying goal is to find a topic that will set your brain on fire. The truth is, there is not one topic. There are potentially thousands, once you suspend your fear of being wrong and asking questions that at first might feel stupid. Asking those kinds of questions allows a researcher to stumble into topics that no one really knows the answers to and to ask the questions that everyone is dying to ask. As you dive into a specific subject, you may also see the world more clearly and in a more complex way. As you learn how to organize a subject, to deeply understand it, your brain becomes better able to deal with a contradictory and yet coherent universe.

Throughout this book, I will refer to the words RELAX, REFLECT, and RESEARCH, which describe a three-step process of (1) relaxing and clearing your head to make space for reflection, (2) reflecting to observe what thoughts and questions emerge, and then documenting those thoughts in writing, and (3) researching to investigate and learn more about your questions and reflections. You're not finished, however, when you reach step three. Rather than doing each step once, the three phases will happen over and over again through a recycling research process in a mode that is called *recursive*. In other words, you use each piece of the process more than once, responding to what you have discovered and written.

The Question of Objectivity

The practice of starting with the researcher is a departure from traditional research methods within higher education. The scientific community in the Western world has traditionally upheld an ideal of *objectivity.* Objectivity – an impersonal, distanced approach to inquiry that tries to take the researcher out of the research – has been a useful goal to help scientists and writers from all disciplines step back to view their subject matter from a new perspective. This book, however, departs from such research models and instead begins from the *I*, the subject of the research process.

Objectivity, an inheritance from the Enlightenment era, empowered scholars by stressing that anyone – not just a cleric or a king – could create valuable knowledge with the correct standardized techniques. This viewpoint has brought about significant advances and world-changing discoveries in scientific understanding. In addition, the vital ideas of seeing one's own biases and acknowledging one's conflicts of interests are important inheritances from this world view. In fact, they form the basis of many activities and readings in this book.

However, no method for generating knowledge is flawless. In fact, educator Parker Palmer writes that objectivism created problems of its own: "As people became convinced that objective answers to all questions were possible – and as specialists emerged who were glad to give those answers – people began to distrust their own knowledge and turn to authorities for truth" (Palmer, 1998: 53). In other words, even the search for objectivity can become a replacement for using one's own powers of analysis.

One critique of the objective ideal is that it can conceal the way real people do research – as well as their reasons for doing it, the results they discover, and what effects this research has on the world. As author Ian Cook writes,

> Research can be a tricky, fascinating, awkward, tedious, annoying, hilarious, confusing, disturbing, mechanical, sociable, isolating, surprising, sweaty, messy, systematic, costly, draining, iterative, contradictory, open-ended process. But you wouldn't necessarily be able to tell that from the way it often has to be written up.... (Cook, 2005: 16)

Cook calls for the research process to become more transparent – for the benefit of the reader, the researcher, and the research.

Today, researchers in fields such as physics, anthropology, geography, mathematics, and media studies also study the negative consequences of pretending that researchers do not interact with their subject matter. This separation can produce research results that are out of touch with human beings and the human and real-world effects of research. An alternative is to acknowledge that each researcher is specific and *situated,* approaching research from his or her background, point of view and biases, locations and limitations, and quirks and interests. While many would categorize this stance as *subjective*, it can also generate different methods for gaining distance and perspective. An alternative to traditional objectivity, multiple perspectives can be combined to create *intersubjectivity*, "the method of connecting as many different perspectives on the same data as possible. These multiple sources encourage the fieldworker to interpret patterns and interrelationships among various accounts alongside the researcher's own account and to leave other interpretations open as well" (Sunstein and Chiseri-Strater, 2007:131).

Each researcher's situation and background can become fertile ground for research ideas and inspiration. Researchers take into account their *fixed* positions, "the personal facts that might influence how you see your data – your age, gender, class, nationality, race – factors that do not change during the course of the study but are often taken for granted and unexamined in the research process" (Sunstein and Chiseri-Strater, 2007:131). Researchers also take into account "life history and personal experiences" and finally look at how the research and writing processes affect what the researcher creates (Sunstein and Chiseri-Strater, 2007:132).

Becoming aware of what and how you think can have another benefit: *perspective*, or *detachment,* which Tobin Hart defines as the ability "to observe the contents of our consciousness rather than simply being absorbed by them" (Hart, 2004: 1). The framework of objectivity was set up to aim for a similar goal, yet awareness practices approach the goal from the opposite direction. How might detachment emerge as you learn about yourself? The greater awareness a researcher has of her or his own biases and patterns, the more clearly he or she can observe connections to these biases and patterns in his or her work. Self-knowledge and disclosure about one's attachments to research can present a much clearer picture for readers to understand the motivations of the research and its results. Finally, an inquiry into one's interests can help a researcher see what subjects and questions are driving a research agenda, and thus can allow a researcher to slowly explore his or her own blind spots and assumptions. Seen from this perspective, the stance of objectivity is a fantasy that in some cases hides more than it reveals.

Beginning the Search

This book will not focus on the correct method for source citations, though a style guide is included in the index and the ethics and practice of quoting are covered in later chapters. Many excellent resources are available for the nuts and bolts of locating sources. Instead, this guide begins with that daunting assignment: *Write about anything*. Maybe an instructor has already assigned you an open-ended paper, or maybe you are a writer with a need to find a new and compelling subject. Either way, you are the beginning of this search. This guide will help you evaluate your level of curiosity, an essential ingredient for a seeker of any kind, and then point you in the direction of following that curiosity.

In this book you will also find some unusual exercises designed to build a bridge between your real life and the words you put on the page. One method for building this bridge is to look for connections between your experiences and larger ethical and social questions. You will find in each chapter a section called GRAY MATTER devoted to this challenge. The name implies, obviously, the gray matter between your ears, and I hope some of the questions fire up that organ. The word "gray" also makes reference to the common saying: "It's not a black and white issue." In other words, any truly interesting question or topic has more than two opposite answers. As you engage in your writing and research tasks, ethical questions will arise, and their resolution will often change depending on the context. There isn't a right way to solve these research dilemmas, but you will get better at addressing them as you identify and think about the challenges brought up by your writing and research.

Throughout this book, I also use the term *freewrite*, first described by writing teacher Peter Elbow. To paraphrase Elbow, freewriting is writing – usually with a time limit – in which your only goal is to keep your pen or fingers moving, letting loose on the page with whatever comes to mind (Elbow, 1973: 3). Writing Experiments throughout this book will require you to freewrite or compose responses to discussion questions or other prompts, and I encourage you to keep these pieces of writing together in a *research notebook*. This is ideally a three-ring binder filled with loose leaf paper, though you can also use a composition book or a spiral notebook.

Your research notebook will contain a growing list of potential topics for your writing, as well as the topics for many other research projects that come your way. You will also learn to use the notebook for recording and reacting to pieces of information and research. Keeping these notes in one place will help you direct your own research agenda; researchers often refer back to old notes to trigger new ideas or to reflect on new ways to see old subjects. Ideally, this notebook of ideas will be a collection of thoughts you return to for future writing projects, in your current class and beyond.

The Mind as Research Tool

This book will focus on external tools like the research notebook, but another major focus will be the way you use your mind in the early stages of research. The brain functions so well to filter and sort information that the process of problem-solving seems almost automatic. But a truly BACKWARDS look at research requires a look at this piece of lab equipment used to gather impressions and make sense of the world. Thinking a bit about the brain itself can reveal important steps in the research process.

The brain is lightning-fast, and the normal range of processing speeds falls between 20 and 100 milliseconds. That's a lot of speed and a lot of capacity to deliver images and associations. When you first start paying attention to what's actually going on between your ears, it can be a bit alarming. The latest count indicates that there are a hundred billion neurons in the brain, each of which can send and receive signals. Researchers have described this sea of activity as an evolutionary advantage; our genetic ancestors were busy talking to themselves, working out problems, imagining, making meaning, reviewing past experiences, and reacting to the present. It's difficult not to take this lightning-speed multi-tasking for granted.

The brain is sometimes described as a computer, but this meta-phor doesn't capture the brain's true nature. While a computer reacts to specific input and commands, the brain can fire at will. The brain's neurons light up in a manner that seems wild and al-most random; some researchers have used the analogy of "white noise," the background rush of the ocean or traffic, to describe the constant activity of the brain.

Patterns of this inaudible "noise" investigated by brain researcher Alex Pouget indicate that the randomness makes advanced compu-tation of probabilities possible (Mysterious "neural noise" actually primes brain for peak performance, 2006). You might look like you're sitting quietly at your desk during a class, but your brain is always working to mull over complicated problems and assimilate new information in a constant sea of electrical impulses. The brain is abuzz with meaning-making tasks, according to neuroscience research summarized by Norman Holland. Each person's brain ex-hibits a unique cognitive style and pattern, which some researchers connect to an individual's sense of identity (Holland, 2006).

What does all of this have to do with research? Paying attention to the brain is one of the main ideas in this book; the brain's "chatter" can reveal subjects, ideas, and passions just waiting to be investigated. After bringing patterns of thought to conscious awareness, more formal analytic and reflective tools – including conversations and questions – can expand and focus these storms of inspiration. Learning to monitor our own thought processes and reactions – using techniques of *mindfulness* – can turn research in exciting directions, with more satisfying research experiences for the researcher and a more relevant reading experience for the audience.

Thinking about Thinking

In one of her untitled poems (numbered 632), Emily Dickinson meditates on the brain and its capacities:

> The Brain – is wider than the Sky –
> For – put them side by side –
> The one the other will contain
> With ease – and You – beside –
>
> The Brain is deeper than the sea –
> For – hold them – Blue to Blue –
> The one the other will absorb –
> As Sponges – Buckets – do –
>
> The Brain is just the weight of God –
> For – Heft them – Pound for Pound –
> And they will differ – if they do –
> As Syllable from Sound –

Dickinson, like many before and after her, was awed by the seemingly limitless power of the brain: it seemed to be able to contain conceptions of the world and the self and to absorb an ocean of material, leading Dickinson to wonder how the brain differs from God.

You may have heard that there are vast areas of the brain that go unused and that only about ten percent of our brain's capacity is used at any one time. This statistic implies that a brain using all of its power might think its way into the stratosphere. Actually, the idea of "spare brain" is a kind of urban legend of neurology. Research on the brain has demonstrated that all brain resources are used to think and navigate the world – just not every second. Different areas of the brain have different specializations, and several areas are firing in a complex symphony of electric impulses as you read and process the information in this sentence.

The brain does have enormous untapped potential, but researchers today understand this potential in a different way. In fact, researchers are demonstrating that the brain can grow and adapt based on how it is used. This amazing trait, *neuroplasticity*, helps the brain change physically in response to experience (Nicholson, 2007). The first part of this book will focus on a specific brain change: the skill of learning to notice the brain as it is thinking.

Noticing: The First Research Skill

What are you thinking about? This question often produces a mysterious sensation and asks a person to tune in to a swirling sea of internal activity – images, pieces of dreams and worries, flashes of concepts, all whizzing around like corn in a popcorn maker or sleepily bumping into each other like boats on a river. Decoding this swirl seems impossible, so if you are asked to sum up your thoughts, a typical response to the question is, "I don't know.... Nothing much." But that response often means "Too much to describe!"

Even when the brain is not focused on a specific task, its neurons and signals are in constant motion. To see this activity, first try to see into the window of your brain for just ten seconds. Close your eyes and, instead of drifting off into semi-consciousness, try to become aware of your thoughts. Are there any loose threads of thought sticking up, demanding attention? Try to catch the first one you can. Maybe it's "My neck is stiff," "It's cold in here," "I want chicken for lunch," or "That perfume sure smells good."

Every other activity requiring contemplation builds on this one simple skill of noticing your thoughts. This view into the mental window is available at any time, but it does take an extra effort. In the same way that learning a new dance step or a soccer kick might require concentration and feel like a workout, practice can develop this powerful ability. The skill of noticing the brain's activity can then help with something as practical a research project or as lofty as trying to understand yourself.

People in many cultural and religious traditions value the contemplative or meditative state as a route to gaining insight, and some people who have worked hard to develop this mental skill can maintain awareness even with their eyes open while they go about their everyday tasks. While the word *contemplative* might have religious connotations for some, the word's synonyms include *thoughtful* and *reflective*; a contemplative state can be accessed by anyone who has a brain.

As with any sport, it is best to develop a new ability through short exercises and gradually build up your brain muscles. Get ready for some heavy lifting while (seemingly) doing absolutely nothing. The following chapters will build on this simple activity with more use of contemplation as research.

Experiment 1.2: Just Sit

Length: *Short*

Timer: *4 minutes*

Discuss: *Recommended*

This exercise can be done anytime, but try it for the first time in class with a timekeeper. Everyone else gets ready to do nothing

– with one important exception. You will close your eyes for two minutes. Your job is to do one thing: notice your thoughts.

You may find that when you close your eyes, you initially face a dark void, and you might say, "Aha! See, there is nothing going on." That's fine. Maybe you really will have no thoughts for two minutes. On the other hand, you might see splashes of images – friends' faces, lists of homework to do, memories from this morning or the night before, strange and random pictures from childhood – or you might find yourself looping back around to one persistent thought.

Step 1. As you sit silently, make a mental note of your thoughts; don't try to control the direction these thoughts take.
Step 2. When the instructor says, "Stop," write down a list of everything that flashed through your mind's eye. Take a few minutes to complete this list.
Step 3. Look back over your list. Go around the room and share your list with your classmates. After everyone has shared their lists, discuss what you noticed as a class.

Conclusion to Chapter 1

The skills and framework discussed in this chapter – including the simple ability to sit back and RELAX at the early stages of the research process – form the basis for the work you will begin in Chapter 2. Although your past research experiences might not have involved sitting quietly and observing your thoughts, repeated attention to this skill and others will allow you to approach research in a new way, using tools of *awareness* to REFLECT and to observe connections between your thoughts and larger questions demanding further investigation.

Capturing your thoughts and responses to the Experiments in a *research notebook* will allow you to see that as you practice, you will be able to excavate a wonderful and surprising range of ideas, most likely more than you would ever be able to use in one class. As you begin with the exercises in Chapter 2, remember that you are focusing on your own interests and experiences not just to rehash what you already know about your life. Instead, you are framing this raw material in a new way, looking with the tool of awareness and searching for connections between your experiences and the larger world.

2   Meet the Author: You

Being the researcher so influences your fieldwork that it would be deceptive not to include relevant background information about yourself in your study.
— Bonnie Stone Sunstein and Elizabeth Chiseri-Strater,
Fieldworking
(Sunstein and Chiseri-Strater, 2007: 131)

Introduction to Chapter 2

This chapter is devoted to you. The exercises in this chapter and beyond include questions to help you generate a detailed and even surprising profile of yourself and your interests. Each activity will also require you to think about the world you live in and how you see it, which will lead to questions for research. As the researcher, you are the foundation for any research project you might complete.

At the beginning of an open-ended research assignment, you might experience a sense of free-fall. What to research? What to choose? The brain fires in a million directions and casts about for ideas. Because anxiety is not an emotion most people prefer to stay in, the easiest course of action is to choose the first thought that comes to mind: elections, the Internet, dating – whatever.

To address this anxiety, first RELAX and realize that what you are doing is normal. This is what the beginning of an open-ended investigation feels like. See Conversation 1 with Ben Vogt for an excellent example of the feelings associated with the open-ended research quest.

Focus on the strange sense of unease that emerges at the beginning of a research project, which often feels as if you are walking out into a fog-filled field, hoping not to fall into a deep hole. This unease seems to be about more than grade anxiety or completing a paper to meet a deadline. Instead, the brain is generating a flurry of concerns, questions, and anxieties, resulting in a sense of dislocation.

How Not to Write a Research Paper

A common method for ending *topic anxiety* as quickly as possible is to choose the most controversial topic imaginable in the hopes that if there's controversy, there will surely be enough information for an assigned open-topic research paper. This approach – gaming for enough information – results in paper topics that take one of two opposing viewpoints on any number of well-worn public issues (Should athletes use performance-enhancing drugs? Is abortion wrong? Do video games cause violent behavior in children?). These are perfectly fine research topics, but the questions they address are so complex that there's almost no hope of covering such a massive topic in a short paper. Writers put pressure on themselves from the beginning by choosing topics that are too broad or just plain boring. Sometimes the research topic itself – too wide and intimidating – causes a writer to procrastinate; the writer has the correct sense that the topic is unwieldy.

The techniques for ineffective writing are well known, and every writer has tried these at one point or another: the all-nighter, the last-minute frenzy, and the desperate blundering into lofty language. Many writers claim they work well under pressure because they have never tried to work another way. Then all of a sudden, the paper is due and it's too late to turn back. The spelling errors are fixed, the heading's at the top of the page, and the final copy sits in the printer.

Days later, the writer might read the paper and feel as though it was written by someone else. When the graded paper is returned, the comments in the margin might include: "Connect this to your topic" or "Focus," and notes near the introduction and conclusion include, "So what's the point?"

That's the problem: the writer did not *reflect* on where the paper was going, and the time to do this is not at the end but at the very beginning, before the topic is chosen. The way you spend those early minutes of thinking can make a huge difference later in the writing process. Choosing the first research topic that comes to mind is a little like craving orange juice, cutting an orange in half, and then only squeezing until there's one drop in the glass. Hardly satisfying! Instead, commit to spending one half hour squeezing that orange – your brain – for good ideas. In this case, spend one half hour in a state of pure, productive *doubt*.

What Thinking Feels Like

The physical sensations of deep thought and wondering can be easily confused with the sensations of anxiety, fear, and doubt. The beginning of a brainstorming session brings with it a strange feeling of free-fall that can easily mimic terror, like a mental flashing red light. If you are not used to the feeling of letting go with your brain in order to jump into free association, that initial leap can feel like an endless void. When students report they have no ideas on a topic or that they are bad at brainstorming, it is a safe bet that they have looked into this endless void for a moment and decided that there's nothing there but empty space.

The first task is to explore this feeling of discomfort, which is actually a normal thought process. Like the burn you feel in your muscles when you lift weights, the brain gives off a little tug of resistance when you fire it up and let it run around at will. This might <u>feel</u> like the pain of worry or anxiety, but it is similar only in the sense that the brain is working. Once you identify that first sputter of brain-work, you can begin to look at it as a positive and necessary sensation.

The brain at work gathers momentum as it moves, like an engine or an athlete. As you begin to identify the sensation of gathering brain-speed, you will also see how important it is to keep this momentum going. For this reason, topic and idea brainstorms should proceed without heed to editing or self-criticism. An engine would not gather much speed if the driver shifted back into first gear every few minutes. Similarly, the brain can produce more ideas if it focuses on the task at hand rather than stopping to edit, criticize, or worry about the quality of those ideas. Since most writers are conditioned to worry about the quality of their output, it can be quite an act of discipline – and a new and unfamiliar skill – to give up control of what emerges on paper or on the screen.

Experiment 2.1: Sit with a Word

Length: *Short*
Timer: *4 minutes*
Discuss: *Recommended*

In this exercise, you will first brainstorm a list of general research topics, which do not even have to be topics you would be interested in researching. Start with the first subjects that come to mind when you think of the phrase "research project." Don't worry about generating something usable for a research project; this is an exercise in investigating how the mind works.

Step 1. Make a list of research topics. Questions, phrases, or single words are all fine, and these do not have to be connected or understandable by anyone but you. Try this for three minutes or even longer.

Step 2. Circle two or three words or phrases that seem most interesting. Close your eyes and sit quietly for two minutes, focusing on one or two of these words. Watch where your mind takes you, and if you start to veer off into a smattering of completely unrelated ideas ("I can't believe Kelly said that on the phone last night!"), bring yourself back to your list. Notice also what questions and tangents are good ideas or unique connections.

Step 3. Write for two minutes about whatever flashed through your mind. What unexpected connections came up? Can you make any connections between two seemingly unrelated images or ideas?

Step 4. Share your ideas with your classmates. What common patterns and experiences emerge?

Freedom of Association

Many students notice a pattern of large and sometimes even bizarre leaps as their minds move from one idea to the next. This is how most brains operate, a natural *associative* process of thinking in which ideas trigger other ideas based on any quality that connects one idea to the next in a spider-web fashion. The leaps between ideas can seem especially random and scattered after an extended focus on linear and logical arguments and expressions as they are usually prioritized in an academic environment. If the brain functioned solely in a linear pattern (like a computer does), it would quickly produce an outline in response to a paper topic; most of us are not blessed with that gift of extreme focus. Instead, ideas trigger other concepts, images, and memories in a branching web of tangents dug through your brain, like the twisting bed of a creek. If you have not paid attention to the stream of thoughts before, the art of paying attention to this wild flow can be a strange feeling for your most complex organ.

Hunters & Gatherers

The division of a research process into a phase of questioning and brainstorming to find a thesis, followed by a phase of research, is a simplification of the real process of research, which is continual and on-going questioning about the subject. A research project often has as many loops as the wire in a spiral notebook, and the researcher will need to reorient and reassess the topic as new information is gathered. Sometimes, a particularly challenging or unique source can take the researcher back to the beginning of the research process, and new basic questions will have to be asked. One benefit of conducting research with self-awareness is that you can learn how to match the various kinds of thinking tasks required of research with your own natural skills and inclinations, which will hopefully also make research a more pleasant or less taxing experience.

What Type of Hunter/Gatherer Are You?

Just as every person cleans a room in a different way, everyone has a slightly different style when it comes to collecting and taking in information. Some people like to collect a huge stack of books and sources and then find quiet time later to digest the material. Others find a single source and plow through it, taking notes during a single reading. Still others do a brief skim of articles or other sources on first discovery, deciding on the spot whether or not the source is truly relevant. Trying to research at a pace or type of attention that goes against your natural strengths and inclinations may be counter-productive. In addition, certain kinds of activities may require more or less concentration for you as an individual. If you know that combing through database entries is something that easily frustrates you, you might save that part of your research task for your best time of day and for a day when you feel you have the most energy and ability to concentrate. Doing a good job at research

– or at any challenge – often involves less innate talent and more ability to understand what you are working with – including your strengths and limitations – and learning how to use them together in a way that makes sense.

Experiment 2.2: Hunter/Gatherer Profile

Length: *Long or Take-home*

Timer: *4 minutes + additional writing and reflection time*

Discuss: *Optional*

Use the table below to draw some conclusions about your research habits. The first column lists common research tasks, although you might not perform them in exactly this order.

Step 1. Using Table 2.1, rank the research tasks listed in the first column from 1- 3. Fill in the second, third, and fourth columns: you will rank each task according to its (a) ease, with 1 being the easiest for you; (b) time required, with 1 being the least time required to do an adequate job; and (c) grade or quality of work you normally produce, with 1 being the task you normally complete with highest quality. Then add up the numbers across each row, and enter the total for each row in the Total column.

Table 2.1: Ranked Research Tasks

	Ease *(1–3)*	*Time Required* *(1–3)*	*Grade/Output* *(1–3)*	*Total*
Brainstorming				
Finding Sources				
Reading & Taking Notes				
Organizing				
Writing				
Preparing Citations				
Revision & Feedback				
Proofreading				

Step 2. To complete the second half of your research profile, consider the following types of cognitive tasks:
- Math and quantitative reasoning
- Abstract thought
- Reading and analyzing
- Emotional thinking, empathy, and communication regarding relationships
- Practical decision-making
- Physical coordination
- Imaginative thinking and brainstorming
- Routine tasks and bookkeeping

Step 3. In Table 2.2 below, use the list of words and phrases above to fill in the times of day you believe are best and worst for the various types of tasks listed above. This is *not* the same as asking yourself when you normally do these tasks. Many students do schoolwork late at night even though they know they are "morning people." Other people know they tend to do better on detail-oriented tasks in the morning and more imaginative tasks at night or in the afternoon, or vice versa.

Step 4. Fill in the final column with the types of cognitive activities you normally find yourself doing at various times of the day, whether through the requirements of your job or school schedule or through habit. You can also put an X through any box representing a time period in which you don't work or concentrate well.

Table 2.2: Research Schedule

Time	Best For	Worst For	I usually...
6 a.m. – 9 a.m.			
10 a.m. – 12 p.m.			
12 p.m. – 2 p.m.			
2 p.m. – 5 p.m.			
5 p.m. – 8 p.m.			
8 p.m. or later			

Step 5. Look at the results in the two tables together. Pay particular attention to those research tasks in Table 2.1 that got the highest numerical total, which correspond to the tasks that are most challenging for you. Think about which of these most challenging tasks you often save for the times when you feel mentally foggy.

Step 6. Write for a few minutes about your best time of day and your most difficult research task, and sketch out an ideal research schedule of when you would function best at various research tasks (assuming you had no other responsibilities).

Watching the Brain During a Brainstorm

During the brainstorming process, the element of surprise is a benefit rather than a hindrance. One question triggers others, but you don't have to worry about the distance or connection between ideas. Sometimes, too, the train of thought can lead to a dead end that suggests a leap into a new topic. This is fine; if you notice a tangent, resist the impulse to focus and follow the thoughts to see where they lead. Associative thinking can sometimes land you in completely new and interesting territory: from new shoes to a space satellite in three easy but mystifying steps!

At other times, however, associative thoughts all seem to lead to the same destination. If you're worried about paying for college tuition and maintaining a scholarship, a well-worn track of associations beginning with an idea for an English paper can lead to the worry about what will happen with the paper, to the worry that you'll fail English, to the worry that you'll bomb the semester. When you're in this state of mind, what's most important is that you *notice* the track of your thoughts. Noticing your thoughts – also called becoming *mindful* – is a practice you may already know well if you have ever kept a journal or a diary.

People who write in a journal every day and then read back over their entries are often surprised to see what was worrying them even a week ago. The catastrophe of one day becomes past history the next. Yet over time, paying attention to the concerns and interests that appear in writing can provide a surprising and complex picture of one's personality, including worldview, habitual reactions, expectations, daydreams, and worries. Even if you're not able to put the brakes on these worries, noticing that your tangents and associations all run in the same direction is huge progress, because it helps your brain become aware of its own patterns – and its own roadblocks for research and organized thinking.

Noticing your thoughts and feelings has another important benefit. You might notice that you're feeling anxious in every writing class. Once you learn this about yourself, you can start asking questions and putting your mind's energy to the task of understanding that emotion – and maybe even changing it. But it's difficult to address a problem if you don't know it is there!

The brain can provide critical feedback about itself, and this most important piece of lab equipment can also be studied by gathering information through external research. Most people use methods of informal external validation every day: asking a roommate whether shoes match or clash with a shirt, wondering aloud with a coworker whether something smells like it's burning in the kitchen. Using that method, you will ask your friends and peers questions that might feel silly and ridiculous. In the process, you will gather useful information about yourself to generate new perspectives on your interests and your possible research topics.

Obsessions: Fuel for the Fire

A new acquaintance asks, "What do you do for fun?" or "What is your favorite movie?" If you were to write out a complete list of answers, the document might be many pages long, yet in the moment when the question is posed, you might find yourself struggling to answer something so basic about yourself. A human being is tough to sum up in a sound-bite; the overwhelming nature of the question can lead to a kind of temporary brain-freeze.

The brain is a web of baffling complexity. The most richly treasured ideas, goals, and experiences are those with the most neural links, associations, and bits of memory. Flashes of past experiences meld with abstract ideas, images, and sensory information, and new connections are constantly being made. In a way, your most important experiences and ideas are probably the most difficult to sum up in a few words; there are so many associations to sort through in order to identify what is at the center. "What do I care about most?" is a complex question of values that requires reflection. Most people do not have this list tucked into their wallets. Generating this list can give you huge insight into your character, but it's not something you can discover by pressing a button. Choosing a topic for an open-ended research assignment can be like answering a question such as "What do I like?" or "Who am I?" because brain-freeze and desperation together can lead to a choice based on the first random idea.

Paying attention to what you like, wonder, and want is a skill, and many people shut off or stop listening to the internal voice that reacts and raises questions. The world-weary cynic is a stereotype of cool. In contrast, confessing likes, wants, and questions raises a problem; in many subcultures it is not cool to be excited, make mistakes, or confess ignorance.

Absorption and commitment to something – to anything – are what create beauty and knowledge. If you've ever seen a guitarist rocking out on stage, completely absorbed in the moment of creating music, contorting his or her face and body without caring what expression comes next, you've seen a fearless version of cool: complete concentration in an activity that demands both passion and attention. In the world of research, you can create worthwhile questions and unique explorations by following those activities and topics that light your fire. As Anne Lamott writes, "There is ecstasy in paying attention.... If you start to look around, you start

to see" (Lamott, 1994: 100-101). Practicing the skill of brainstorming – and staying with the practice long enough to understand its
challenges – helps us to understand our range of possibilities.

Brain Chatter and Brain Grooves

It would be fantastic if sitting quietly for a moment allowed immediate access to a chorus of wonderful ideas. However, you might
have noticed that when you focus on the chatter of your mind, you
can turn up the volume on an inner monologue that plays over and
over, a song as repetitious as a commercial jingle: what you'd rather
be doing and who or what is causing you discomfort. The mind is
busy but rarely focused, and it can be extremely discouraging to
begin paying attention to your thoughts if the expectation is immediate inspiration.

However, it is relatively easy to trick the mind into skipping out
of the worry or discomfort groove and to direct it toward questioning. This ability to refocus is invisible and internal, yet it is the
basic action that creates the conditions for curiosity. To refocus the
mind onto the track of curiosity, you can compile a list of topics
that easily trigger your mind toward interest in something beyond
the worries and concerns of the present moment. As you work
through the exercises in this chapter, you will see how a growing
awareness of your interests allows you to distract yourself away
from distraction. In other words, you will learn how to focus on
topics you care about as a jump-start to brainstorming.

The challenge is that these topics are often as plain as the nose
on your face – and as invisible to you without the aid of a mirror.
What you care about can be so obvious and intrinsic to your identity that you can't even see it. For that reason, it can be helpful to
start a list of obsessions and interests by taking a step back and
collecting a profile of your subject matter – you – from a crew of
those who observe you day in and day out.

Experiment 2.3: Interview Your Friends

Length: *Take-home*
Timer: *None*
Discuss: *Optional*

Friends and family might be able to provide helpful information about you and what you seem to care about because they see you in ways you cannot see yourself. Make a few copies of the interview worksheet on the next page, and ask two or three friends or family members to complete *Worksheet 1: Interest Inventory*. The topic is <u>you</u>. This might seem like a strange exercise because your friends will want to know whether you've come down with a case of amnesia. You can tell them your teacher is making you do it, or you can explain that this is a technique for exploring the gap between self-perception and others' perceptions of self.

Step 1. Fill out a copy of the worksheet for yourself.
Step 2. Ask a few trusted people to fill out a worksheet about you. Don't share your answers with them, because you want them to answer without being influenced by your answers.
Step 3. Your first reaction when you receive the completed worksheets may be disappointment or disbelief: How can my mom/my significant other/my best friend/my lab partner know so little about me? You might be tempted to correct the worksheet and hand back failing grades to everyone. Resist that urge. Instead, look at this as valuable empirical information. Fill an abbreviated version of each person's answers into *Worksheet 2: Interest Inventory Responses*, using one column for each respondent.
Step 4. Look at the responses to each question, and circle the three or four words that seem most surprising or interesting.
Step 5. Freewrite for three minutes, starting with one of the words you circled. What surprises you about this? What

associations do you have with this word or phrase? What questions might someone have about this trait or activity? If the word is a character trait, how does this trait arise, and what caused it in your personality or behavior? If the word is an activity, what questions might you or others have about this activity? If you were describing this activity or trait to an alien visiting from Mars, what questions or confusions would the alien have about this trait or activity?

Step 6. Repeat this activity for three more words on your chart.

Worksheet 1: Interest Inventory

- Please answer the following questions about _____.
  If you don't know what this person's response would be, give your best
  guess. There are no wrong answers.
- After you've finished, circle the three answers you are least sure about.
- Finally, mark the three answers you are most sure about with a star.

  1. This person is most calm when _____.
  2. This person is most agitated by _____.
  3. This person is annoyed by _____.
  4. This person's favorite activity is _____.
  5. This person's favorite possession is _____.
  6. The two or three causes or public issues this person cares about most
     are _____.
  7. The personal experience that has had the greatest impact on this
     person is _____.
  8. This person has been heavily influenced by this role model:
     _____.
  9. This person's "personal style" could best be described as ____
     _____.
  10. Something this person doesn't value enough about himself/herself is
      _____.
  11. Other people tend to value this quality most about this person: ____
      _____.
  12. The place you can most regularly find this person is ____
      _____.
  13. A place this person would not be caught dead is _____.
  14. This person's musical tastes could be described as _____.
  15. This person's would most like to spend a two-week, all-expenses-paid
      vacation to _____.
  16. If time and money were not concerns, this person would most like
      to learn _____.
  17. In conversations, this person is often _____.
  18. This person's favorite childhood activity was (or might have been)
      _____.
  19. This person often acts this way in a large group: _____.
  20. This person is most likely to laugh at _____.

Worksheet 2: Interest Inventory Responses

Question	My Response	Person 1:	Person 2:	Person 3:
1. Calm				
2. Agitated				
3. Annoyed				
4. Favorite activity				
5. Favorite possession				
6. Public issues				
7. Significant experience				
8. Role model				
9. Personal style				
10. Overlooked quality				
11. Quality others value				
12. Regular hangout				
13. Place to avoid				
14. Music				
15. Vacation				
16. Desired skill				
17. Conversation style				
18. Childhood activity				
19. Large group behavior				
20. What's funny				

The Interest in the Obvious

As you freewrite on the words you have circled on your chart, you may begin to see a trait or favorite activity in a different light. Seeing yourself through the eyes of other people – even using a simple device like the survey worksheet above – can spark respect, interest, and wonder about one's traits and personalities. These lists often lead naturally to questions: What is the reason for a gap in perceptions? Why do others seem to make consistent observations? Although each brain is vast and complex, each person plays a role in various social networks. Wondering about these roles can provide a wealth of information about possible research topics.

As an example, the people who completed worksheets for you might focus on one community or trait – say heavy-metal music – in defining you. You might find it surprising that a simple musical preference dominates the way others see you, and that in the eyes of others, this interest overshadows other interests and preferences. This might cause you to wonder why people have certain perceptions of fans of heavy metal, how these stereotypes are communicated, and what traits are assumed to be a part of this stereotype. In the process of exploring one of these serious questions, you might learn something that relates tangentially or directly to a question in your own life.

Excavating the Obvious

Separating objects from their environment to study them can often make these objects – and their owners – visible in new ways. Taking a random and yet representative sample of any subject matter is one of the mainstays of scientific research. It is equally possible to take a random scoop or sample of stuff from your life in order to gain greater distance from and perspective on your current subject matter: you.

Experiment 2.4: Five Objects

Length: *Take-home preparation; Short in class*
Timer: *4 minutes*
Discuss: *Yes*

Step 1. Choose five objects from your bedroom or the place
where you spend the most time. These should not be strange
objects designed to stump or trick your classmates. Don't
think too much about the selection of the objects. Just
grab what means something to you – instead of something
anonymous like a pen or candy wrapper. Bring these objects
to class and trade your objects with another person.

Step 2. Look at the objects you have received from your partner.
On a piece of paper, complete these responses: (1) Describe
each object in detail; (2) List possible qualities of a person
who owns or cares about these things; and (3) Brainstorm
possible questions inspired by each object.

Step 3. Trade back your responses with your partner, and circle
or underline any questions or responses that surprise you or
that you might not have thought of. Then take four minutes
to list questions for each object that are triggered for you
by your partner's questions and responses.

Making the Familiar Strange

One technique and goal of scientific inquiry is to change perceptions about subject matter in order to create insight and reveal
patterns of information. For example, an archeologist conducting an excavation of a site will set up a grid of strings to divide a
large area of earth into smaller sections. Each smaller section is
then painstakingly excavated, and whatever is found in that area
is tracked by its place in the grid. The grid provides information

about location and also allows the excavation team to proceed carefully from one section to the next. The regular series of squares prompt the excavators to focus on each segment as a separate project, each worthy of the same attention and each a location for potential discoveries. In the same way, taking objects out of the jumble of your environment allows you to focus on them and to see them in a new way. It is easy to take the scenery of life for granted, and sometimes it takes a series of special techniques to make this material visible.

The Gray Matter: What We Don't Want to See

When you go to a job interview, you naturally talk about your positive qualities rather than the biggest mistakes of your life. In some sense, a healthy dose of self-promotion is necessary in a culture that evaluates people on the basis of success and accomplishment while not always rewarding humility or reflection. However, many cultures and subcultures value behavior that others might see as self-denigrating or overly modest. Some communities believe that if a person brags or makes an external display of success, that person is in danger of attracting the "evil eye" (Spiro, 2005: 62). Some religious groups value modesty and believe that a focus on one's accomplishments can lead to vanity.

Depending on your background, you might have well-developed or not-so-developed abilities to see the areas of life that contain room for improvement. This piece of self-awareness, and the muscles required to stay in touch with this view of ourselves, can also generate ideas for inquiry. On the other hand, if you're not used to looking at your own faults, you might be missing an important category of research ideas and even a tool of self-awareness.

Experiment 2.5: Room for Improvement

Length: *Long or Take-home*

Timer: *3 minutes + 4 minutes + 2 minutes + 3 minutes =*
          12 minutes

Discuss: *Optional*

Step 1. Take three minutes to list anything you've heard about
        yourself – once or repeatedly – that seemed to be critical
        or constructively critical. You might focus on your habits,
        the quirks about your behavior that provoke laughter or
        discomfort in others, and the traits, challenges, and prob-
        lems that friends give you advice about.
Step 2. Look at your list and circle one topic that might be true
        for a whole group of people, then do a four-minute freewrite
        on how you might frame this topic as a research question.
        For example, you might tend to date a certain kind of
        partner repeatedly in a pattern that results in predictable
        unhappiness. You might ask yourself what group of people
        engages in this behavior and then phrase the question about
        the causes of this behavior for this group.
Step 3. Now write down one word: the single trait that might
        be your biggest fault. Procrastination? Self-centeredness?
        You might even notice how stressful it is to write that one
        word on paper!
Step 4. Do a two-minute freewrite about this word.
Step 5. Do a three-minute freewrite to turn these associations
        into research questions.
Step 6. Give yourself a pat on the back for delving into an area
        that most people spend a great deal of effort to avoid. You
        may also discuss your findings from Step 5 in small groups
        or as a class.

Conclusion to Chapter 2

It is not easy to challenge and excavate one's self-image; the brain often actively wards off such thoughts in order to create a positive and unified self-image. Skilled researchers know to pay attention to and REFLECT on exactly those uncomfortable and personal feelings – the very stuff you might think is the opposite of empirical research – because those very feelings are often shared by many and connect to some of the biggest dilemmas in life.

As you can see, starting with a specific object, or a specific trait or activity in your life, can often produce a research question that is focused and has some personal connection. The personal connection – the sense of a link between your own experience and your subject matter – adds fuel to the research process as well as motivation to get you through those times when you might find a generic research project a little dull. Another benefit of starting from your own life is that it is also pretty easy to generate interesting and broad questions – including some controversial ones – that nonetheless have a direct connection to you.

So far, you have used material from your life to investigate the gaps between your own knowledge about yourself and the perceptions of others, using those gaps and responses to generate research questions. These questions will have an extra element of creativity because they are specific and because they come from life itself, rather than from a canned list of common research topics. The process of finding answers to these questions may bring excitement rather than anxiety, because the questions themselves are relevant to your life. You can also use your own interests and past to weigh the research you gather, continuously testing your material against your number one case study: your life. Throughout this process, you have begun to see the ways in which good and complex questions relevant to many people are hidden in the cracks and corners of your specific life. You have begun to practice the habit of paying attention to small details or patterns in your life in order to come up with research topics, thus developing the habit of *mindfulness* – the REFLECT step – as a way to generate ideas and to see how large issues and questions are contained in and expressed by small occurrences. The next chapter will help you further develop the art of generating questions from your own life in order to expand and focus your research agenda. By the end of the next chapter, you should have a strong list of research ideas that connect to your interests, background, and concerns – including items in these categories you might never have considered!

Conversation 1 with Benjamin Vogt: Wandering Research

Benjamin Vogt earned his Ph.D. in poetry and creative nonfiction at the University of Nebraska-Lincoln, where he teaches English and serves on the editorial staff of *Prairie Schooner*. He is the author of two poetry chapbooks, *Indelible Marks* (Vogt, 2004) and *Without Such Absence* (Vogt, 2010) as well as a forthcoming full-length collection of poetry. He is writing a memoir on gardening and family. This conversation took place via email.

You're currently working on Morning Glory: A Story of Family and Culture in the Garden, *which is a memoir about your family and gardening. What has been your research process?*

Vogt: There are three steps to the researching process in my mind, at this minute: 1) Obsessing; 2) Collecting or researching the research; 3) Actual research (reading, taking notes, organizing notes, merging notes from various sources). I don't remember what one event or time marked a beginning in my topic for a book – I probably should. But I obsessed because I obsess about everything. This is how I research each piece of material – thoroughly, slowly, deliberately, thoughtfully. I don't like this slow process, but I love what I learn and the new places I end up.

What types of material has this topic led you into? What types of research have you conducted so far?

Vogt: My first piece of research – at least that I'd use a capital "R" with – was the book *Landscape Design: A Cultural and Architectural History*. It's a heavy, oversized mass reminiscent of high school history textbooks football players would use in the weight room. And so many fields feed into landscape design: art, history, agriculture, biology, chemistry, philosophy…. Landscape design is sort of like English: you can do anything with it, bring anything to it, and it takes on new dimensions. I recently read a book entitled *This Sacred Earth: Religion, Nature, Environment* in hopes of gaining some base knowledge of how various religions around the world practice spiritual environmentalism.

I think it's important to start out with vague passion and deep interest, earnest excitement, and genuine hope for a subject. Anything more, and you might cut short the "light bulb" discoveries in research that redefine and refocus the project. That said, later on in researching there are definite questions I needed answered: What is the size of the watershed where my childhood home was located? What plants are native to south central Minnesota? What's the life cycle of ruby-throated hummingbirds? What do Buddhism and Islam have to say about our place in nature? What was my mother's relationship with her father really like?

For me, research includes any visit to my parents to observe family dynamics, but also especially gardening in my yard. At first, I sort of used gardening out back as a crutch, half-heartedly believing its value at the time because I was going through a dry spell in my writing and research – too many other events were distracting me from working. But now, gardening very much is research. It focuses me – how I try to garden sustainably, what native plants I choose for this region, even the physical and psychologically restorative effects it has on me. I have time alone with my thoughts. I end the day with a prayer, which is gardening. It's very much research.

The great aspect – the greatest – about writing is you discover what it is you meant to say, what you really believe in, but didn't know you did. Working on these answers, then, I recall why I decided to write this book, or what tipped the balance for me: my parents were building a new house and set to move in a year or so. I grew up in the house they are leaving. I can tell you where every squeak in the floor is, where the best hiding places are, what each noise is late at night. I was a teenager here – those wonderfully/awfully troubling years are imprinted on those walls and spaces. As I thought about my home, I began to think outside the house and my love for gardening and nature that started in my mom's garden. And they were going to just move? Toss this all away? Would my wife ever see my home, feel it like I did? Would my kids relish life in these bright rooms some day? So, maybe writing this book (and keep in mind research is also writing, perhaps the writing) was an act of sentimental posterity.

But it's changed since then for two reasons: I'm beginning to be forced to know my mom in new ways that are hard (but very good) for an introvert like me, and I've now begun my own large garden, which feeds into the credibility of what I'm saying about nature and gardens and ecology and environmentalism and religion and…. I will never then be able to research all I'd like to, but since the book is a story about my evolving/fluid relationship with my mother, I won't have to, either. That's what keeps it interesting for others to read: learning new things (research) while being engrossed in, I hope, a good story propelled and focused by the research.

Could you describe your research process?

Vogt: I think I have a slow, far too methodical research system that's also too messy. As I'm reading, I take down short notes on a separate piece of paper. Occasionally, I'll also write in the books I own. After I'm done reading, I'll go to the computer and read through the notes one at a time, and refer back to the page in the book, seeing if that's really something I might find useful or interesting. Then I'll type up either the quick glob of information, my reflection, or a direct quote that I feel I might use when writing. The quote is the biggie; the very last thing I want is to be writing and have to stop to find a strong quote in the book, and I sure won't do it later while editing – I'll have lost the organic moment while writing, I need the quote now, ASAP. I'll also do this process for online articles I've read or any other source, and eventually read through all my notes again and try to consolidate them into outlined topics or subjects before I settle down to write. I find that this does one huge positive thing for me: makes me remember, so that when I'm writing I know what I want to say and where it was, and won't have to stop the writing process for as long.

I can't write fast enough, I lose ideas faster than I can write, so I don't need to be organizing my notes while writing. I want to come into writing with as much authority and confidence and knowledge as possible, not because I have an inferiority complex, but because I'll be able to write faster and be able to follow new thoughts more richly.

The only times I felt over my head, which is good – it means I've got something to write about – is when I'd Google a topic or went to Amazon (I love researching there) and saved about 20 books I thought would be interesting or helpful; that's a problem, as I only need a few. I've bought more used books than I need. I've been to more presentations then I can count. I've typed up more notes than I need (three times the length of my book manuscript). I'm in way over my head. I love it!

How will you know when you have enough material?

Vogt: Research never ends, but I think at some point the act of reading material can finally be overkill, a crutch for the fear of writing, even though every new article adds to your knowledge and focus and excitement, and even gives you new ideas for chapters. Eventually, I've noticed, the research gets circular – talking about the same things in only a slightly different way, research informing research instead of your own writing; that's when you know it's time to stop, have faith, and just write.

What are the most important misconceptions or mistakes made in thinking about research?

Vogt: Can I use a list form? It helps me think sometimes, and sort of resembles outlines I make for essays.

1. Thinking too hard before doing. As Yoda says, "Don't try, do." (I love *Star Wars*). Focus comes from research. You need that focus to begin the essay, where you can then spin off into a hundred different things if you'd like.
2. That every source has to be super-academic, and thus stuffy and stilted.
3. That every source should be a statistic. (47 percent of writers believe this!)
4. That every source can be a song lyric or a quote from some anthology o' quotes or something you heard a stranger say at the bar.
5. Research is boring, awful, excruciating, physically painful, of no worth to your life or anyone else's.

So many times a student will be reading her paper in a workshop group, and at the end, someone will say something like, "That quote on page two was incredible – I didn't know about that, had never thought about this before, it made your essay, and now I want to go read that book." Yes!

3 Areas of Expertise: Using What You Already Know

> *Research is a creative process. And just like other creative pro-cesses, research gets hampered when we close down its possibili-ties, narrow too much our definitions.*
>
> – Bill Roorbach, *Writing Life Stories*
> (Roorbach, 1998: 107)

Introduction to Chapter 3

This chapter will focus on you as an expert. Even if you haven't mastered arc-welding, solo mountaineering, or French cooking, you might discover that your low-key and everyday activities contain fascinating questions. Who would care, you ask, that you're a master hedge-clipper or maybe the queen of the perfect grilled cheese sandwich? For now, let's set the bar low and assume that if you've developed a skill, there's a reason for it and it means something. As you have developed this skill, you have collected information and experiences that give you a sort of databank to draw on as you examine your life for possible research questions. Assume that your skills have meaning and that they will reveal the seeds of questions to research. All you have to do is to reflect and experiment with framing these skills in a new way.

Experience – in all its sensory detail and the richness of memory and physical experience – provides complex and fascinating data for analysis. Each experience, because it is shaped by history and circumstances and personalities, can defy, shape, and challenge your expectations. Take one simple activity that you enjoy for the purposes of relaxation, and you will see how complex this activity becomes when you consider all the data you have gathered through your experiences.

As an example, maybe in real life you occasionally enjoy zoning out and reading fashion magazines. First, consider any skills that are required in subscribing to and reading a glossy woman's magazine. That sounds like a joke, right? But let's stick with it for a second. What about: the ability to look at a haute couture dress with a price tag of $3,970 and mentally piece together a similar outfit from ingredients found at the thrift store and your boyfriend's closet? Or maybe your skill is that you somehow don't get envious looking at these jet-set women and their purchasing power. Your research question might be: What exactly do women get from reading these magazines? Is there something going on that is more complicated than envy and self-hatred? Maybe looking at those aching feet in stiletto heels and the made-up faces helps you realize that you're happier wearing tennis shoes to work.

Now this is starting to get interesting, and you might pay attention to yourself as you read a magazine like this – maybe noticing annoyance as you page through the ads with the women looking slightly emaciated, their shoulders hunched over in a weird posture that makes their chests seem to cave in. Why do the poses look similar, and where does that look come from? What's with the dark circles painted around the eyes of the models, and how does "heroin chic" get to be chic, anyway?

As another example, let's take something as simple as sleep. Everybody does it, and if you can fall asleep anywhere, you might even claim to be a nap expert. Yet once you start looking at this simple process in terms of what it adds to your life and what it takes away, you might be amazed at sleep's complexity. You might ask about dreams and their necessity for waking sanity or the interpretation of dreams in different cultures. You might use your own experiences as a trigger for questions: If you find yourself waking up tired the morning, or consistently waking up at 2 a.m. to worry, you might wonder how common these phenomena are, and you might look into causes and solutions. Do you find yourself wanting a nap each afternoon around 4 p.m.? If so, should you nap or stay awake, and what might be the causes of your afternoon weariness? Does your significant other complain about your snoring – and if so, what is the cause of a snore? Is it merely annoying or a threat to your health?

Many productive research topics start with a question far removed from the researcher's day-to-day existence. Those are wonderful research ideas, but in neglecting life experience, it is easy to overlook the material you have already been researching in a sense through your own life. A challenge to look at your own life can produce topics and questions that connect your interests with larger issues, subjects, and contexts.

Experiment 3.1: Activities and Questions

Length: *Long or Take-home*
Timer: *None*
Discuss: *Optional*

Step 1. Start by drawing two lines down the middle of a page in your notebook, creating a total of three columns. Label the left-hand column *Activity*, the middle column *Skills & Abilities*, and the right-hand column *Questions*.

Step 2. In the left-hand column, list your hobbies, no matter how significant or minor they might be, with one entry per line. If you don't feel like you have hobbies, list any activity you do to unwind or relax.

Step 3. Now add to that list anything else that you've done in the past week that gave you a feeling of satisfaction or pleasure.

Step 4. Now move to the middle column. For each entry on the left, list the skills required for or developed by this activity. If you do yoga, for example, flexibility is probably a skill or activity that corresponds to that activity. A second skill might be the ability to be patient with yourself as you gradually improve. A third skill might be the understanding and experience that breathing is an important part of the exercises.

Step 5. Now comes the fun part – the questions. Using the skills and abilities column as a way to focus on the specific action involved, generate something you don't know about each activity and write at least one general question in the third column for each activity.

No Such Thing as a Stupid Question

As you formulate questions, you will become gradually more skilled at spotting the habitual hiding places of research topics. Many researchers have a mental list of categories they ask themselves in order to generate questions. Often, these lists are not consciously articulated by a writer or researcher; instead, they are a way to break apart a topic into components. Each writer's method for doing this will emerge from his or her specific values, interests, and past experiences.

Through REFLECTION and observing my own writing and research process, I have found that I tend to examine a topic by asking the types of questions influenced by my interests and training in areas of anthropology, sociology, and ecology. My framework for questions falls roughly into these categories:

1. Origins of the activity
2. Process of doing the activity

3. Goal of the activity
4. Intended and unintended side-effects of the activity – on families, on communities, on the natural and built environment, on other activities
5. People who practice the activity around the world
6. Communities who practice the activities around the world

If you are using yoga as an example, you might use the list above to generate questions like this:

1. Origins of the activity
   - When and where did the practice of yoga emerge?
   - How did it develop?
   - How did it become popular in this country?
   - Who are the major people who introduced yoga practice to this country or this region?
2. Process of doing the activity
   - How do you know you're doing the yoga pose "downward dog" correctly?
   - What might be the unintentional side effects of doing this pose incorrectly?
3. Goals and outcomes of the activity
   - Are there different philosophies about the goal of yoga?
   - Was it originally intended to be for the purposes of health and relaxation, or for spiritual development?
   - Are these two goals complementary?
   - How long does it take for the positive effects of yoga to manifest, and how long do these effects last?
   - Do these positive effects continue after a person has stopped doing yoga regularly?
4. Intended and unintended side effects of the activity – on families, on communities, on the natural and built environment, on other activities
   - What health benefits have been observed in yoga practitioners?

- Does yoga have a positive impact on emotional or psychological issues, or on the immune system and the ability to ward off illness?
- Does a long-term yoga practitioner have any health side effects to worry about, such as wear and tear on the joints?

5. People who practice the activity around the world
   - What do individual yoga practitioners say and believe about how this practice affects their well-being and their lives?
   - How do they fit yoga practice into their schedule?
   - How does it intersect with and influence other areas of their lives?
   - What distinguishes the short-term yoga practitioner who abandons a yoga practice from one who maintains it?

6. Communities who practice the activities around the world
   - What communities have adopted and embraced yoga, and what are reasons for resistance to it in other communities?
   - What regions of the world show highest and lowest concentration of yoga practitioners and why?
   - How has this configuration changed over time?
   - What socioeconomic groups tend to practice yoga and why?
   - How do stereotypes about yoga practitioners inhibit the spread of the practice?
   - How are stereotypes about this group maintained and spread?

For more practice with this REFLECTION skill of breaking down activities into components, you might continue the "Activities and Questions" Experiment in this chapter or return to the material that emerged in your *Interest Inventory* in Chapter 2. Look at your lists of favorite or habitual activities and try to come up with at least one question for every activity. If one topic seems particularly fascinating, take a whole page and list as many questions as you can. Pay attention to those moments where you're writing small to fit all of your questions in, or curving your sentence onto the margin of the page. That's a signal that you might be onto something that interests you.

Nothing to Brag About

It's likely that you also have skills in subject areas that don't seem especially valuable to you. One of my colleagues calls this process "inadvertent skill acquisition": You may know how to do things that are not hobbies or ways to relax. Instead, you may have developed these skills without ever enjoying the activity or without even paying much attention to the activity. These unseen or even unwanted skills are some of the most interesting topic areas because they can also help you develop a picture of yourself as you function in your daily life.

Paid employment is a great category for these types of explorations. Consider this example, which is taken from the book, *Work as a Spiritual Practice* (Richmond, 1999), about a box-packer named Johnny who worked at a warehouse. Johnny was able to:

> laugh, talk, listen to the radio, fool around, and all the while his hands shaped the box, laid in the goods, wrapped the tape, sealed and stapled, without a miss. He rarely had to back up and do anything twice. Even in the way he laid down the stapler he had a strategy…. Johnny knew instinctively what many artists, athletes, and craftspeople carefully cultivate, a balance between paying attention and letting attention go. (Richmond, 1999: 41)

There are many different definitions of the words *efficient* and *productive*, depending on the values and priorities of the person performing or managing the action. My definition of *productive time on a research activity* might include an hour-long walk in which I don't crack a book or take notes on anything. Yet according to my definitions, reflection is productive productive. A walk, therefore, in allowing me time for reflection, fits into the category of productive work. Both *productive* and *efficient* are value-laden words defined by your ultimate goals. Johnny, by the way, ended up with the highest productivity scores for box-packing, but he never looked like he was breaking a sweat. So appearances can be deceptive, and some of those things you or others miss about yourself and your aptitudes may be the things you accomplish with most proficiency. Since we tend to take our own experiences and skills for granted precisely because they become invisible to us, REFLECTION on our activities is necessary in order to reveal what we know but don't consciously <u>know</u> that we know.

For the next exercise, you will create a three-column grid on a piece of paper to list the skills you have that might be annoying, taken for granted, or just not particularly exciting. Maybe your list of activities includes: avoiding housework, making jokes at serious times, and composing an outfit in two minutes. Part of the challenge is to identify the actual skill that comes with each activity. For example, what skill could possibly help to produce and support the general activity of avoiding housework? If you break this general state of being down into its components, it's clear that one requirement is the ability to either ignore or accept clutter: the skill of looking at a sink full of dirty dishes and not feeling particularly bothered by the mess. You might argue that possible skills involved in this activity are: the ability to accept mess and not be disgusted by rotting food, the ability to use one dish and one pot to make a meal because all the rest are dirty, or the ability to distract yourself so you don't feel bad about the mess in the sink. These might seem to be hair-splitting ways to enable a slob or a shirker to build a resume, but the deeper function of analyzing these activities is to generate questions. Why exactly do young people living on their own for the first time so often avoid washing the dishes? Is it because they are lazy, because they are rebelling against the expectations of house-cleaning they saw at home, or because they always had their dishes washed for them and therefore honestly don't know how to wash dishes? Is the downfall a lack of dish-washing routine, or are there positive elements about avoiding housework? Does the need to make a mess eventually prompt a young person to discover for himself or herself which types of mess are acceptable or comfortable and which are not?

Experiment 3.2: Catalogue the Unseen Skills

Length: *Long or Take-home*
Timer: *3 minutes + reflection*
Discuss: *Optional*

Step 1. Draw another three-column grid and again label the columns *Activity, Skills & Abilities*, and *Questions*. Now take three minutes to list general types of boring activities you have participated in. Maybe these happen every day, or maybe they happened at a certain time in your life.

Step 2. Take as much time as you need for brainstorming the skills you have developed for dealing with each of these challenging, annoying, or boring situations. For example, what skills have you developed for dealing with work tasks? With people who annoy you or test your patience in some way? With chores? With making major life decisions? Are you good at looking busy? At keeping a straight face?

Step 3. Now add to your list of activities and skills by writing down the things you do that aren't necessary or productive. Can you tie a cherry stem into a knot with your tongue? Do any magic tricks? Remember every joke that's been told to you? Although it might seem difficult at first, identify a specific skill that is developed or required for each of these activities. Honing in on the skill is what helps to see this activity in a new light and connect it to other activities. For example, maybe you come up with inappropriate one-line jokes in response to items on a meeting agenda or a course assignment. There's something about the seriousness of a meeting or class that might bring out your sense of humor. A possible skill here might be "Breaking workplace tension."

Step 4. Look back at your results from Experiment 2.3 in Chapter 2, in which friends and family members completed the survey about you. Did someone say you're good at managing your time or solving problems? What specific skills might be involved with these general activities?

Step 5. Now come with at least one question for each set of skills and abilities. If, for example, your activity is "dressing for work or school in two minutes" and your skill is "finding the minimum acceptable clothing to meet any dress code," you might ask questions like, "How have school dress codes changed over time? How do instructors' appearances affect student clothing choices? Do student clothing choices affect learning outcomes? Why do certain students dress up and others dress down, and how are these choices related to the student's social class, ethnicity, or size of the students' town or city?"

The Gray Matter: Decisions as Experience

Although the first part of this chapter focused on common and everyday experiences, single and significant events can also provide fodder for research. In terms of significant life experiences, you probably have so much material that it can be difficult to know where to start. To narrow down the wide range of material your life presents, let's start with ethical dilemmas and difficult decisions as examples of complex experience in your own life.

Tough Choices as Research Questions

An open-topic research assignment often immediately evokes questions drawn from the most polarized and visible debates that grip our culture or society. Although these topics provide the stuff of conversation and debate in the news and among friends, framing these topics as research is somewhat challenging. One of the disadvantages of choosing a hot topic from the daily headlines is that the topic often comes packaged in our minds with two or three simplified positions on the issue: are you "pro" or "anti," "yes" or "no"? This common framework for discussing public issues is grounded on the idea of opposing viewpoints, in which two positions are built as if they were competing to win a debate competition. In a formal debate, the differences between the positions are sharpened until there is very little middle ground. Judges award points to teams whose members can dismiss or refute the opposing side's arguments. Although debates develop skills of logical thinking and building support for an argument, complexity can be pushed aside as attention is focused on areas of disagreement.

In real life, in contrast, there are no judges awarding points for rhetorical skill. Very few issues – especially those that are interesting, complex, and involve the lives of real people – can be broken into two neat pieces. If you have lived through an experience that is in some way connected to a major debate, you might have found that it is difficult to communicate your own experience without reference to these major and polarized viewpoints. If you have a family member who is the victim of a violent crime, for example, it might be assumed that you have strong and clear feelings about how the perpetrator should be treated. In real life, your feelings probably often don't fit into neat boxes, especially after you've lived through something and become aware of all the complexities.

A little brainstorming about real-life ethical dilemmas can reveal good, complex questions. These quandaries need not be huge or headline-making, but the choices and reasons for your choices will most likely connect to larger debates – because it is likely that others have faced the same decision. Maybe, as one example, you wrestled with what to do when you saw a classmate blatantly cheating on an exam. Or maybe you accepted a summer job and told your bosses that you weren't going back to school, knowing full well that you would be gone by August. In each case, your personal experience was probably repeated by others, and the behavior raises questions connected to large public issues.

Experiment 3.3: Choices, Choices, Choices

Length: *Long or Take-home*
Timer: *3 minutes + reflection*
Discuss: *Optional*

Step 1. In three minutes, list the ethical dilemmas or challenging choices you have confronted, either in the last few years or over a longer period of time. Focus on those moments where you were actually stymied, those big questions you faced and those times you had to ask for outside advice, or when you made first one decision and then changed your mind. For example, you might have faced a dilemma regarding a friend who was regularly plagiarizing assignments for a class. This might have been a bothersome concern that irritated you, but you might not have felt compelled to get involved in an active way until you were confronted with a specific situation: the friend asked you for your research paper from History class last semester and offered to give you $100 for selling it to his friend.

Step 2. Look over your list and circle the questions or phrases that are appropriate or interesting for further research. Feel free to skip over topics and questions that might be too personal or too confusing to turn into research at this moment.

Step 3. Draw a new three-column grid, with the headings of *Decision or Dilemma, Deciding Factor*, and *Questions*.

Since you might not have developed a practiced skill for dealing with such a rare dilemma, focus instead on your decision-making process. Write your list of decisions or dilemmas from Step 2 in the first column. For example, in considering the plagiarism situation, the decision or dilemma would be whether or not to sell the research paper.

Step 4. In the second column, list an element, person, or moment that helped you face and make each big decision. For example, maybe you talked the problem over with a trusted friend who shared a new way of seeing the situation and put your mind at ease. Or maybe you saw that despite your misgivings, a decision had to be made – and one consequence in one direction began to seem like the most important or most prominent factor. In the plagiarism example, add a significant wrinkle: you need $100 because your car is in the shop. If you don't fix the car, you can't get to class. You might be tempted to sell the paper with the argument that you had no choice and needed the money. After talking it over with your best friend, however, you might decide that selling the paper actually decreases the worth of your own grades, which you're working for honestly. So you decide to get a ride with a friend to campus and pick up an extra few shifts at work to cover the car repair. The deciding factor for you in this example would be the long-term consequences of plagiarism for your own education; plagiarism downgrades the value of everyone's education and hard work if anyone can buy a diploma or a grade.

Step 5. Now see if you can turn each of these deciding factors into a general research question. You might ask, for example, what motivates students who decide not to plagiarize? What are the ethical arguments in favor of plagiarism? How do students and other people who run plagiarism businesses and research paper mills defend their actions, and what arguments do they construct to do so?

Choices and Outcomes

Turning an ethical dilemma into a research question allows you to see how real-life complexity points toward research complexity. The plagiarism example raises many issues beyond the simplistic question of whether it is right or wrong in an absolute sense. Evaluating an issue around a question of right or wrong requires a reference to a specific set of values, so a research project on that topic can really only outline the opposing viewpoints. A research question that emerged out of *reflection* and personal experience, in contrast, can reveal connections and complications: What happens to the students who plagiarize? Has anyone done a study about whether getting caught plagiarizing caused a significant change in behavior or values? Do plagiarists continue to plagiarize even if they have received warnings and consequences? What about the consistent presence of high-profile plagiarists in the headlines – did these people get off easy early in life with previous plagiarism charges? Are there qualities of a plagiarism judicial process that provide greater or fewer learning opportunities for the student, and what is actually learned?

Outlining your own values is important, but a statement of values and idealized behaviors usually glosses over the important gray area that led to the ethical dilemma. Ignoring the complexity means side-stepping all of the fascinating and real-life questions that lead people to act the way they do.

Conclusion to Chapter 3

Chapters 1, 2, and 3 prompted you to develop a long list of personal experiences and a beginning list of possible research topics. You may have noticed that a key to exploring these topics is to momentarily RELAX and not worry at all about such questions as "Will this get me enough information for a research paper?" Relaxing your focus on the outcome of the research assignment is not actually a suspension of analytic thought or a rejection of intellectual activity. Instead, focusing on personal experiences, interests, and memories allows you to create a *process-driven* research agenda in which you see questions emerge from these experiences, interests, and memories by using the process of REFLECTION. The ability to relax expectations about outcomes is a mind-tool, and reflection is another mind-tool for re-seeing with the help of analytic frameworks such as the grids you completed in the various experiments.

Now that you have examined a wide range of personal experiences and skills, you will move beyond these in the next chapter to build the questioning muscle that you began to work with in the Experiments. You will continue to use a combination of the RELAXATION mode of thought to create space between a practical issue and its constraints – its connection to your life or the requirements of a specific research assignment. You will then gain experience in additional REFLECTION techniques to generate questions about this topic, which will lead to complex and focused questions for research.

As you continue with this process, you might imagine yourself as an apprentice Questioner in order to appreciate the new range of skills you are developing. You might imagine the Questioner as a person who goes through life generating good research questions every day, noticing and confronting everything that seems confusing or interesting. The Questioner uses awareness to see moments of personal confusion as signals for future research projects. In that way, confusion is a vital tool for every experienced researcher and an essential part of the research process.

4　Living and Loving the Questions

Have patience with everything unresolved in your heart and try to love **the questions themselves** *as if they were locked rooms or books written in a very foreign language.*
　　　　　　　　– Rainer Maria Rilke, *Letters to a Young Poet*
　　　　　　　　　　　　　　　　　　　　(Rilke, 2001: 34)

Introduction to Chapter 4

A serious question can be annoying or even maddening. Questions can trigger anxiety along with the uneasy sense that life is an essay test without any study notes: "What am I going to do with my life? Will Person X or Y ever go out with me? Why is Person Z such a pest or a mess?"

The poet Rainer Maria Rilke, in the quote at the beginning of the chapter, encourages a young friend to "love the questions," but developing affection for life dilemmas is a long-term goal. Part of what he means is that each serious question is like a valuable seed, holding the potential for much change and redirection. The questions can be frustrating because the answers are unknown, but their value comes from their potential and also the focus they provide. In this chapter, you will brainstorm a list of the itchy, up-in-the-air, nagging questions that wake you up at night or make you wince or sigh – with the ultimate goal of using these questions for research.

Rilke urges his young friend to see a persistent question as a window of opportunity. Rilke realized that this might require a shift in perspective; the normal view is to see a question as a task to complete or even as akin to failure. Many cultures place a high value on certainty and confidence. Depending on your background and your role models, you might be conditioned to believe that asking a question is a sign of ignorance. Parker Palmer writes that students and teachers are sometimes "afraid of failing, of not understanding, of being drawn into issues they would rather avoid, of having their ignorance exposed or their prejudices challenged, of looking foolish in front of their peers" (Palmer 1998: 37). Our question-asking abilities are influenced by our views about questions themselves and by our ability to be vulnerable, to make mistakes, and to admit to not knowing everything. The next freewrite will help you to investigate your assumptions about the questions and the questioners who ask them.

Experiment 4.1: Questions and Questioners

Length: *Short*
Timer: *2 minutes + 3 minutes*
Discuss: *Optional*

Step 1. In your notebook, write the phrase "The Person Who Asks Questions." Then take two or three minutes to write every thought, sentence, word, or association triggered by that phrase.

Step 2. Look back at your freewrite and circle the adjectives that seem most vivid or that are repeated more than once.

Step 3. Write for three minutes on your findings and connect your assumptions to your own behavior. Are you a questioner? Or do you shut down the question-asking ability in yourself in response to messages from around you or within you about the value of questioning?

Questions in a Culture of Answers

Did you write about a friend who asks prying questions? Or a peer in class who asks questions the instructor has just covered in a lecture? Like any other expression or communication, questions can be honest or self-serving, inane or insightful.

Maybe you wrote about a childhood memory: the annoyance or confusion on your parents' faces as you pestered them with questions like "Why is the sky blue?" or "Why can't I paint the cat?" If you have spent any time around young children, you know how difficult it can be to answer these questions. Some require a background in optics and physics, and others require ethics discussions about our relationship with animals. By the time you have formulated a simple and clear answer, the child has already run outside to play or the child's cat has already been thrown in the bath. Some questions are challenging because they require justification for automatic behavior, uncover explanation for hidden assumptions or stereotypes, or threaten to expose choices and actions that are illogical.

Questions slow things down and can be seen as an annoyance in a culture that values productivity and task completion. Pausing to ask why or how can also be seen as a fruitless departure into abstraction. Some researchers know that as they start asking questions, they will feel an internal kick of anxiety, like a reflex acknowledging that they are going against the grain and challenging taken-for-granted assumptions. Others even learn to take this kick of anxiety as a sign that they are moving in the right direction. They learn to follow the feelings of confusion, to love the questions themselves.

Using Questions to Generate Research Ideas

To start this phase of your research planning, focus on the feeling of confusion that most people find easy to access. Sit quietly for a minute or two and guide your mind toward one or more subjects that make your stomach churn. For you it might be the practical question of finding a new apartment or paying off a credit card, or a personal challenge like getting more exercise or dealing with a health condition. Now focus on one of those topics. If you imagine the anxiety as the outer layer that surrounds each topic, you can picture the knot of questions and dilemmas as the core of each topic. For many people, the topic itself might not cause much anxiety. The fear is often caused by all of those swarming, looping questions. The sheer number of unanswered dilemmas – each with more than one right answer – can be overwhelming.

To turn confusion into research material, first separate the strands or themes into specific questions. For example, you might start with a feeling of anxiety about a stray dog that showed up on your doorstep. Before listing your questions, you might have a clear experience of frustration, the mixture of stress that comes from adding a new and unpredictable element into your life.

As the saying goes, identifying the problem is the first step toward a solution. If you give yourself the task of listing specific questions, you might ask: How much will the vet bill cost if I keep the dog? Is my landlord going to evict me? How big is she going to get? And so on. Even phrasing them as questions can result in a new way of looking at a problem and can even indicate steps to a solution.

Your first impulse may be to see this dog as a hassle – even if she is cute. You might then challenge yourself to see the situation in a way that opposes your first instincts, and generate questions based on experience. You might wonder whether it is accurate that pet owners have lower blood pressure or research the use of therapy dogs in hospitals. You might research dog breeding or ask yourself why humans bond with dogs at such an emotional level.

Since the new dog is not a global problem, she might not seem like a very good source for controversial or challenging research ideas. But research ideas also come from taking your own situation and imagining who else it might affect. How many dogs are abandoned in college towns when their student owners move or can't take care of them? Have spay-and-neuter public awareness campaigns made any difference in the number of strays?

Thinking about pets and the costs of their upkeep might then bring you to another issue – maybe it's a statistic that the United States spends more on pet food than on children's healthcare. You might wonder where you heard that and ask whether this is urban legend or exaggeration. In trolling the Internet to answer that question, you might find the mention of pet food expenditures topping $17 billion in 1998, as compared to the amount required to vaccinate every child in the developing world, $7.5 billion (World Health Organization, 2009).

And all of these questions come from one stray dog.

Experiment 4.2: Questions without Answers

Length: *Long or Take-home*

Timer: *4 minutes + 3 minutes + 3 minutes + 3 minutes + 3 minutes = 16 minutes*

Discuss: *Optional*

Step 1. Do a four-minute freewrite about all to the questions you wish you had an answer to. This can include those hypothetical questions that would require sorcery or super powers to reveal (When will I die? Why were we born? Am I a good or a good-enough daughter or son?) and those urgent, mundane, or embarrassing questions that honestly plague you (Why am I such a bad cook? Is it possible to stop drinking so much coffee?).

Step 2. Choose one question or topic and take three minutes to list specific questions that emerge from that topic. As an example, let's assume you do not enjoy cooking and wonder why that is the case. Starting with life experience, you might reflect on the fact that your mother cooked many fantastic meals but also, as a working mother, created her share of instant dinners and box meals. You might wonder whether children of working mothers have a penchant for packaged meals that became popular as more women entered the workforce? Other questions: Is fear of killing someone with undercooked meat a neurosis? Do you not enjoy cooking because of the memory of cooking failures, or because family members don't like your favorite foods? How does the culture of recreational cooking – with celebrity cooking shows and extreme cook-off battles – affect the person who doesn't care about cooking?

Step 3. Highlight or underline the sentences and phrases that could immediately be used as research questions. Then circle the phrases that could easily be turned into a research question with a bit of tweaking. For example, if you dislike cooking because you are afraid of undercooked meat, you could easily turn this into a series of questions about the practical dangers and incidence of these situations in home cooking.

Step 4. Go back and choose two additional "questions without answers" from Step 1 and then repeat Steps 2 and 3.

What Makes a Good Question?

Some of these questions will be more satisfying than others as research projects. A whole research project on what happens to someone when they eat undercooked meat might make you nauseous. But maybe you could turn this concern into a project you really would enjoy, such as the practical reasons for vegetarianism

among those with culinary challenges. Or you could research traditional food-preparation practices in various cultures that prevent
food poisoning.

As you generate questions, be aware that some are more suitable
for truly engaging projects. If your question is phrased in a way
that asks for a true-or-false or multiple-choice answer, you will
probably be tempted to locate facts in an encyclopedia and stop
when you've gotten your results. Questions like "Which state is
most famous for excellent barbeque?" or "Does sex education lead
to a lower rate of teen pregnancy?" often have a fill-in-the-blank
type of answer, and as you try to answer them, you might move
away from the complexity in those topics. The complexity might
come in when you see that people disagree about <u>how</u> to answer
the question and what criteria to use in coming up with an answer.
Another way to head toward complexity is to ask for solutions and
origins, causes and effects; so you might ask, "What programs and
classes have been found to cause lower rates in teen pregnancy?"
or "How might a person evaluate excellent barbeque?'"

A Healthy Dose of Skepticism

To get your questions still more complicated and yet more interesting, you might aim for the point of *maximum conflict*. Reporters use
this skill to hone in on dramatic story angles, a sort of go-for-the-
jugular, sling-from-the-hip story idea generator. Reporters tend to
develop their sense of what is news by analyzing the day's events
with equal parts skepticism and curiosity. Curiosity is half art and
half habit, and you can consciously stoke that skill throughout
this guide. Skepticism, however, is the doubting – and sometimes
paranoid – cousin of curiosity.

For example, if someone makes a claim ("I've invented an air-
powered car!"), the skeptic's first response is to go for the weak
points and problems in this statement, which might target concerns
about a person's self-interest, the truthfulness of the claim, and any

possible hidden agenda. Using the example of an air-powered car, you might wonder whether this person was truly the first, whether an air-powered car can be useful on the highway and compete with gas-powered vehicles, and which individuals or organizations funded this person's research. What does this person stand to gain from this discovery, and what might be the negative side-effects of introducing air vehicles into the marketplace?

If you already have a healthy sense that the world might be out to get you, skepticism can be your best friend in generating research ideas. From a skeptic's perspective, the question about why you don't enjoy cooking might lead you to many research questions. If you are a woman, you might wonder how many women share the "hate-to-cook" guilt. How much of a role does gender socialization play in these concerns? How do the makers of toy kitchen sets and instant dinners capitalize on this guilt to sell their products? What other social forces contribute to this guilt and perpetuate it?

Adding Fuel to the Fire

As if your own initial and pressing dilemmas weren't enough, many additional questions can be generated based on some standard categories for viewing and analyzing your life. These are questions that might not necessarily be on your "need-to-know" list, but generating questions is a skill that improves with practice. Brainstorming the non-urgent questions can help you see beyond the immediate concerns into your patterns of interest and areas for potential research that you had not even acknowledged.

Experiment 4.3: Two Hundred Questions

Length: *Take-home*
Timer: *None*
Discuss: *Optional*

The twenty categories below are each described with a few triggering questions and phrases to get you started, but your goal is to list any question that occurs to you that is connected to the topic. You might notice that if one good question emerges, others will follow and branch off from that starting point. The key to this activity is not to worry about whether or not you are generating good questions. Simply ask, and in the process of brainstorming and building your comfort with this skill, you will no doubt come up with a few (or more) excellent questions.

Since this list is quite extensive, you might want to allow at least a week to complete it. You can also break this list up and complete it over the course of a few weeks, or have a class work on sections of the list and pool your findings after completing your work. However, it's a fascinating challenge to see how many of these you can complete on your own, and you might surprise yourself.

1. The Body and Mind

What questions do you have about how the mind works? What is intuition? How does the heart function? What has recent research revealed about the function of dreams? Is there a cure for diabetes?

1.
2.
3.
4.
5.
6.
7.
8.
9.
10.

2. Family

What questions do you have about your family history? What do you wonder about a friend's family history? Why did a family member make a certain choice or pursue a certain line of work? How did your family's ethnic background affect the lives of individual family members and the choices they made?

1.
2.
3.
4.
5.
6.
7.
8.
9.
10.

3. Memory

What significant memories in your life connect to unresolved or interesting questions? Do you have a family event that members of your family remember in different ways? What other questions do you have about how memory works or what you remember and don't remember?

1.
2.
3.
4.
5.
6.
7.
8.
9.
10.

4. Friends

Which of your friends have interesting skills, traits, habits and backgrounds, and how can you turn these into research questions? Which of your friends' jobs or areas of study would you like to know more about? How have your friendships influenced you? How do friendships change over time?

1.
2.
3.
4.
5.
6.
7.
8.
9.
10.

5. Land & Geography

What can you ask about the land or geography of the place where you grew up? Where you live now? What geography or landscapes are you attracted to and repelled by, and why? What landscape changes, land uses, and particular areas of land are most interesting to you, and how can these trigger research ideas? What displaced population or immigrant community has always sparked your interest, and what might you ask about that group?

1.
2.
3.
4.
5.
6.
7.
8.

9.

10.

6. Objects

What objects are most significant in your life, and where do these objects come from? How were they designed and made, and how has their construction changed over time? Who buys these kinds of objects, and what is spent on them? What are the benefits and drawbacks of these objects for people who use them? What are the political and cultural meanings and social importance of these objects?

1.

2.

3.

4.

5.

6.

7.

8.

9.

10.

7. Origins

What habits, practices, or social groups mystify or interest you? Where do these subcultures come from, and who is a part of these institutions? What art forms, types of music, political groups, technological innovations, folk practices, or business innovations have you wondered about?

1.

2.

3.

4.

5.

6.
7.
8.
9.
10.

8. No-Such-Thing-as-a-Dumb-Question

If you can list ten questions that you might worry are "dumb," then you can give yourself an A+ for developing the skill of questioning your internal critic.

1.
2.
3.
4.
5.
6.
7.
8.
9.
10.

9. Overheard

If you open your ears for a week, you will hear at least ten good research ideas through eavesdropping – like a woman I heard in a local coffee shop who asked for a quadruple espresso shot and told the clerk that the caffeine was the only thing that straightened out her heart palpitations. You might wonder what effect massive doses of caffeine have on the heart, and whether it is possible to treat (or cause) heart rhythm irregularity with caffeine.

1.
2.
3.
4.

   5.
   6.
   7.
   8.
   9.
   10.

10. International

What country do you know the least about? What would you need to learn and do to move to another part of the world? What international conflict have you heard about and pretended to understand? What was the cause or basic background of a current conflict or issue in the headlines? How has a headline-making issue in the world affected daily life or young people in that region? How were major chain restaurants able to spread all over the world? Where do people live who have hobbies similar to yours? How big is the online gaming community in the Netherlands?

   1.
   2.
   3.
   4.
   5.
   6.
   7.
   8.
   9.
   10.

11. Outrageous

List the crazy and un-ask-able questions that you normally would not consider seriously but that might make good research. Who has survived a tornado and what does it feel like? How many circus clowns hate their jobs? If you sneeze with your eyes open, will your eyeballs really fly out of their sockets? Has Walt Disney really been frozen? What happens to bubble gum when you swallow it?

1.
2.
3.
4.
5.
6.
7.
8.
9.
10.

12. Religious

What religious or spiritual practices are you curious about? What conflicts in your own religion have always confused you? What conflict between two faiths or faith communities might spark questions? What effect do religious practices have on the health, lives, and life choices of their members?

1.
2.
3.
4.
5.
6.
7.
8.
9.
10.

13. Practical

Think about the inefficiencies and bothersome tasks in your own life, and wonder about how to optimize or avoid them. Ask about the tasks that people must take care of and how they carry them out and/or avoid them. What happens to your recycled waste, and how efficient are local recycling programs? What is it like to work for a moving company? What do tax accountants do when it's not tax season?

1.
2.
3.
4.
5.
6.
7.
8.
9.
10.

14. Process

Think about the production of any object, performance, or experience that you enjoy. How was it created or produced? What does it take to put on a rock concert in an arena, and how much electricity is used? How is decaffeinated coffee made? How have children's cartoons changed in the last fifty years?

1.
2.
3.
4.
5.
6.
7.
8.
9.
10.

15. Career

What are the costs, concerns, prospects, and challenges for any field of work? Do fast food workers suffer high rates of obesity? What job entails the highest rates of verbal abuse from customers? What are the most important skills needed for becoming a zookeeper? How do elementary school teachers deal with students with behavior problems? Do fortune tellers read their own fortunes, and if not, why not?

1.
2.
3.
4.
5.
6.
7.
8.
9.
10.

16. Future

What future scenarios or predictions alarm you, and why? What looming decision or situation in your future causes you the most anxiety or the most excitement, and what do you wonder about that situation? What do you wonder about the future-planning practices of individuals or institutions? What age is your generation slated to retire, and why? What are the various plans for addressing budget shortfalls for retirees' pensions? Do farmers plan for climate change, and if so, how?

1.
2.
3.
4.
5.
6.

7.
8.
9.
10.

17. Government & Political

Include here any questions you have about local, national, or in-ternational political issues and processes. How has your county decided where and how to develop recreation centers? What issues of corruption have been notable in the recent history of your town, city, or state, and have they been addressed? Why do people run for political office? Why has a certain government risen to power or remained in power for an extended period of time?

1.
2.
3.
4.
5.
6.
7.
8.
9.
10.

18. Historical

Think about periods in history that you might have learned or heard a bit about and that sparked your interest. How was your town or city first established, and what brought people to live at that site? What conflicts or situations affected your current way of life? What local or regional history needs to be documented or is in dispute? What are the historical origins of current celebrations or holidays?

1.

2.

3.

4.

5.

6.

7.

8.

9.

10.

19. Food

What is the origin of something you ate yesterday, and what is its cultural history? What political issues can be connected to that piece of food? Who profits from that piece of food? How has production or marketing of a specific food changed over time? Where did your diet or eating habits come from?

1.

2.

3.

4.

5.

6.

7.

8.

9.

10.

20. Culture & Leisure

Why do certain groups of people enjoy certain leisure activities? What's the role of a particular sport in the life of a community? If nobody reads anymore, how or why are so many books being sold?

1.

2.

3.

4.

5.

6.

7.

8.

9.

10.

After you have completed this exhausting exercise, you might be sick of generating questions for a while. But the positive side-effects of this question blitz might include a temporary or long-lasting ability to see questions everywhere. You might find your brain spontaneously generating other questions out of your daily experience, and you might also discover that you have a storehouse of possible research topics for any future open paper assignment – not only for your English or writing class but also for your other classes as well.

Conclusion to Chapter 4

You may never again want to generate that many questions, but you have hopefully seen that question-asking itself is a type of brainstorming. Once you RELAX the expectation that your first question will be your chosen writing topic, you can loosen up and generate many possible options, then weigh each of them for the degree of interest and the challenge each one poses. You have also seen with this exercise how REFLECTION on your own life experiences – including brief encounters, observations, and the overheard conversations from yesterday or the hobby of your next-door neighbor – can lead to good research questions when you pursue a topic in the direction of your curiosity and the limits of your knowledge. The outcome of your research has everything to do with *your ability to ask a creative question.*

Section II
The Inside Meets the Outside: Paying Attention
as Research

5 Learning to See

Our most important research tool...was our own self; self-observation and self-awareness were not to be suppressed in the work of observing and gaining an understanding of others.
– Deborah Bird Rose in *Extraordinary Anthropology*
(Rose, 2007: 88)

Introduction to Chapter 5

Deborah Bird Rose, an anthropologist who studied and lived with Australian Aboriginal people, learned from her mentor, Jane Goodale, that "good field learning is a whole person experience" (Rose, 2007: 88). As Rose studied and became immersed in life in the Northern Territory of Australia, she found herself developing a close friendship with one of her subjects, a woman named Jessie Wirrpa who was a skilled hunter living in the Victoria River Valley. Although some would view her relationship with Wirrpa as less than objective, Rose describes Wirrpa as a "teacher and friend" rather than just an interview subject or informant. As Rose observes her findings in the field, she also relates the changes that occurred in her own life as the result of this entanglement. She proposes that, in general, the web of relationships surrounding research is an ethical requirement that leads to creation of knowledge. Rose's research findings grow directly from her awareness of her own reactions, attitudes, instincts, feelings, entanglements, and judgments.

As Rose describes it, the researcher's self-awareness is an essential element of knowledge creation. But paying attention to personal reactions and thoughts while engaging in research is no simple feat; it requires essentially a double focus, outside as well as inside. In that spirit, some simple exercises will get you primed for collecting some inner research – with the ultimate goal of making you a much more savvy, productive, thoughtful, and original researcher. The first task is to practice separating observations from judgments in order to collect more data and information from the world and to pay closer attention to what you see.

Experiment 5.1: You Are Here

Length: *Short or Take-home*
Timer: *None*
Discuss: *Optional*

Step 1. Look around right now, wherever you are, to absorb the details of your surroundings. Then write a list of seven or eight objects you see.

Step 2. Now look at your list. For each object, reflect on the subconscious judgment you might have made about it: good/bad, desirable/undesirable, calming/annoying. For example, you might look at a dirty spoon on your desk and get frustrated about the cleaning you need to do. Or you might look at a vase holding fresh flowers and feel gratitude for the person who put them there.

Step 3. Look again at each object and record a detail about it that does not directly relate to your judgment about it. If you can, try to come up with an association or connection that runs against your snap judgment of this object. The dirty spoon: well, maybe you used it to eat something good for you, like yogurt. The flowers: they're lovely, but maybe they make you sneeze.

Step 4. Choose one of your objects. Take three minutes to write about it, beginning with the association that goes against the grain of your first judgment (for example, the dirty spoon and what nutrition it delivered). Pursue this line of inquiry by writing anything else that comes to mind. You might also write about why it is challenging to view this object in a different light than you are accustomed to.

Contemplative Research

Thoughts tend to sweep along in a torrent that collapses time. If you have tried to catch a thought as you're thinking it, you might wonder what in the world about your breakfast led you to think about a trip to Boston seven years ago. Watching the mind zip along at lightning speed is a surprisingly challenging skill, and it takes practice. The discipline of watching one's own thoughts is central to the practice of many who practice *meditation*. Meditation and other *contemplative practices* play an important role in almost every worldwide religion, but meditation does not have to have an explicitly spiritual focus.

The principles of contemplation have been applied to everything from boosting the immune system to reducing stress. And these skills can even apply to research; the brain is a busy place, and the better you get to know it, the better you get to know – and to wonder about – the world you live in. Seeing shifts in thought – from an object to an opinion or judgment, from a face to a memory – is vital to understanding how you see the world. If you can begin to untangle these strands, you can look to your own associations and contradictions as the seeds for research questions. This second experiment is an expanded version of a previous exercise.

Experiment 5.2: Take Three

Length: *Long or Take-home*

Timer: *3 minutes + 3 minutes + 5 minutes + 2 minutes =*
13 minutes

Discuss: *Optional*

Step 1. Set a timer for three minutes, or find a time-keeper to let you know when three minutes have elapsed. Sit quietly with your eyes closed and try to watch the train of your thoughts, paying particular attention to the series of associations that trigger your thoughts, if possible. It sounds easy, but you might find that the blur of thought is faster than a speeding bullet! If you can catch one or two associations in process, consider this time well spent.

Step 2. Write for two or three minutes about your train of thought. Describe any connections you see between two ideas or a string of ideas.

Step 3. Take five minutes to brainstorm about any general questions that emerge from your seemingly random associations. Your task is to wonder why one idea led you to the next. You might wonder where a certain idea or judgment came from, and how you were influenced to hold that opinion or thought. Or you might wonder about the causes, side-effects, origins, or connections between two thoughts.

Step 4. Take two minutes to brainstorm any research questions that can be pulled from these general questions. For example, if news about a cousin's experiences in medical school led you to a negative association, you might wonder what it is really like to be in medical school, how the experience of medical school is changing for a new generation of students, or how the use of the latest technology is affecting how medical students learn medicine.

Student-Driven Research

Starting with a deep look at your own concerns might seem like a self-centered approach to research, but your interests can create connections between you, your subject, and your readers. This contemplative approach has been used in student research for decades.

Ken Macrorie, author of a groundbreaking book on college composition called *The I-Search Paper*, encouraged his students to pay attention to their own reactions as they researched and wrote to create *I-Search* (as opposed to "re-search") papers (Macrorie, 1988). For this type of paper, students choose topics that connect to their own lives in some way and use their connection to the topics to pull them through the research process. In the finished I-Search paper, the author explains (1) what the author knew before the start of the research; (2) why the research was done and why the author wanted to do the research; (3) what was discovered – as Macrorie describes it, the "story of the hunt"; and finally, (4) what was learned or not learned (Macrorie, 1988: 64).

In addition to creating a research project you care about, the I-Search process has benefits for your reader. Telling your research as a story draws the reader into the drama of the hunt and creates suspense. And when the author explains a personal desire for research or information, the reader can identify or empathize with the author and see why that information might be important to someone's life. Rather than barraging the reader with a flurry of facts and a definite thesis, the I-Search paper starts with a question and takes the form of an explanation and exploration. In telling simply why it interests you, you are making the case (potentially) about why it might matter to someone else.

Brain-Watching and Field Notes

Associations, questions, and ideas zip through your brain constantly – not just when you're sitting quietly for three minutes in a classroom. Once you get used to watching your thoughts, you can then practice catching your thoughts in action as they are triggered during an average day. This next level of brain observation can produce constant research ideas.

The challenge is that these research ideas and thoughts are often half-formed or under the surface. Thoughts move so quickly that they are phrased in a short-hand and don't seem like questions at all. Instead, you can study the tracks of the thoughts as though you are following an animal through a forest. Sometimes the tracks are so faint that you have to collect any details you can find along the way. This requires a time commitment, but it does not require you to do much analysis. Your focus is on noticing, so don't worry about the task of figuring out the patterns and meanings of the details you collect.

Obsession Notebook

The following exercise is borrowed directly from the teaching of the wonderful and talented Bill Roorbach, featured in Conversation 2. Bill has a habit of showing up to his writing class with a plastic bag full of multicolored little notebooks. He passes one notebook to each student, leans back in his chair, looks at his students with a smile that twists up one side of his mustache, and says, "Fill it up. You've got a week." Bill uses this exercise as a way to help authors generate ideas for creative nonfiction essays, but it is also useful for coming up with research ideas that are woven into the fabric of our lives.

You might find that you start carefully choosing your words and subjects, but as the days pass, you become more haphazard in what you write as the deadline approaches. This is actually part of the idea; the deadline of a week forces you to get beyond self-editing and to write without thinking much about quality or judging what you put down. Include ramblings, deep thoughts, drawings, grocery lists, names of rock bands you love or wish you were in, favorite foods, sketches – whatever. Carry it around with you for a week and fill the whole notebook. Eavesdrop. Wonder. Get bored and write anyway. Record your dreams and describe the kinds of donuts in the bakery display case.

Try to avoid these pitfalls: (1) putting off the notebook until the night before and then attempt to fill it up; (2) writing one huge letter or word on each page; (3) getting desperate and making a "flip book" drawing of a little man who runs around when you flip the pages. These are tried-and-true methods for avoiding the assignment. If you mess up or lose the notebook, start again with a fresh notebook and a new week.

Many students who complete this exercise are surprised to see how much they actually care or worry about certain topics. Other students who have done more than one of these *obsession note-books* report that they are surprised at how quickly one obsession can be replaced by another.

Experiment 5.3: Obsession Notebook

Length: *Take-home over one week*

Timer: *None*

Discuss: *Recommended*

Step 1. Buy a small notebook (about the size of a deck of cards). It can be bound together in any way, but make sure the pages are thick enough to write on both sides.

Step 2. Fill it up in one week. Write anything that you think about in order to fill the pages; you will probably have to carry it around in your bag or backpack to get this done whenever you have spare moments.

Step 3. After you've finished, review your notebook and highlight or circle any themes that you wrote about more than once.

Step 4. Write for a few minutes about the surprises that you discovered when you flipped through the pages. What topics surprised you? Did you sound like a different person than you believe yourself to be? What concerns or questions returned to the pages? What observations or incidents struck you as interesting?

Step 5. Make a list of persistent, nagging issues, questions, and themes that your mind seemed to be drawn to in the notebook. Don't worry if they seem mundane. Issues of managing daily life – eating healthy, balancing relationships, getting exercise, finishing school and work responsibilities, wondering about personal and professional dilemmas – are naturally what take up a great deal of most people's everyday focus.

Step 6. Which of these contain the seeds of a research project? Take one theme and write as many research questions as possible that draw from that root or seed. For example, if you wrote more than once about being exhausted, you might have the opening to a whole range of research questions: What causes insomnia? Why are people getting less sleep? How much sleep does the average college student get, and why? Where did the tradition of the all-nighter homework session come from?

Shared Obsessions and Public Issues

A lone individual who cares about a certain topic is often considered quirky or nerdy. If two people care about the same topic, they have a shared hobby or concern. When you find ten friends who share the same interest, you have the beginnings of an organization or interest group. Every public issue and community concern starts out with individuals who care passionately about a topic. They find each other, talk about why their obsession matters to them, and pretty soon they are reaching out and finding still more like-minded people. You might very well have one or more topics in your research notebook that have also raised concern and interest for other people. What you see as a private interest might actually already have an organization, national studies, and lobbying groups behind it, or there might be huge online communities and message boards devoted to this topic. If your subject matter makes for good research, you will be able to find articles and books on the topic in your nearest library or using an Internet database. You can consult traditional research guides for help in finding this information or ask a librarian to help you formulate a search on this topic.

Good research can also come from those who have committed themselves to a cause. This assumption might challenge the rules you have learned previously about reliable sources. In many contexts, a person or group that cares passionately about a subject is assumed to be *unreliable* for research purposes because the commitment to that subject is seen as clouding rational judgment.

Using a fictional group, Students for Free Tuition, as an example, imagine that you are interested in a research project on a proposed tuition increase on your campus. Some researchers would worry that SFT members might not be able to give you an objective or balanced view on the pros and cons of a tuition hike. So you have a dilemma: who to trust? The good news is that researchers don't have to make these broad assumptions based on unreachable ideals of objectivity. You can observe the full range of opinions on a topic – including groups and individuals with a specific point of view.

For this exercise you will start your research in a way that might seem backwards. Instead of pretending you have no opinion on your topic and then finding outside sources on every possible angle, you will start from your point of view and your interests. If you are obsessed with the issue of financial aid and tuition, you probably already have a set of opinions on the issue. Brainstorm what would happen if you found a group of people who shared your beliefs.

Experiment 5.4: The National Association of Yo-Yo Aficionados

Length: *Long or Take-home*

Timer: *5 minutes + additional untimed writing*

Discuss: *Recommended*

Step 1. Review the causes and topics you wrote about in Step 4 of Experiment 5.2. Now write down the name of an imaginary national organization devoted to one of these issues or topics. You might also know about a real group that meets these criteria, and you can also use that organization as a model in answering the questions below. But in either case, don't research the answers to the questions below. Instead, use your imagination.

Step 2. Write your answers to these questions in your notebook:

    a. What might be some of the resources this group would offer to its members?

    b. If there were personal stories to raise awareness of this issue on the group's website, what kinds of stories would be best?

    c. If this group were to support legislation or other political acts, what might these look like?

    d. If this group were to offer its members ways to get involved and contribute, what might they be?

    e. What other organizations, if any, might this group work with and/or support?

    f. What kinds of organizations, if any, might have goals or public statements that would challenge this organization?

    g. If this group were involved in a public controversy, what might it entail?

Step 3. Hopefully the list of questions above revealed that any topic might conceivably generate a range of opinions and even controversies. Circle the answers to a few complex questions or dilemmas in your list from Step 1.

Step 4. Now conduct an Internet search to find one or two organizations or individuals that share the passion or commitment to an issue you wrote about above. Use that online source to answer the questions below.

    a. What are the main obsessions and interests for the source you found?

    b. What proposals or goals are listed for this organization?

    c. In what ways are your concerns from the list in Step 1 similar or different from those articulated by this source?

    d. How much detail does this organization provide about current controversies, and how many links from this page allow a reader to find and consider complex questions?

Step 5. For five minutes, brainstorm a list of possible research questions that come from this comparison of your concerns and the concerns of a source or organization. For example, you might wonder why there is no national group devoted to lowering college tuition, or what factors influenced a particular legislator or other influential person or body to sign on to a campaign. You might wonder what a certain organization does to further an issue and whether they are effective. You might ask why there are so many chess enthusiasts and why they are so deeply divided on the issue of whether a computer could beat a human chess champion.

Group Think

People who care deeply about an issue spend a lot of time thinking about the complexities of that issue. These complex questions are often more interesting to research than a simple yes-or-no, right-or-wrong choice. Formulating a research question based on your honest interests does not mean you are going to produce a hopelessly biased paper. It will mean that you will have to carefully consider opposing arguments. In looking at an organization's web site or a current public controversy, you are more likely to discover multiple complex and real-life positions, rather than an over-simplified "right" proposal and its barely-considered "wrong" opposition.

Rather than simply avoiding sources from any group or organization that seems to have a clearly defined point of view, a mature researcher will often evaluate a source based on that source's acknowledgment of the complexity in an issue. If a source or organization paints the issue as an either-or choice, the organization is ranked a bit lower as a reliable source. But if the organization or source provides and acknowledges complicated questions, opposing arguments, and unanswered dilemmas, this would raise the source a bit in a researcher's estimation as a good site for locating research topics.

The Gray Matter: No Right Answer

For some complex dilemmas, there are simply no right answers or solutions. Acknowledging this doesn't mean you have no standards or values; some might say that the ability to see these conundrums is the hallmark of reaching adulthood. Indeed, true research often operates on exactly the questions which seem so thorny that they are beyond the realm of opposing viewpoints and simple answers on one side or another. Being truly curious about the world also requires an approach to the world that is open to these dilemmas and is focused on learning and observing before making judgments about right and wrong. Complexity and even contradiction are some of the qualities that might draw a person to a research obsession. But it can be a challenge to turn these complex and often fascinating topics into research proposals. A research paper often states the author's position before explaining any background or argument, as if proving right or wrong were more important than examining the evidence.

If you need to turn a complicated question into a thesis statement, there are several strategies you can use for taking a position that gets beyond a dualistic "yes" or "no," right or wrong. Although a moral response – that gut-level commitment to a set of principles – sometimes guides a researcher in choosing a topic area, true research aims to get beyond these questions. The researcher's goal then changes from trying to prove a stance correct or incorrect (the arena of debate and public relations) to producing new knowledge, new understanding, and new ways of seeing problems and possible solutions.

Rather than examining a solution that you feel to be right or wrong, you as a researcher might consider the impact, appeal, awareness, causes, and consequences of a problem or solution on a group of people. For example, if the topic is sustainable agriculture, you might examine the groups of farmers who might be most and least likely to adopt a certain pesticide-free growing practice. In this way, you are able to see your subject with a bit of distance. You're using your analytical power to examine the evidence, but your theories aren't grounded in a familiar moral framework that supplies you with an automatic answer. Instead of asking "yes or no?" consider asking questions that require more elaborate answers, such as "Who? How Much? When? Why? or Where?"

Experiment 5.5: Real-World Research

Length: *Long or Take-home*
Timer: *None*
Discuss: *Recommended*

Choose one of your research topic ideas that is connected to some form of publicly debated question or well-known controversy. In this exercise, you will consider who wants what regarding this issue, and why they want it.

Step 1. Make a list of possible organizations and groups, types of supporters and opponents, and possible solutions or proposals regarding this issue. You might even make a chart where you list the possible issues and/or solutions across the top in each column, and the groups down the side, then mark how each group would feel about each issue and/or solution.

Step 2. Figure out the possible standpoints for each group. What proposal or solution is most likely to appeal to Group X? Why did this proposal or solution appeal or not appeal to Group Y?

Step 3. Write research questions about your issue that ask about the "Who, What, When, Where, Why, and How?" of this public debate. Here are some examples:

a. Why did Solution Y get so much attention at a certain time?

b. Who are the most powerful supporters of Effort Z?

c. When did an organization first formulate Proposal A, and why?

d. What were or could be the unintended consequences of Solution Q?

f. Why did Group X support or not support Proposal W?

g. How did Group Z build support for its proposal?

Open Questions

In examining complexity, these types of questions invite you to use your own creativity and analysis to arrange your argument. They are like complex puzzles rather than simple "yes or no" questions. In addition, they invite a reader to examine the evidence with you and to consider your analysis. Your reader will likely welcome a fresh look at a familiar topic, a welcomed change from the ever-present shouting match of opponents trying to convince each other that their position is the only correct one.

Instead of choosing a subject based on its level of conflict, experienced researchers often head directly for the point of *maximum unknown*. They consciously choose topics that bother them or that seem to contain a sense of personal danger. This doesn't mean that they research while rock-climbing. Instead, their research topics aim for the questions that seem to threaten the sense of self and identity that we all hold dear. For example, a writer who has been a committed stay-at-home mother who home-schools her children might consciously write about her doubts about this choice and then investigate these. A politician might examine the nagging concerns he has had about the effects of a policy he proposed. Looking at a nagging or unresolved issue in your own life is a great way to create interest for you and for your reader – and a good way to get personal benefits from an academic or professional research project.

Experiment 5.6: Real-World Research, Part II

Length: *Short*

Timer: *5 minutes*

Discuss: *Recommended*

Step 1. Choose a topic that you have strong opinions about and that is in some way connected to your sense of yourself, your identity, or your place in the world.

Step 2. Take five minutes to write. List the concerns and questions you have about your position, the cracks in your armor, the doubts, questions, or fears you have about your position on this issue.

Step 3. Go over your freewrite and circle any phrases that might contain *third positions*, or areas between the two commonly cited opposite positions in a debate on public issues. Is there any possibility that others might share your concern? You might even do a few Internet searches to see if like-minded individuals or groups have articulated these issues and complexities. While you might not end up with a clear-cut research idea from this short exercise, you might very well develop a position or complex view that is between two clichéd opposing viewpoints. And that is progress!

Conclusion to Chapter 5

Your work in this chapter represents a bridge between the REFLECT and RESEARCH steps of a complex research project. As you have continued to use your RELAX techniques to gain distance from your first reactions and to brainstorm many possible research topics, you have broadened your awareness of the range of possible complex topics available for research. Asking questions that consider real-life scenarios, groups of people, political and social issues, and public controversies invites and paves the way for finding external information to engage with. Because you have taken the time to brainstorm and REFLECT on your initial responses and ideas, you have most likely come up with sharp and interesting questions for research.

Rather than muddling around with a sea of opposing viewpoints, your crafting of careful questions has prepared you to engage with information on the topic in an informed and *aware* manner. By becoming aware of your own position on your research issue, you can begin to understand how multiple positions on that issue are constructed. Now is the perfect time to begin engaging with other sources of information, which you will do in Chapter 6.

Conversation 2 with Bill Roorbach: Immersion Research

Bill Roorbach is the author of several books of nonfiction, including *Temple Stream: A Rural Odyssey* (Roorbach, 2006), and two books of fiction, *Big Bend: Stories* (Roorbach, 2002), which won the Flannery O'Connor Award, and *The Smallest Color* (Roorbach, 2002), a novel. The 10th Anniversary Edition of *Writing Life Stories: How to Make Memories into Memoirs, Ideas in Essays, and Life into Literature* is now available (Roorbach, 2008). He's also the editor of the Oxford anthology *Contemporary Creative Nonfiction: The Art of Truth* (Roorbach, 2001). For more information, go to: <www.billroorbach.com>. This conversation took place via email. Photo of author: John L. Buckingham.

Have you always come up with good ideas for research projects? Any horrible ideas, say, from high school? Any memory of the first time you researched something and got into it?

Roorbach: I never set out on a research project, ever. What I set out on is a writing project, and generally most of the way through a rough draft, or all the way through, when I finally know what it is I'm going to need, I go to the library and get to work. I'll take out several dozen books on interlibrary loan, graze the stacks, come home with huge piles of books, cull them for the ones I really need to read, and then I (a delight) read. Along with books, every periodical reference I can find (usually right in the library, taking notes, and recently not forgetting to note bibliographical info), and quotations, and stuff from today's news, all stuffed into a paper file, the best of it typed into the machine, later to be typed into the manuscript.

After I've done my book learning, I interview people on the subject at hand. That way I know what I'm talking about, and I know when they don't. Final step is to Google my way through everything, looking for the most current sources and juicy bits I'd otherwise miss, also leads for more study. And I'll keep researching right up to the time I finally have to say "Done."

What's the most difficult thing for you about conducting research? The most enjoyable?

Roorbach: I guess just getting going is hard. And I don't particularly like contacting people for interviews, though it usually turns out fun. Most enjoyable is just getting immersed, making myself something of an expert on whatever subject.

How often during the research process for Temple Stream were you either overwhelmed by the task, by the information, or by the thought of making it all cohere?

Roorbach: Fairly often. One of the early drafts was 600 pages. The final draft was 300. I really got involved in studying beavers for that book, and it threatened to turn into a book about beavers. They are so cool. Do you know they mate swimming under the ice? That all beavers are born in May or June?

6　Responding to Reality

Curiosity is, in great and generous minds, the first passion and the last.

> – Samuel Johnson, *The Rambler 150*
> (Johnson, 1846: 231)

Introduction to Chapter 6

You may have grown up in a home where the daily newspaper arrived in a rubber-banded roll on the front step. Or maybe you passed by newspaper boxes on your way to school and glanced at the headlines and pictures signaling the top stories of the day. Maybe a newspaper subscription is not in your budget or schedule, but you pick up a section left on the bus to glance at the paragraphs that draw your interest. Or maybe you read the headlines online and click through to stories that interest you or listen to the television news as you cook dinner.

Interaction with the daily news might be your only contact with the world beyond your immediate experience and circle of friends, family, and acquaintances. Yet this news – often bad, contradictory, fragmented, and confusing – can easily be blocked out altogether because it deals with tragedies taken out of context. By the time a person reaches early adulthood in a media-saturated society, he or she is probably skilled at the art of tuning out or dismissing such news. In some ways, this is a survival strategy for navigating the seas of information while still being able to function. But at a certain point, this decision to limit your attention becomes automatic, and you might end up missing new ideas and questions to pursue.

The newspaper – in its old-fashioned physical form – is a wonderful launch pad for research because of its random comprehensiveness. An online newspaper technically has the same content, but clicks and separate nested screens allow the viewer to completely bypass topics and articles without even scanning the contents. The practice of reading the newspaper does not require a person to read every article. However, to read a newspaper the old-fashioned way, a person flips through each page, scanning the headlines and snippets of key text at a rapid pace, occasionally slowing down to read something that seems interesting. For this reason, the hard copy of a newspaper is a more random and multi-topic experience that exposes the reader to a greater degree of un-sought information. And that can be a good thing. The physical newspaper is a sample of a community, a scattershot selection of portraits and moments capturing shared experiences.

Experiment 6.1: Reading the Newspaper with Scissors

Length: *Long or Take-Home*
Timer: *5 minutes + 5 minutes + 5 minutes=15 minutes plus reading time*
Discuss: *Optional*

Step 1. Purchase the print version of a daily newspaper. Don't use the library copy or borrow a copy that someone else wants back, because you are going to destroy this one.
Step 2. Taking as much time as needed, browse through each section of the newspaper. Cut out any and every article,

review, event listing, photo, or graphic that makes you pause to read or to look. You can either read these pieces as you cut them out, or cut first and then go back to read.

Step 3. Lay out the pieces you have selected. Then choose three, making sure that one of these pieces addresses a topic you don't know much about.

Step 4. Freewrite for five minutes about your reactions to each of these newspaper articles. Don't worry about making coherent thoughts or arguments related to the topic of the piece. Instead, include questions about what you don't understand or what seems boring in this article. Rant on what frustrates you about this topic and what you wish you understood. Record your opinions or write about why this topic has never interested you.

Step 5. Go back to look at each of your three freewrites, and circle any possible seeds of research questions that emerge.

Step 6. Make a list of three research questions from each freewrite; think of research in this situation as a way to get your honest questions and confusions answered. For example, if you have a difficult time understanding the names and controversies in an article about relations between Hong Kong and China, you might phrase a research question like this: "What are the most important causes of the tension between Hong Kong and China?"

Boring Topics

Take a random topic: shipping regulations, kite-flying technology, or the function of the inner ear. An outsider to these topics might assume that these subjects are boring because they involve specialized knowledge, or because they seem to have no immediate connections to our lives. Yet sometimes – say, in flipping channels and in catching a piece of a television documentary – you may find yourself captivated by a conversation, image, or issue related to a topic you might otherwise dismiss. For a moment you are drawn into another world, with players, conflicts, and concerns that appeal partly because of their drama, their foreignness, and their specificity. That lovely catch of attention is called *curiosity*. It is a natural human impulse, a function of a brain at work, gathering information, enjoying discovery, and even taking pleasure in learning.

That feeling might remind you of the free-form exploration of childhood. When children play, they are hard at work developing and growing the vital skill of curiosity through experience and repetition, as described by child psychologists:

> When the child explores, she discovers. A wonderful cycle of learning is driven by the pleasure in play. A child is curious; she explores and discovers. The discovery brings pleasure; the pleasure leads to repetition and practice. Practice brings mastery; mastery brings the pleasure and confidence to once again act on curiosity. All learning – emotional, social, motor and cognitive – is accelerated and facilitated by repetition fueled by the pleasure of play. (Perry, Hogan, and Marlin, 2000)

In adulthood, time, money, and a to-do list conspire to push play to the sidelines. Competitions for power, status, and resources all force adults to develop expertise and areas of authority. Adults gain influence through expertise, so it becomes imperative to prove what you know and to say it with confidence. As adulthood progresses, the ability to say, "I don't know" – and the ability to see not-knowing as a positive thing – is shelved far back in one's heads with dolls and toy cars. Over time, not knowing becomes equated for many people with being stupid. Instead, many people cultivate a sense of mastery over certain areas and subjects, specializing – sometimes very early in life – and veering away from topics that present the feeling of a wide-open unknown.

Given this set of assumptions, it's easy to see how panic and discomfort result when a student is asked to formulate a research topic he or she knows nothing about. Every example of expertise, produced by serious study or casual interest, starts with learning.

And <u>not</u> knowing is essential for learning to occur. A learner has to admit his or her own ignorance, to become willing to learn, and occasionally to fail in the pursuit of knowledge. Instead of studiously avoiding unfamiliar topics as threats to one's sense of self, the researcher first identifies and then moves toward those areas of the Great Unknown.

Experiment 6.2: Don't Know Much About History, Biology, the Economy...

Length: *Long*

Timer: *5 minutes + 5 minutes + 5 minutes = 15 minutes*

Discuss: *Recommended*

For this exercise, choose a section of the newspaper you normally avoid. If you are an avid stock-trader, pick up the arts section. If you only read the sports page, go for the business news. If you generally avoid the newspaper, try the front section.

Step 1. Look through the entire section and glance at the articles.

Step 2. Choose one article – boring or interesting, familiar or unfamiliar – to read carefully. One caveat: do not choose articles with subjects related to entertainment or sports scores, movie reviews, recipes, celebrity/gossip, or horoscopes. An arts story is fine, but the goal is to find what would be classified as *hard news*: an in-depth article which required original reporting with quoted sources, and which takes on an issue that affects the lives of some group of people.

Step 3. Do a five-minute freewrite about your associations and random thoughts related to this news item. If you find the subject matter dull, you might also write about why this topic does not seem interesting, why you would normally not read this article, or why it is difficult for you to understand or relate to. Or you might connect the news item to something in your life.

Step 4. Do a second five-minute freewrite in which you try to analyze and understand your reactions. Imagine you are looking at yourself from the outside, and comment on the relationship between you as a person and this piece of news. For example, if you chose an article about an explosion at a sugar refinery, you might ask what possible connections could be drawn between your life and the life of this subject or topic. Looking at the connections between your life and the refinery, you might note that you are a college student who consumes a lot of sugar in the form of candy and soft drinks. Does the sugar from the local sugar refinery go into your snacks, or is it used for some other purpose? Does anyone in your town work at the refinery? Write down possible connections even if they seem strange.

Step 5. Do a final five-minute freewrite on the sensory details included in the article and your associations with them and/ or the sensory details and experiences you imagine that are in some way connected to this topic. Using the example of the sugar refinery, you might wonder if the air in a refinery tastes sweet, what it is like to feel the crunch of sugar every day under your shoes, what it feels like to work there on a hot day, what the refinery looked like after the explosion.

Connections

The previous exercise might feel a bit strange; how could imagining sensory details ever lead to an academic research topic? You might be surprised at the extent to which getting close to your subject – even imaginatively – triggers scholarly research ideas or general questions. But imagining the details of a subject down to the level of its physical reality can begin to show you all there is to know about a subject from multiple points of view. It is easy to follow in the tracks of previous researchers and writers and to focus on what has already been written about a topic, but the truly groundbreaking researcher often starts with the basics and approaches a topic from a new direction. Reminding yourself of the physical details of a topic is a great way to break out of the ruts dug by other researchers.

The Portable Researcher

Continuing with the idea that sensory information can trigger good questions, the next step in focusing the skill of curiosity is to take it outside for a walk around the block. Some of the best ideas for research and inquiry arrive by accident, and the history of almost any field of study is filled with stories of those bursts of inspiration triggered by everyday or unexpected events, such as sitting in a bathtub of water (Archimedes' insight about calculation of volume), an apple falling from a tree (Sir Isaac Newton's meditations on gravity), or a daydream about space travel (Einstein's visualizations about the speed of light).

Experiment 6.3: Research in Motion

Length: *Take-home*

Timer: *5 minutes + 5 minutes + 5 minutes=15 minutes plus additional time*

Discuss: *Recommended*

For this exercise, you will visit a place that is either familiar or unfamiliar and simply pay as much attention to your surroundings as possible.

Step 1. Choose your destination. The place you have in mind might be as specific as an exhibit at a local museum or as general as the downtown area of your city or town. If you are having trouble coming up with a location, you might do a two-minute freewrite to list possible destinations that are easily accessible; maybe these are places you have wondered about but never visited, or they may be places you pass by every day.

Step 2. Plan your expedition. Most likely you will only need a notebook and pen. You might consider carrying a camera to take pictures, which can be useful as fuel for thought after your walk. The most important part of your preparation is to make sure you have a period of time (probably an hour, maybe with additional commuting time) sufficient to allow you to relax and observe everything about your destination. Do not try to multi-task and complete this activity while running errands or when you only have fifteen minutes to spare, because this will require your full commitment and attention.

Step 3. Head toward your destination. First browse around your destination in a manner that might seem aimless. Look at anything that draws your interest, and write down any questions triggered by your experiences. Pay attention to and record the sensory information you notice.

Step 4. Once you have studied this environment in a general way, choose one point of view or object to focus on. Position yourself so that you can see this object or point of view easily and comfortably. You might also consider sitting down to write if that is an option.

Step 5. Take five minutes to describe this object or point of view in as much detail as you can. Be specific and include any questions you have about the object.

Step 6. For another five minutes, write wildly about anything this object or point of view triggers in your head. Does the painting in the gallery remind you of a jungle scene, and is that splotch of yellow a lion? Circle any words or phrases that might lead to research questions.

Step 7. For your last five minutes, imagine that you are studying yourself at a distance. Try to describe yourself and your relationship to your object as if you were an anthropologist or newspaper reporter viewing yourself as part of the scene. For example, if you are doing a freewrite on a rock-climbing wall at a local fitness center, you might imagine yourself there and wonder if you fit the profile of a typical rock-climber. This might lead you to ask whether the fitness center sees more college-age climbers, more women than men, and why rock-climbing as a hobby might appeal to some individuals or types of people or groups more than to others.

Post-Walk Field Notes

Curiosity is the ability to see things in new ways and to wonder about them. For this reason, Steps 5, 6, and 7 ask you to disrupt your normal way of looking at a scene by first focusing on something specific, then including your own free associations in that view, and then finally seeing yourself as part of this scene. These mental calisthenics can break up the habitual pattern of noticing either what you normally see or seeing only what directly connects to your interests and experiences.

Once you have gathered your data, review your notes. Using a highlighter or colored pen, mark any element of your notes that catches your attention and indicates the potential for future writing or research. You might try to brainstorm research questions connected to the objects or sights you were most drawn to. What surprising insights came out of this exercise? Which of the three points of view (Steps 5, 6, and 7) was most productive for generating ideas and observations?

The Gray Matter: Beyond the Edges of the Newspaper Page

Using a walk or an issue of the daily newspaper can be a wonderful way to trigger research questions and to investigate and broaden interests and areas of inquiry. Taking these exercises a step further, you can generate additional questions by remembering that the presence of something also indicates the absence of many other things. For example, a scene of children playing might seem pleasant and stereotypically uninteresting until you notice that the children are all of one race or that they are all playing one activity. The obvious research question is, "Why?"

Journalists, scholars, and scientists constantly switch back and forth between two mental modes: (1) observing and (2) asking themselves what they are not seeing. The "what's missing?" mindset triggers the viewer to question the *framing* of a news story, a museum display, or a work of scholarship. Another way to think about framing is to visualize a picture frame. If you were to hold the frame in front of you so that you could see part of a scene – such as a busy outdoor market – you might be leaving out the six-lane overpass nearby in order to capture the most picturesque part of this moment.

In a similar way to a picture frame, anything you might make or write has limitations and a focus. These limitations mean that some important topics are not addressed. Sometimes the framing of an exhibit or news story is caused by limitations of space or time, and sometimes the frame has only minor effects. In other cases, the framing might reflect biases and prejudices of the author and might be a subconscious or intentional effort to influence the audience.

Experiment 6.4: Reading Between the Lines and Beyond the Screen

Length: *Short*

Timer: *5 minutes plus additional reflection and writing time*

Discuss: *Recommended*

Step 1. Return to the section of the newspaper you examined in Experiment 6.1 or find a news article on the Internet or on television.

Step 2. Choose one news story for your analysis. Make a list of possible subjects, sources, and complexities that were not addressed in the story. For example, if you see a short segment about a new playground built in a park, you might wonder how many other playgrounds were built in the city, what surrounds the playground, what sort of neighborhood the playground is built in, and what the playground might look like in five years. You might ask what happens to the old or outdated playground equipment, or you might wonder why certain areas of the city get new playgrounds and others do not. Developing this ability to "see the invisible" is a powerful tool for generating both awareness and research ideas out of thin air.

Step 3. Do a five-minute freewrite about the gaps in the news story. Could your questions have been addressed in a short news article or broadcast, or are they complex enough to require lengthy explanations? How does the format of the news limit what is covered?

Another way to see how framing affects the presentation of a news story is to examine the coverage of a story from the perspective of two news outlets. A reporter, like any other researcher, uncovers many more facts than can be included in a news story. Space limitations and the presentation and focus of a news story both require that cuts be made. No story can tell the "whole" story, and every news story comes packaged with an implicit or explicit perspective. This is not at all to say that one is more accurate than the other, though some readers might feel that leaving out certain points of view creates such a blind spot that the story is only partially correct.

Experiment 6.5: Comparing Two Frames

Length: *Long or Take-Home*
Timer: *None*
Discuss: *Recommended*

Step 1. Choose an issue that has received coverage in multiple news outlets, preferably a local or regional issue, and print out two articles of about equal length (both less than a page) on the topic. Make sure that these articles are not directly taken from the same source, because many newspapers use *wire services* for their international, national, or state coverage. You can tell if the story is from a wire service by looking at the byline, which might have an acronym like AP, which is one popular wire service.

Step 2. Starting with one article, underline the key perspectives, facts, and topics covered. As you find each topic, opinion, or viewpoint, check the other article to see if that viewpoint is mentioned. Circle the opinions, views, or fact mentioned in the first article that are not mentioned in the second article. Then read through the second article again and circle the viewpoints not mentioned in the first article.

Step 3. Do a five-minute freewrite about the gaps in coverage between the two stories. How did the two stories differ? How would your impression of the event have been different if you had read only one?

Conclusion to Chapter 6

Your work in this chapter has moved you beyond brainstorming and into an engagement with the outside world. You have seen that even browsing through a newspaper section or walking to a place in your town can be valid and fruitful research. Rather than leaving your tools of RELAXATION and REFLECTION behind, you have brought them along with you in order to generate responses and questions to the information that real-world sources present. Locations and unintended sources of information are important triggers for questions, because they help reveal the ways in which a questioning and reflective mindset generates questions out of almost anything it encounters. Rather than searching for a topic, your growing skills of RELAXATION and REFLECTION allow you to see a full range of possible research ideas in any situation, giving you many more options on your research quest. As you have seen, engagement with outside information is useful not only for obtaining pieces of information but also for generating more questions. These questions, rather than random quotes or facts, are what will guide your research in the next chapters.

7   Uncharted Obsessions

*Over the long run, the people with the interesting answers are
those who ask the interesting questions.*
>   – David Bayles and Ted Orland, *Art & Fear*
>   (Bayles and Orland, 1993: 113)

Introduction to Chapter 7

Author Steve Almond, profiled in Conversation 3, decided to put
his normal life on hold in order to travel across the country in
search of a candy bar. The journey broadened into a sugar-soaked
saga and became a book called *Candyfreak* (Almond, 2004), but
the story started because he really, really liked one brand of candy
bar. Along the way, Almond tracked down mom-and-pop candy
producers, tasted confections straight off the assembly line, had
a sugar crash, developed a multi-layered theory of "freaks," and
used corporate candy production as an unexpected case study for
the toll that economic globalization has taken on local economies.
But he started with a caramel and chocolate candy bar called the
Caravelle and wound up at about 250 pages.

Although the book can provoke quite a chocolate craving,
Almond (2004: 1) also encourages his readers to develop a larger

desire to discover their inner *freak*: "We may not understand why we freak on a particular food or band or sports team. We may have no conscious control over our allegiances. But they arise from our most sacred fears and desires and, as such, they represent the truest expression of our selves."

Obsession comes with a price. For Almond, a close look at his freakdom also required an excavation of the dangers and downsides, including questionable nutrition, financial costs, and the social risk of boring his friends at parties as he ranted about the demise of a favorite candy bar. He also wondered about the ultimate causes of his obsession, which led him to look at unmet childhood needs and family dynamics. Although Almond tells the story with humor, there are moments darker than the darkest chocolate bar.

Nerddom and the Kingdom of the Geeks

At some point in your life you were hopefully delighted beyond the bounds of reason. You were overjoyed at the win of a sports team, thrilled by a toy, unable to stop talking about a song or a rock group or a beloved book. Most likely, someone responded with disbelief, doubt, or annoyance: "Are you crazy?" You learned that your obsession was uncool, too earnest, and wrong. The passion – or at least the public expression of it – fell by the wayside in the universal quest for social acceptance. Peer pressure and unspoken social codes often provide a confusing message; what you like might be the problem, or maybe it's the fact that you're too enthusiastic in general. If childhood is marked by visible joy, the easiest way to achieve coolness is to put on a blank expression of world-weary cynicism and pretend that it's impossible to be surprised or impressed.

In the transition to adulthood, you might have temporarily mislaid the many subjects, activities, and topics that brought simple curiosity and excitement. Following Steve Almond's lead, try in this next exercise to reach back into your childhood to see the obsessions from your younger years, and then to discover whether they have any resonance for you today.

Experiment 7.1: Geek, Nerd, Freak

Length: *Flexible (Short or Take-home)*

Timer: *4 minutes + 5 minutes = 9 minutes plus time for reflection*

Discuss: *Optional*

Step 1. Take four minutes to review your *freak autobiography*. Make a list of as many possible obsessions, present or past, as you can. What activities brought you the most joy as a child, and why? What subjects did you yearn to know about, what did you collect, and what did you pester your family about? You might also need to put this freewrite aside and let your memories float to the surface over a day or two. Sometimes it can take time and work to remember what we have pushed away as undesirable or uncool about our own past.

Step 2. Review your complete list. If you took a break to reflect, add anything else that came to mind, whether it was the passion of years or the focus of a particular month or two in elementary school.

Step 3. Now review your obsession notebook from Chapter 2. What seem to be your current obsessions? What topics do you think a lot about but might not list as obsessions? Add any current obsessions to your *freak list*.

Step 4. Choose any interesting item on this list and write about it for five minutes, following any tangents and questions that come to mind.

Intuition as Research

Your list of obsessions can be fuel for hilarious conversations with friends; most likely, the fads and trends of decades past are contained like time capsules in your memory. On a deeper level, becoming aware of your quirks, interests, and passions can also train your brain to focus on its own reactions. If you focus on hearing that small voice inside you, you will develop the ability to listen to yourself, to tune into areas of the associative right side of your brain and to monitor signals that might otherwise be dismissed as irrelevant in the face of louder external and internal stimuli. If you can focus on the feeling of following and remembering past obsessions, you can strengthen the cognitive muscles that sense interests or thoughts running against the grain of common knowledge, logical thought, or so-called "normal" behavior.

This *self-listening* can be described as an unconventional research skill. In the book *FieldWorking*, authors Sunstein and Chiseri-Strater (2007: 134) describe this practice as "checking in," which they say "will heighten your awareness of the extent to which the instrument of your data gather is not statistical information or a computer program or an experiment but *you* – with all of your assumptions, preconceptions, past experiences, and complex feelings."

Sometimes the inner voice – including its strange quirks and interests – can get steamrollered by the force of popular opinion, loud voices on the car radio, and the demands of everyday life. Such forces can even lead a person to forget that he or she has a unique response to almost every moment and experience in life. However, small tasks – like an inventory of present and past interests and thoughts – can sharpen the ability to listen to that inner voice. And as your self-listening ability improves, it becomes easier to access what many people call *intuition*.

Intuition is often described as an immediate flash of insight or feeling. Because so much of the brain's functioning is still a mystery to researchers, both the processes by which a person intuits as well as the validity of this intuition are not measurable. Since an intuition cannot be weighed, tracked, or correlated to an external event or cause, some researchers dismiss the product of intuitions as emotionally-driven wishful thinking, or as a waking dream unconnected to reality. Other researchers, including psychologists, theologians, and philosophers, note the pervasive presence of intuition in human experience and argue that ignoring such a phenomenon means, in effect, ignoring data from the brain. Some note that what we experience as intuition might be the result of cognitive processes which are so rapid that we cannot track the thoughts or trace the path of logic, analysis, and sensory information and connect it to the intuition.

Intuition is not usually described as a research method in the sciences, but most biographies of scientific and artistic pioneers record leaps of thought that bring amazing insight when the brain is seemingly at rest. Striking images, seemingly unrelated events, and dreams have triggered any number of empirical breakthroughs. It may even be true that the brilliance of many researchers – even those whose careful research resulted in advanced scientific discovers – lies partially in their ability to listen to signals from the unconscious mind.

Tobin Hart, an educational researcher and college professor, describes the two sides of research. The familiar side is "[r]ational empiricism," which "trains us to pay attention to some things and not to others, discounting hunches or feelings" (Hart, 2004: 5). The other half of research, Hart (2004: 5) explains, is contemplative, contained in "shadowy symbols, feelings, and images as well as in paradoxes and passions." Why bother paying attention to the half of our mind that sounds so vague and confusing? Hart (2004: 5) writes: "Understanding expands as we learn to listen to the unique ways our inner life speaks to us and integrate the voices of the analytic and the contemplative."

Hart uses the word *passions*, which might sound strange in the context of research. Yet Almond's passion for candy bars led to months of empirical research as he gathered first-hand

and second-hand data. Almond's big connections began with the creative impulse to follow his obsession and to believe that there was something worthwhile in that study – even if he had no idea where it would lead. Instead of choosing a topic based on what other people told him was important, he followed his gut – in more ways than one.

Bubble Charts

It can be helpful to visualize connections between related topics by making a bubble chart – also called clustering. To make a bubble chart, start with a topic in the center of a blank sheet of paper. Draw lines branching outward from this center and connect to related ideas as you brainstorm connections between your topic and other questions, issues, or current events. This will end up looking like a spider web or a bird's nest of lines; neatness is not required. Draw lines to link ideas and concepts even if they come from different spokes or areas; this can help you identify which areas have the most connections and to see which topics you are most interested in. An example of a bubble chart – this one on the topic of collecting blank notebooks or journals – is below.

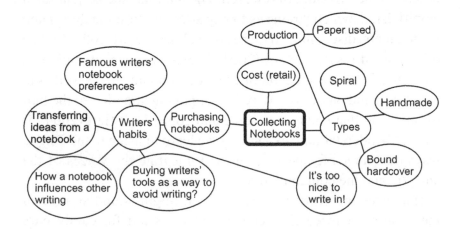

Figure 7.1: Bubble Chart

Experiment 7.2: Outward Bubbles

Length: *Flexible (Long or Take-home)*

Timer: *None*

Discuss: *Optional*

Step 1. Look again at your list of obsessions. Choose one that seems interesting or complex. Write it in the middle of a piece of paper.

Step 2. Make a bubble chart. For the first level of connecting topics, list as many themes, phrases, questions, or subjects as you can, even if they seem wildly unrelated. Then try to generate at least a few second-level bubbles branching out from each of these, becoming more and more specific as you work outward. The goal is to visualize many different ways a topic can be approached and to stimulate you to see one subject from multiple perspectives.

Step 3. Circle any questions or topics that seem to be possible research ideas or that interest you.

Step 4. Make bubble charts for two or three other topics from your list in Experiment 1. You may find it difficult at first, because this method uses different cognitive muscles than the practice of choosing a broad topic and narrowing it down. Instead, you are taking the first step to broaden your interests outward and see the connections to the rest of the world.

Beyond Bubbles

You might quickly find that the clustering idea becomes second-nature, especially if you are a visual thinker or in cases where you are used to seeing a topic from a certain point of view and only need a jump-start to brainstorm other perspectives. However, in some cases the clustering approach may prove frustrating, particularly when you know little about your subject and do not see the various possible sub-topics that could branch off your main idea.

The phrase *six degrees of separation* describes a mathematical concept that has moved into popular usage: the idea that almost everyone on the globe can be shown to be connected through a chain of social networks and relationships that link every individual by no more than six steps to every other individual. Although no theory transfers the six degrees idea to research methods, the exercise below can be used as a research challenge to envision your topic in a new way.

To do this exercise, make a list of five or six big world issues or questions. You might take these from today's newspaper, or for an extra challenge, brainstorm these ideas off the top of your head. Alternately, you might brainstorm words and phrases in a group of peers, write them on index cards, and then draw your words from a common pile. For example, your six degrees list might include: *Sri Lanka, Condoms, Georgia O'Keefe, Platypus,* and *Third Graders*. Although this list is completely random, the challenge of this six degrees list will be to connect one or more items on it to the word or phrase in the center of your bubble chart in six steps or less.

Start with the center word or phrase from your bubble chart and connect it to one word from your six degrees list. Using the example of the bubble chart from Figure 7.1, you can connect Sri Lanka to two of the topics from that bubble chart: *Paper used* and *Production*. If you think about paper production and any overlap these topics might have with Sri Lanka, for example, you might come upon the question of *forestry* or *deforestation*. Either word could make a successful connection between the center word of *notebooks* and *Sri Lanka* through the topics of *paper* to *deforestation* to *timber industry in Sri Lanka* in less than six bubbles. You could ask these questions: "Is deforestation a problem in Sri Lanka? Does it have a timber industry? What kind of paper is used and sold in Sri Lanka?"

Take the topic of *condoms* as another example. Starting with *Collecting Notebooks*, you could draw an easy connection to a new bubble: *Collections and Collectors* and then add the bubble: *Does anyone, anywhere collect condoms?* or *Do condom manufacturers have a museum?* We might even make this connection in more than one way: *Collecting notebooks* could connect to another new bubble: *Journaling*, which could connect to another new bubble: *Does journaling about safe sex methods result in higher degree of usage for teenagers?* or *What do teenagers write about safe sex?*

This method moves in the opposite direction from the traditional method for brainstorming research ideas. Instead of choosing a broad subject area and waiting for a specific question to fall into your head, you start with a specific idea and then move outward toward seemingly unrelated topics. Now that you have tried *broadening*, you might try to generate a new set of six-degree topics for this or another core obsession. If Steve Almond was able to connect a chocolate bar to economic globalization, what connections can you discover between world issues and your tiny topic?

Experiment 7.3: Six Degrees

Length: *Flexible (Short, Long, or Take-home)*
Timer: *None*
Discuss: *Optional*

Step 1. Choose one of your bubble charts from Experiment 7.2.
Step 2. Make a list of five or six big world issues or questions.
Step 3. Look at the core topic from your bubble chart and its web of immediate brainstormed connections from Experiment 7.2. Is there any way you can, through multiple connections, reach one of the topics in your six degrees list?
Step 4. After completing the web, you will see that you have generated some very interesting and very specific research questions that are in some way connected to one of your obsessions.

The Gray Matter: Why We Love What We Love

Steve Almond was so curious about his candy obsession that he followed it across the country while seeking its roots in his own heart and mind. He collected memories from his childhood that evoked or stemmed from candy (and there were many). Almond knew that if he wanted to truly understand his subject, he had to examine the way it functioned in his own life. If he had decided to leave himself out of the story, he would have been ignoring the interview subject with the most information available!

Was this a case of self-obsession to the extreme? Some might see it that way, but Alan Wallace, author of *Contemplative Science* (Wallace, 2007), describes the mind as a research tool that we have to explore and know in order to use. Wallace (2007: 56) asks us to imagine the mind as a new piece of lab equipment presented to scientists, who would have to "examine its nature, including its strengths and limitations…. Only after they had understood the design, functioning, reliability, and capacities of the instrument could they confidently use it to collect data."

Every mind is different, except for one common trait: none of them come with an instruction manual. You can, however, look at your own life and choices as a way to see how your mind operates. Studying the mind of the researcher can indicate what kind of research will be produced. While traditional standards of objectivity focus on keeping the researcher separate from the research, recent work in fields from literary theory to quantum physics suggests that humans are inextricably intertwined with whatever they study. Rather than aiming for an illusion of objectivity and ignoring your mind, you might approach your research with the goal of awareness, hunting not only for your subject matter but also for greater perspective on how that subject affects and is affected by you.

In the final Experiment in this chapter, you will try something that might feel strange: adding yourself right into a bubble chart. Figure 7.2: Double-Bubble Chart shows how this will look, using the example of my own experiences as they connect to the topic of collecting blank journals and notebooks. You are connected at the center to your topic, and connections will branch off both from your bubble and from the bubble of the other main topic you choose. This may be quite a challenging exercise, because it requires you to see the ways in which your life might intersect with a subject that feels somewhat random. As you do this, you will need to reflect on past experiences, interests, and memories to examine your connections to the topic at hand. The outcome of this exercise is very useful for writing and research; it provides a visual map to help see the ways in which you may have unique connections, biases, or expertise on the subject. This is helpful especially in cases where the connections are taken-for-granted or otherwise invisible to you. As you begin to research a topic seriously, a *double-bubble chart* like this can also help you mine your memory for personal anecdotes to illustrate a point or to use past experiences and impressions as a way to generate research questions.

Experiment 7.4: Double-Bubble Chart

Length: *Flexible (Short, Long, or Take-home)*
Timer: *5 minutes + 5 minutes = 10 minutes plus additional reflection and writing time*
Discuss: *Optional*

Step 1. Choose another topic from your list of obsessions in Experiment 7.1.

Step 2. For five minutes, freewrite about how this topic connects to your life, your experiences, dreams, and desires. You can also do this step in the form of a double-bubble chart with yourself as one of two central words or phrases. See Figure 7.2 below for an example of how you might visualize a bubble chart that focuses on your relationship to your subject.

Step 3. Add to your freewrite or double-bubble chart the experiences, questions, evidence, and subjects from your own life that might serve as connectors between this core subject and you. Also add in any other specific topics that seem to help connect you to your core idea.

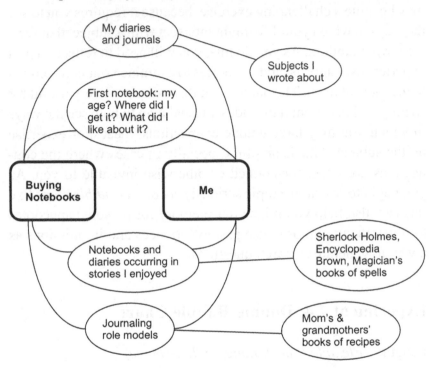

My diaries and journals

Subjects I wrote about

First notebook: my age? Where did I get it? What did I like about it?

Buying Notebooks

Me

Notebooks and diaries occurring in stories I enjoyed

Sherlock Holmes, Encyclopedia Brown, Magician's books of spells

Journaling role models

Mom's & grandmothers' books of recipes

Figure 7.2: Double-Bubble

Step 4. This double-bubble chart may give you new ideas for general research questions; you might see experiences that trigger interests and ask whether such triggers are a pattern among people in general. If you see possible research ideas on your chart or in your freewrite, put a star next to them.

Step 5. Freewrite for five minutes on how your past experiences might influence your current approach to or view of your topic. Experiences can create blind-spots or areas in which it is difficult to see the differences of others. For example, if you have positive experiences in keeping a notebook, you might assume that it is a universally easy or pleasurable activity. If you come from a family that loves to cook together, you might miss the range of negative associations with cooking. On the other hand, experience can also create a great deal of specific knowledge that gives us extra insight into a topic or extra motivation to study it.

Step 6. Look at the freewrite from Step 5 and use this material to write at least three general research questions for further study. Does a certain experience lead to a certain view toward subject X? Which experiences lead to a favorable view of subject Y?

Conclusion to Chapter 7

In this chapter, you have taken the RELAX element of brainstorming to new limits. In completely letting go of the need for a specific topic, you have instead branched outward with completely random words and phrases and then tried to discover any connections you find to the research idea at hand. This might have felt like quite a series of mental calisthenics, but the goal has been to strengthen your ability to see *connections* between your research topic and almost any other topic you can think of. Using REFLECTION to discover these intermediate steps between two unrelated topics often reveals very specific questions for research. Although this might seem paradoxical, the pattern is quite predictable: if you narrow a topic by looking at its areas of overlap with any other topic, you have drastically narrowed the range of potential questions that can be asked. Thus, you have started with a subject that was overwhelming in its vagueness and ended up with a very specific and real-world question that you might never have come up with on your own – and all this through the power of searching for connections. Congratulations on generating an impressive range of specific research ideas. In the next chapter, you will make the leap into investigating and researching one of these topics, using strategies that continually draw upon your skills of RELAXATION and REFLECTION to keep an open mind and search out connections as you proceed.

Conversation 3 with Steve Almond: Freakdom

Steve Almond is the author the story collections *My Life in Heavy Metal* (Almond, 2003) and *The Evil B.B. Chow* (Almond, 2006), the novel *Which Brings Me to You* with Julianna Baggott (Almond and Baggott, 2006), and the non-fiction books *Candyfreak* (Almond, 2004) and *(Not That You Asked)* (Almond, 2008). His newest work of nonfiction is *Rock and Roll Will Save Your Life* (Almond, 2010). This conversation took place via email.

How did the research process start for you in Candyfreak*?*

Almond: My basic take is that everyone on earth is an expert on one thing or another, even if your expertise feels sort of embarrassing. So the fact that I've always been obsessed with candy and kept tabs on all the various new bars and could talk about candy for literally hours on end – this didn't feel like expertise. It felt like freakdom. And like nothing I would ever write about. It was too immature. But I also believe that our freaks, our obsessions, if thoroughly investigated, pretty much tell the story of our lives.

That being said, the only reason I started writing about candy was because I didn't know what else to do. I'd written a book of short stories, which had gotten some nice reviews but tanked. I'd written a big, long, awful novel. I literally had no idea what to do. So it was desperation, really. I just said: What do I love enough to write a book about? To get me through all the lonely decision-making. And the answer was (duh) – candy. Then I started visiting the factories and any doubts I had were immediately erased. The larger truth to emphasize is that everyone has their areas of expertise, whether it's video games or a sports team or competitive origami. Whatever.

Did the book start out with a question that you wanted to get answers to?

Almond: If there was one question I wondered about, it was: why did my favorite candy bar (the Caravelle) disappear? Why do some candy bars go extinct? But this question led to an examination of how the confectionary industry operates, which, in turn, led to an examination of late-model capitalism, and the death of regional commerce, and the homogenization of the marketplace. Not only did I get an answer, in other words, but that answer led to a broader exploration of the culture. It wasn't just about the Caravelle anymore.

Did you have any concerns initially about this project? Any fears about whether there would be <u>enough</u> material or whether you could make it interesting to someone who wasn't already fascinated by the subject?

Almond: I was racked with doubt throughout the process, so much so that I had trouble finishing the manuscript. I just thought: this is silly. Nobody gives a shit about this stuff but me, and I'm certifiably nuts. This kind of doubt is pretty natural for self-doubting, depressive types like me, for a lot of writers, I suppose, regardless of the genre. It's the reason you have to be stubborn and sort of suspend your own disbelief. And you also need a few good readers who can put a spur in your ass when you're stalled.

How much of what you gathered – quotes, impressions, other material – ended up in the book?

Almond: A pretty small fraction. Maybe a tenth or something. That's typical. The whole trick with a non-fiction book is to gather a lot of material, decide what the good stuff is, and get the hell out of the way.

In your opinion, what advantages does a subjective researcher – or a research project with a narrator – have over a traditional work of nonfiction? What disadvantages, if any?

Almond: Readers tend to get attached to desire. They come to books (any art, really) because they want an intensity of feeling absent elsewhere. The more honest you are about your desire, your personal involvement, the less objective you become. Which is fine. That doesn't mean that you have *carte blanche* to lie, to mess with the facts of history, or your own experience. It means that your job is to be radically subjective about objective events.

Was there a low point in the research process, a point at which you got the feeling that this all wasn't going to cohere into anything meaningful?

Almond: Many. In fact, I sent the first few chapters to a bunch of agents (Dumb!) and they all said, "We don't know what this is. We don't know where this would go in Barnes & Noble." And I was so discouraged I shoved the manuscript in a drawer for two months. I only dug it out because friends of mine urged me to. I also had lots of doubts during the writing. But the fact that I'd done all this research made me feel like I needed to complete the book.

What's your organizational system for keeping track of all the research you collect?

Almond: "Organizational system" is overstating the case. I transcribed all the interviews onto my computer. That was the main thing I did. Organization isn't my strong suit.

What for you personally is the most challenging part of conducting research? What is the most enjoyable?

Almond: The best is going out into the world and seeing cool stuff and talking to people who are as freaky as you are. The hunting and gathering. The writing itself – decide what matters – is the part that I find excruciating.

Why do you think students have a tough time coming up with research topics?

Almond: Like I said, students aren't used to looking at their own obsessions as potential academic material. It's way too personal, and they may in fact be embarrassed to reveal the stuff that matters to them most deeply. That's a lot of being in college: you're so self-conscious. So they stick with the subjects that supposedly feel important and that remain at the level of rhetoric, rather than challenging them to reveal something about themselves. One thing I've done with classes is to just force them to write about their obsessions. To plug into the expertise that's already inside of them. The basic rule is that the more into it the writer is, the more into it the reader's going to be.

Have you always come up with good ideas for research projects? Any horrible ideas, say from high school?

Almond: I don't remember writing any research projects in high school. I will say that pretty much anything is fascinating if the person telling you about it is obsessed. There are no horrible ideas, really. Only uninspired narrators.

8 Beginner's Mind

Wabi-sabi is not about gorgeous flowers, majestic trees, or bold landscapes. Wabi-sabi is about the minor and the hidden, the tentative and the ephemeral: things so subtle and evanescent they are invisible to vulgar eyes.

— Leonard Koren, *Wabi-Sabi*
(Koren, 2003: 50)

Introduction to Chapter 8

When you choose a topic to research, you might feel as though you are looking out into a wilderness blanketed in fog. The truth is out there somewhere, but getting enough direction to take a clear position or construct an argument might seem impossible. The beginning of any research trek can feel baffling and a little overwhelming, even for the experienced researcher. Many students try to get rid of this discomfort as quickly as possible, maybe by typing the topic into an Internet search engine to find out what others have written or copying whatever is provided on the Wikipedia website. In fact, this feeling and even discomfort or fear of *not-knowing* is the key to successful research. The state of not-knowing itself contains a certain kind of insight that can provide direction and even wisdom as you hone in on your topic.

The quote at the beginning of this chapter describes a Japanese artistic concept of *wabi-sabi*, which has been translated as a kind of "rough beauty." The quote suggests that the beautiful is seen not in a full-grown tree but in a bare branch with a few buds (Koren, 2005: 50–51). Thinking about the beginning stage of research as a tentative, new growth – a bud or seed of an idea – may help you separate the anxiety of an unknown or new topic from the opportunities and possibilities that the topic offers. The beginning is an unavoidable stage that offers its own beauty. Knowing the specific qualities of a new research project allows you to use those characteristics to your advantage.

For the Experiments and discussion that follow, you will need to have chosen a research project topic – big or small, complex or simple – to work with. The next level of skills in RELAXATION, REFLECTION, and RESEARCH will deal with the ways you can approach this specific topic. If you don't yet have a topic you are excited about, now might be a good time to go back through the entries in your notebook, including the freewrites, the obsession notebook, the charts of brainstorms, the bubble charts, the interest inventories, and the lists of topic ideas and questions prompted by specific Experiments. Mark the topics that seem to capture your attention. As is usually true with research, you don't need to feel completely committed to this idea, and you may find you need to alter it or change it later. But for now, choose a topic in order to get started with the specific challenges and opportunities of a research project. You might want to start out by writing down everything you know about the topic, and everything you have questions about. This stage can be daunting, so the next Experiment will address the moment in which a researcher confronts his or her own lack of knowledge about a subject.

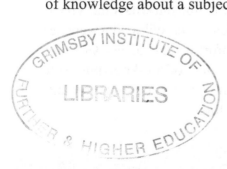

The Discomfort of Not-Knowing

You have probably heard the adage "Knowledge is power." We see experts and authorities as powerful because they possess and master information in their field; not-knowing is by definition weakness. Given that cultural baggage, it is understandable that throwing oneself into a voluntary state of ignorance induces some stress.

If you have had the unfortunate experience of a particular *block* or difficulty in trying to learn a new skill, if there's a subject you've repeatedly tried to understand that eludes you, or if you have had trouble with a certain topic in school, you might have extra anxiety regarding the experience of not-knowing. In addition, anyone who has high standards for themselves or who has picked up new skills easily in the past can develop frustration when a research goal fails to unfold as planned. Because research requires careful attention to the process of knowledge acquisition, a desire to rush through the process and to answer only the easy questions can directly determine the quality of the knowledge produced.

It is important to realize that your level of anxiety about the task of research has no bearing on your ability to do research. But learning to tolerate and even welcome this anxiety is in some sense a requirement for successful research. Think of research as a type of strength training. If you are interested in building muscles, you assume that your workouts will cause a specific and concentrated type of discomfort but will benefit your body and your mind. After you gain certain skills and incorporate the strength-training routines into your life, the discomfort will fade into the background as you experience the wide range of benefits that come from your effort.

While the research workout won't give you a brain that bulges out of your skull, you will find yourself gradually freed from the crushing sense of panic that can accompany beginning research. You find yourself able to brainstorm questions and make a research plan, to even enjoy the research. And if you are not watching for these benefits, you can easily take them for granted and forget that the training was what led to these lasting, and in some cases permanent, results.

For the first Experiment, turn your attention to the experience of not-knowing as a way to understand how social, cultural, and personal attitudes toward ignorance, learning, and not-knowing might shape your approach to research. Gaining awareness about your research traits will help you to know your own habits as a researcher and to learn about your research instruments – including your mind and identity – in order to adjust for your particular quirks and adapt them to your research project.

Experiment 8.1: I Don't Know

Length: *Long*

Timer: *5 minutes + 4 minutes + 3 minutes + 5 minutes = 17 minutes*

Discuss: *Recommended*

Step 1. For five minutes, freewrite on one or more experiences in your life in which you were frustrated or challenged as you attempted to learn a new skill or absorb new subject matter. You might write about how you responded to these challenges, what you thought about yourself, what fears and anxieties the experience provoked, or how long it took you to become more comfortable with the skill or subject. Were there any experiences in which the beginning phase was so difficult that you abandoned the subject or skill altogether? What skills or subjects do you typically describe as "I can't do that" or "I'm not good at that"?

Step 2. Choose one of the skills or subjects from your first freewrite and write for four minutes on the teacher and/or the learning environment in that situation. Was there anything about the method of instruction or the teacher that added to your frustration? Consider the time in your life and your age; were you ready to acquire this skill? Also write about how peers, classmates, and adults responded to your attempts.

Step 3. Look back over your first two freewrites and see what insights emerged, then freewrite for three minutes about any patterns that run through these experiences. What general obstacles do you confront when you learn new skills or subjects? Are there specific subjects or types of skills that come more easily, or not so easily, to you?

Step 4. Now freewrite for five minutes on as many things as you can remember learning with joy and enthusiasm. Think particularly about early experiences with activities, people, or subjects you immediately felt connected to or skills you acquired with little effort.

Know-It-Alls and Beginner's Mind

The Know-It-All is someone you might have encountered at a party or in a class. He or she would have you believe that there is nothing surprising in the world, and that he or she possesses boundless information on almost any subject you might bring up. Part of the reason this type of person is so annoying – and so often a source of unintentional humor – is that we recognize the impossibility of the Know-It-All's claims. Yet most of us live in a Know-It-All culture. Facts and figures, graphs and charts, are cited as reason and justification for national and local policy. *Empiricism* – the approach to knowledge that seeks to measure and quantify external reality – is prized above all other sorts of judgment and insight. Committees and commissions often address problems of public policy by issuing a report after gathering as many facts as possible in order to reach a decision.

These efforts are essential, yet a collection of facts does not necessarily point toward a solution. Certain types of questions – those that draw connections, that come from thinking "outside the box" and that seem to come from nowhere – are often those that hold the key to new insights and that often generate surprising and innovative projects. Instructor Richard Brady writes: "My students are so conditioned by a culture that constantly judges and evaluates their answers that they want to ask only good, expert questions. How many of these students had any difficulty asking questions when they were five years old?" (Brady, 2004: 9). Five-year-olds grow up and quickly learn that asking too many questions causes annoyance, discomfort, and other negative repercussions.

Most successful researchers – and artists, writers, and scientists in many fields – have the ability to be comfortable in the state of not-knowing. The beginning of knowledge comes with a sense of wonder and excitement that provokes innocent and basic questions and that builds as a subject area is mastered and more questions are generated. Robert Tremmel, a teacher, writes: "In order to stay alive, to grow, to stay on the journey it is necessary to…go back to school, to go back and reconnect with the mind and energy of the beginning" (Tremmel, 1999: 96). In this sense, the beginner's energy and outsider perspective are a kind of insight: the fundamental questions asked by the outsider are often invisible to the expert who is fully immersed in his or her field.

Japanese Zen master Shunryu Suzuki writes about the value of "beginner's mind," which he described as "an empty mind and a ready mind" (Suzuki, 1973: 21). Suzuki explains that a beginner's mind is free of the tendency to see only what it expects to see. He writes: "If your mind is empty, it is always ready for anything; it is open to everything. In the beginner's mind there are many possibilities; in the expert's mind there are few" (Suzuki, 1973: 21). In this profound observation about the trade-off between knowledge and possibility, Suzuki implies that the more we think we know about a topic, the more readily we surrender our ability to question the fundamentals and assumptions that form that area of knowledge. This is not to say that expertise and advanced knowledge have no value. Suzuki is merely pointing out that as expertise in a particular subject area develops, so too does the tendency to see the subject as framed by the boundaries, rules, and expectations of that particular discipline.

Experiment 8.2: The Power of Not-Knowing

Length: *Flexible (Short, Long, or Take-home)*
Timer: *5 minutes*
Discuss: *Optional*

Step 1. Write your topic idea at the top of a piece of paper.
Step 2. Choose five words from this list:

Origins	Causes	Effects	People
Environment	Economy	Culture	Conflicts
Solutions	Innovations	Changes	Legacies

Write the five words you have chosen in a column down the side of the page.

Step 3. For each word, brainstorm a question or something you don't know about your topic that connects somehow to that word. Write one or more simple questions next to each word. For example, if your topic is automobile racing, next to the *Solutions* category you might ask, "What problems could or does automobile racing solve (maybe racetracks bring in revenue for towns with racetracks and with few other industries or attractions)?"

Step 4. Now get even simpler. Take five minutes to channel the voice of your inner five-year-old. What would a child want to know about your question or topic? If it helps, you can brainstorm these child-like questions based on the five categories or go off on a tangent. List as many questions as you can that connect to your topic in some way. What happens to the tires after they're done being used by the race cars? When have various forms of automobile racing reached a peak of popularity in various countries, and why? How often do people die in crashes during races?

The Work of Not-Knowing

As you might have realized by now, channeling your inner five-year-old is not child's play. Developing open-minded and complex questions about the world is a skill we often neglect, and those who are able to retain and enhance the skill of "not-knowing" have particular strengths when it comes to finding a career. Journalists, researchers, inventors, scientists, doctors, and artists (among others) all use persistent and innovative questioning as a way to push beyond conventional expectations to find novel approaches to a problem.

Many employers have realized that cultures in their workplaces can stifle this questioning skill. Daniel Goleman, who has written extensively on mindfulness, psychology, and the brain, observes with co-authors Paul Kaufman and Michael Ray in *The Creative Spirit* (Goleman, Kaufman, and Ray, 1992) that employers can "encourage 'naïve' questions that call attention to unexamined assumptions in the workplace. Such questions, though they may seem naïve, are never 'dumb' – they challenge people to examine the habitual mindset that makes work routine and uninspired" (p. 129).

A careful researcher can ask seemingly naïve questions and be off to a good start. An imaginative researcher can take this one step further to picture the hazy outlines of questions that are still invisible, along with the people, places, and things to provide answers to those invisible questions. A good journalist, as one example, knows that every subject under the sun connects to a whole culture devoted to this subject, populated with experts who each know different facets of that world. In newsroom lingo such a reporter is described as having a *nose for news*. And the news often comes from unexpected directions: a third-generation dairy farmer reveals family arguments about the best way to treat chapped cows' udders. A Blues musician reflects on the lower incidence of depression among his fans. A schoolteacher reveals unexpected predictors of success among low-income schoolchildren. For every topic there are experts – and most of them are not full-time authors or employees at universities and think tanks.

Good reporters and researchers pay close attention to exactly what they don't understand. They collect data and observations, anecdotes and stories, and they know that each expert will have a slightly different view on their topic. They aim for a complicated, diversified, and well-rounded view of a topic rather than a simple answer, and they know that the more they learn, the more questions will be revealed.

Open vs. Closed Questions

In the textbook *FieldWorking: Reading and Writing Research*, Sunstein and Chiseri-Strater advise students on the research process (Sunstein and Chiseri-Strater, 2007). They draw an important distinction between *open* and *closed* questions in an interview. (More will be said about interviewing and questions in Chapter 11.) Thinking about the types of questions you ask can also be helpful as you craft and choose questions that will launch a research project.

A *closed* question can usually be answered without much elaboration: *What is your name? How many pets do you have? What's your astrological sign? Do you like horror movies?* These questions ask for a simple bit of data, maybe even just a "yes" or "no" or a simple nod of the head. The term *closed* also implies that such a question is a tiny opening and offers little room to move around. An *open* question, on the other hand, offers you and your interview subject a lot more room to explore. An *open* question does not have one right answer. Instead, it focuses on gathering "expertise, knowledge, beliefs, and worldview" (Sunstein and Chiseri-Strater,

2007: 239-240). Open-ended questions invite a response in the form of a story or a complex explanation: What event has been most significant this year? Why do you like the color blue? Why did your mother not attend college? Open questions don't guarantee complexity; if you ask someone, "How was your day?" you might hear anything from a curt "Fine" to a ten-minute tale of woe or joy. But these questions at least open the possibility of elaboration. With a closed question, it is more difficult to get outside of the box or to leap the fence into complexity.

As you brainstorm your research ideas, you are in effect interviewing yourself as you scan your interests and collected knowledge and look for sites of interest. Students often start on research quests by asking themselves closed questions. This makes sense because these questions offer an entry-level approach to a subject and seem to promise a simple answer.

However, there is a significant downside to using a closed question as the basis for a research project. If you ask, "Is the death penalty right?" or "Who was the best U.S. president?" or "Do art majors get jobs after college?" you will be setting yourself up for a struggle because you are attempting to ask a complicated question in terms of a simple one. The answer to these questions must all start with such responses as "It's complicated" or "It depends on your point of view, your parameters, or your criteria for making this decision." You might then feel like your paper is a failure because you have to jump around to survey the different points of view. As a result, your paper cannot really come to any conclusions because your question has limited the depth of your research. In contrast, an open question can push you to account for multiple perspectives, including the ones that are not obvious at first.

The Gray Matter, Part I: Ethical Questions

You might start brainstorming a research idea with a "yes or no" question, such as whether the death penalty is wrong. You would then quickly discover that this question evokes heated and contradictory responses from different perspectives. Your instructors might steer you away from tackling these questions to help you avoid getting mired in a moral quagmire.

This does not mean that these questions are irrelevant. Moral questions are an essential part of life and are a sister to research questions. Frameworks and systems of values and morality form the foundation for such questions because they allow people to interpret reality. But moral systems are not research topics in and of themselves. If you turn to a moral framework to find a research topic, you are researching an answer instead of a question. Posing and answering ethical questions about right and wrong depends on the moral and ethical frameworks used to create and interpret those questions. Simply put, your background and what you believe will determine and influence the types of moral and ethical questions you ask.

A research topic that explores only two sides of an issue does not leave much room for complexity and real-life complications. If you research a hot-button issue like gun control or capital punishment, you might find yourself repeating highly charged statements of value from people who are deeply engaged in the debate. Western culture – particularly those elements influenced by the practice of debating – places a high value on this kind of strongly worded and opposing-viewpoint sparring, and each perspective presents evidence to back up its ethical stand. Western culture also tends toward a dualistic way of thinking, which frames problems and solutions in paired and opposing categories: right and wrong, useful and useless, interesting and dull. If we approach the world with this framework, we may be seeing certain questions clearly while missing choices and ideas that don't fit within this frame.

Weighing two opposing ethical standpoints requires the tools of philosophy, theology, and faith; to undertake these questions as a research topic is to miss the fruitful seeking and questioning opportunity presented by a research project. An ethical or political inquiry can be searching and research-based, but some arguments based on ethics or politics take a particular stance on an issue and try to convince the audience about the correctness of that stance.

This does not mean that research is divided or separated from ethical life. On the contrary, research is intimately connected with the gray areas of life that ethics explores. All knowledge, even if created for its own sake as with pure scientific research, has an ethical component and an impact on the real world when the knowledge comes into contact with the world. We might develop, strengthen, or reconsider an ethical or political viewpoint in the midst of doing research. Research is more a matter of investigating complex relationships: cause and effect, actions and reactions, choices made, and complex results. A research question can be asked by someone with a strong political or ethical stance, but the research question will be more searching and will steer itself away from questions that can be answered with a simple yes or no. A careful researcher will ask questions that go to the heart of his or her own confusion rather than aiming for the heart of the opposing argument.

Experiment 8.3: Questions to Consider

Length: *Short (or Take-home if all are assigned)*
Timer: *5 minutes*
Discuss: *Optional*

Consider the questions below, and choose one (or more) to address in a five-minute freewrite. Then as you examine your answer, you might see that some of the most interesting research topics could be generated from those very subjects you see as off-limits or too complicated or sensitive to tackle.

1. What topics do you feel very strongly about? How might your ethical views on these topics influence your ability to research multiple viewpoints on this issue?

2. What questions about ethics come up for you on a regular basis? Could any of these be written as open-ended research questions? What groups of people might regularly confront the same moral dilemma, and what might this mean? How do groups of people or individuals respond to these daily moral dilemmas?
3. What issues and topics might you avoid as a result of your moral and ethical views? What topics could you challenge yourself to learn more about that you might normally avoid?

Bias and Conflict of Interest

Researchers must be aware of and acknowledge biases, but weeding them out completely is probably impossible. On the other hand, research projects can share the authors' source of biases in the results and can also correct for such bias in various ways.

Bias can be introduced in any research project when a researcher has a strong emotional, financial, professional, or other tie to his or her subject. The danger comes in when the reader does not know about this tie and the researcher has not shared this information or tried to correct for it. Controversies around *conflict of interest* in research usually arise when a researcher has conducted an experiment without disclosing that he or she has a financial or other tie to the outcome or to the subject matter. A researcher may believe that he or she can correct for personal and emotional ties and other conflicts of interest. But it takes quite an ego to claim that you – unlike most of humanity – can detach from your own life and that you can do this detachment so well that you do not even need to bring it up in your research.

The cause for concern is real, even for beginning researchers. To put it simply, if you already have a strong attachment to one side of an argument or a proposed solution to a problem, you have a more detailed and complex understanding of that part of your research question. As you might already have seen, understanding leads to complexity, to more questions. And so your knowledge about a topic necessarily leads into a desire for further attention to that topic. If the researcher is not being careful to brainstorm all possible questions about a topic, it is very easy to fall into the rut of pursuing one well-known element of a problem. Therefore, even advanced researchers sometimes need to step back from their subjects and do a little brainstorming about subjects for which their depth of knowledge might be obscuring alternative viewpoints.

Experiment 8.4: Question Launch Pads

Length: *Flexible (Short, Long, or Take-home)*
Timer: *4 minutes*
Discuss: *Optional*

Step 1. Look back at the questions you generated in Experiment 8.2. Put a star next to the questions that require more than a few words as an answer.
Step 2. Using your topic idea from Experiment 8.2, brainstorm an open-ended question for each of the categories for which you asked a closed question (The categories were: *Origins, Causes, Effects, Changes, People, Environment, Economy, Culture, Conflicts, Solutions, Innovations,* and *Legacies*).
Step 3. Look at the list of child-like questions from Experiment 2, and put a star next to the open-ended questions.
Step 4. Can you reframe the child-like closed questions into open-ended questions?

Beginner's Mind into Researcher's Mind

The notion of *beginner's mind* is a rich source of inspiration you can call upon whenever you find your interest dulled. This point of view can also help you into the writing process; many writers ask very simple beginner's questions to help them focus on telling their readers the most important parts of their research. Why does this matter? So what's the big deal here? So what?

After you have explored the beginner's perspective, you make a decision to move ahead and set some research goals that will carry you toward the complexity of a real research quest. To judge whether you have built a good foundation for your research, you might ask yourself whether you have pushed your own definitions or expectations of the topic at hand. When you are able to ask intelligent questions that get at the complex parts of your topic, you have naturally and effortlessly moved from Beginner's Mind into Researcher's Mind. Part of keeping this Beginner's Mind/ Researcher's Mind active is to keep asking questions throughout the research process. To ensure that you are not getting off track with your research and to check whether your topic and your questions need to be reassessed, you should stop and reflect on your overall direction after every source. Each source should raise questions, generate confusion, or present new avenues for inquiry. (More about the methods of keeping your questions running will be covered in Chapter 9.)

Experiment 8.5: Research Sampler

Length: *Long or Take-home*
Timer: *4 minutes + additional online research time*
Discuss: *Optional*

Step 1. Choose a research topic that you think you might like to devote some time to, either for a specific course assignment or for the purpose of learning about your research process.
Step 2. Locate two or three good but short all-purpose summaries of this topic, using an online search engine, wiki, or

database. Such all-purpose sources which skim the surface of a field can be a helpful place to start.

Step 3. As you read each source, list the questions that occur to you. These might be terms, events, or processes that are unfamiliar in the text themselves, or they might be subjects that seem connected to the topic but are not fully explored. Try to come up with between six and nine questions in total (two to three per source).

Step 4. Highlight or underline two or three of these questions that are particularly interesting. You might also use a bubble chart to diagram the connections between these questions and to see which point in a general area of inquiry you'd like to follow.

Step 5. Do a four-minute freewrite to mull over the questions you generated, and write about which of these interests you most. What questions and complex issues were raised by these introductions to your topic?

The Gray Matter, Part II: Don't Patch Over the Gaps

As you begin to know more about your topic and uncover useful sources, you naturally become more invested in a particular view of your topic. This investment is an outgrowth of curiosity and a growing familiarity with your subject, as a bit of curiosity added to knowledge and interest grows still more curiosity as the questions become more complex. You move away from beginner's mind as you become more of an expert on the topic. The downside of developing expertise, as Suzuki explains, is that you become invested in one framework for seeing the world.

As you sharpen your own arguments and become attached to certain perspectives or viewpoints, you might encounter sources that refute your argument or your position. Students often ask in these situations whether they are allowed to skip over these sources, because they wonder whether sharing these perspectives with a reader will weaken their watertight argument.

It is common for students – and all writers – to want to ignore a challenging source. It is easier to make a simplistic argument that presents one side of the picture, but then you end up with a simple argument that presents one side of the picture. A slightly more advanced strategy is to present an opposing argument in order to find its weak points and argue against it. This is common in debate-style or opposing-argument papers, where the writer takes a strong position and backs it up with evidence. In these cases, the writer is usually presenting a weak or clichéd version of the counter-argument in order to make a favorite position look better by comparison.

The truly *seeking* researcher – the one who is fueled by questions, not easy answers – will become interested in evidence that seems to point out a weak point or contradiction. The questions inspired by this evidence can take a project in a creative and fruitful direction, and may lead to a path that no one else has considered.

Questions for Thought or Discussion

1. Discuss an experience in which you admitted you did not know something. What was the result? What are the reasons for anxiety when admitting lack of knowledge, in your opinion?
2. How would you address or bring up questions in a research project that you cannot answer? How might you share these questions with your audience?
3. List the types of limitations you might face in a research project such as a paper for a class. How might you address these within the context of the project?
4. What are the causes of a researcher's limitations?

Conclusion to Chapter 8

It might seem strange to delve into Beginner's Mind in the middle of this book, yet in a *recursive* theory of making knowledge, a writer moves forward in a kind of spiral fashion and builds upon what has already been accumulated. The writer moves along this spiral path while returning to previous tools, like RELAXATION and REFLECTION, for understanding and orientation for the next stage of the journey.

The first seven chapters of this book focused on building your skills in the areas of brainstorming and asking questions. These brainstorms led to a range of possible research topics, and the choice to pursue one or more of these. Once you have committed to a research topic, you are halfway through the research process but back at the beginning in another way. Rather than finding a topic, you have to find yourself in relation to your chosen topic. Chapter 8, then, has formed a bridge to the chapters that follow. Next, you will begin to research information about your chosen topic, reflect on that information and your reaction to it, and remember to take breaks to ask yourself where your research quest is headed.

Section III
Big Bang: Form and Structured Chaos in Research

9   Take Note

> **How it felt to me:** *that is getting closer to the truth about a notebook….* **Remember what it was to be me:** *that is always the point.*
>
> – Joan Didion, "On Keeping a Notebook,"
> *Slouching Toward Bethlehem*
> (Didion, 1968: 134–136)

Introduction to Chapter 9

Joan Didion, an American essayist and novelist, flips through her notebooks to remind herself of snippets of past moments, details that connect to stories, and pieces of overheard conversations. In her essay "On Keeping a Notebook," she puzzles over the records she finds herself keeping and wonders why she is drawn to such a practice of gathering and collecting.

As Didion observes, this scribbling about one's thoughts seems, at first, self-centered. But as she traces each memory and phrase, she begins to see that these pieces of life connect to other people, to moments in life she wishes not to forget for the lessons they hold. Although a day's vivid intensity feels burned in our mind, Didion (1968: 13–139) observes, "We forget all too soon the things we thought we could never forget. We forget the loves and the betrayals alike, forget what we whispered and what we screamed, forget who we were. I have already lost touch with a couple of people I used to be…."

The strange part of research is being frozen in a moment of time, doing research with a certain version of "you." Whatever topic you are pursuing is pursued by the person you are right now. But Didion asks us to examine "the couple of people" we "used to be" who might have something to add to the account. Past experiences – even views and theories you once held that you have since discarded – might shed some light on a topic you want to pursue. The life raft for your leap into the unknown of a topic is your research notebook – a collection of materials and ideas in one place, the raw material from which to build a conversation between you and slightly different versions of yourself you used to be and will become.

Didion's experiences in keeping a notebook highlight the *recursive* nature of writing, the way in which we forget facts and memories, accumulate experiences, and come back to our work as a slightly different person than we were the day before. This is an advantage: each day with its changeable events and point of view offers a new perspective on your life and on your topic. If we don't keep track of our reactions to information and to events in our lives, we lose the unique insights offered in each day. For that reason, research is also a process of reacting to and reflecting on what we find – all the way through, from start to finish.

Cut-and-Paste or Mix-and-Cook

Many research projects are not composed in a *recursive* fashion. Instead, they spring from an overuse of cut-and-paste word-processing technology; the author simply drops quotes into a finished document without much thought or reaction. This is like trying to bake a cake by setting a whole egg, a box of cake mix, and a splash of milk into a cake pan. If you put the unmixed ingredients into the oven, what you get an hour later is either an inedible mess of cardboard and goo – or a fire in your oven. The ingredients may have been merged together in some fashion, and they look sort of integrated into a new whole, but it's not the kind of cake anyone would want to receive for their birthday.

Similarly, when you string together quotes without analysis or reaction, you might assume you will make sense of this information when you sit down later to write the paper. But if you wait until the writing phase, you are often concentrating on making your text polished and readable, and you forget to first make <u>meaning</u> by putting original ideas into words. Putting frosting on your mess of cardboard, cooked egg and eggshells and soggy cake mix won't make a nicer cake. Making sure to interact with all of the raw in-gredients – mixing egg and sugar, measuring spices, adding flour in the correct amount, and so forth – ensures that you have more than what you started with. Like the spaces and measurements required to make a cake, the space in your notebook is dedicated to interacting with your material.

Space for Your Research

When you have chosen a research topic, dedicate a section of your notebook to this task. You might insert a divider or a piece of construction paper to divide general notes and brainstorms from the specific research topic. The important thing is that your research project should have its own place in your life, free from other course notes, shopping lists, assignments, and freewrites. The first thing I usually do when I start a new project is to put all of my notes and freewrites on that topic together in one place, which often reveals the development of thought processes about the topic. Having a focused notebook allows connections within a topic to emerge that would not be as immediately apparent if they were not *juxtaposed*, or situated near each other in a way to reveal the contrasts between them.

The next thing I usually do is a series of unstructured freewrites about a topic.

You might think of this as searching your own mind and memories to brainstorm lists of questions, examine your own interest in the topic, and flesh out your confusions. You might even give yourself mini-assignments, asking yourself what you know about a topic, what you have heard, what you don't understand, how the topic connects to your life.

Experiment 9.1: Taking Notes

Length: *Flexible (Short, Long, or Take-Home)*
Timer: *None*
Discuss: *None*

Step 1. Dedicate a section of your notebook to your specific research topic, and mark it off in some way so you have plenty of paper to work on and an area to take notes. If you are using a three-ring binder, add plenty of blank pages for further reflections and notes. If you are using a spiral or composition notebook, make sure you have sufficient pages left for notes and brainstorms. You can also include a pocket folder for material from other sources if you like.

Step 2. Brainstorm your lists of questions and interests related to the topic, using any of the exercises you found helpful in the preceding chapters. Collect pages from freewrites you have already completed in the preceding chapters that connect to the topic. If necessary, use tape or staples to attach other jottings, inspirations, and notes you have collected that connect to the topic on blank pages of your notebook. Weed out whatever doesn't have anything to do with your topic.

Net of Questions

As you brainstorm, you may feel like you've reached the edge of your knowledge, experience, and questions. You're <u>almost</u> ready to start looking for outside sources. Before you do that, you need a net, which is a looser and more flexible structure than an outline. An outline is often taught as a formal organizational structure for a paper, with several levels and a complex numbering and lettering system. Outlines are intended to be helpful for organizing a paper, but some writers find them intimidating and/or confining. An easier way to move from freewrites to research is to make a *net* of questions and topics.

Experiment 9.2: Fishing Net

Length: *Flexible (Short, Long, or Take-home)*
Timer: *None*
Discuss: *Optional*

Step 1. Go back through any notes or brainstorms that you have accumulated on your topic. Using a highlighter or pen, put a star in the margin next to any thoughts that seem to be big ideas and overarching themes, as well as sub-topics that cover smaller categories of ideas.
Step 2. As you review your writing, circle or highlight the question you generated about your topic.
Step 3. Make a pool or group of these topics and questions on a piece of paper in no particular order.
Step 4. Look at the pool of topics and questions. Draw lines to connect the questions and topics that seem related by theme or subject area; the result may look like a net or a spider web.

Step 5. If you like, make a separate list for each of these connected clusters. Put a star next to the one or two lists that
seem most interesting or detailed.

Nets to Catch Facts

You have now generated a little picture of your knowledge and
your questions in a convenient visual format. Your clusters may
also give you a clue about your interest areas; if you have any
clusters that are particularly large or detailed, you might consider
focusing on these to take advantage of your own momentum and
curiosity. You might not have the time or interest to pursue all of
these topics for your research project. Some of your items might
lead in very different directions, but even if you focus on just one
of these, you may be able to return to this list later for inspiration.
And as you begin to collect your sources, you might find a few
other techniques useful for dealing with your research materials.

Double-Column Notebook

Before you start taking notes for a research project, draw a line
down the middle of each page. With one motion you have created
a double-column notebook. Many writers and researchers use such
a system to record facts and observations in the left column, and
to write their questions and reactions to those facts in the right
column. As Sunstein and Chiseri-Strater (2007: 90) describe it,
"the double-entry notes are designed to make your mind spy on
itself and generate further thinking and text." In other words, this
simple act of reacting immediately to what you collect – a kind of
research journaling or REFLECTION – allows you to acquire facts and
figures and also to place these pieces of information in context and
create knowledge (Sunstein and Chiseri-Strater, 2007: 83).

In the laboratory, scientists running experiments may use the left column for recording their planned procedures and the right column for results. In classes, the double-column method is helpful because you can take notes from a lecture in the left-hand column, and jot questions or reactions on the right. Then you can see at a glance the ideas that come from your teacher and those that are your own responses. Still another strategy is to use the left-hand column for recording main ideas and the right-hand column for filling in details.

For research, I recommend this method: copy quotes, ideas, and concepts that you find especially compelling into the left-hand column, along with source citation material. (The following chapters will discuss finding sources in greater detail.)You may also cut and paste paragraphs from articles and print them out with narrow margins (about half the page), then cut out quotes that you like, and tape them into the left-hand column. On the right, react to these.

Here are some ways that you might engage with quoted material:

1. Comment on the quotes in any manner you like.
2. Note to yourself why you went to the trouble of collecting this quote.
3. List your questions.
4. Disagree with the author.
5. Pose problems and point out contradictions and issues not addressed in an article.
6. Make notes about your own experiences and observations.
7. Circle words or phrases you don't understand on the left and draw lines to your questions on the right.

Much as a lab scientist uses the right column for experimental procedures, you will use the right-hand column to test the findings of another author in the laboratory of your mind and your life.

It is important to gauge and record any details about your own reactions to the research material. Using practices mentioned in Chapter 5 about observing yourself and your state of mind, make notes about what sources make you happy or frustrated, what questions give you a headache or where in the research process you find yourself particularly annoyed with something. You might circle or star these reactions, or put them in the margin, so that they are easier to see later when you are reviewing your notes and looking for ways to organize your material or questions to ask about the research topic.

Questions to Focus

Many writers use the right-hand column of their notebooks to list questions and confusions they have about the research notes. You can keep track of your confusion by simply putting a question mark in the right-hand column next to each note that raises a question, although you then have to then go back and figure out what your questions were. Another option is to write one clear, complete question in response to each source after you read it. When the material is most fresh in your mind, ask yourself about something missing or unexplained, or ask a question about a connection between your source and other topic.

These questions might seem to be leading you off the path of your topic, or they might lead you to reexamine sources you've already read. A return to something that is not clear for you is the fundamental practice of *re*-search; as you go back and *re*-see a source in its complexity, you are mulling over trouble spots that likely contain the most intriguing elements of your topic. Listen to your own questions and follow them. Allow yourself to get distracted, and discard the sources that don't interest you. Recognize that you are making a conscious choice to move in a new direction.

Questions that draw your research toward something specific are actually <u>focusing</u> your research. Although it feels like you are going back to the drawing board, you are honing in on a more complex question than the one you started with. You are having a conversation with the research and following a thread to see where it leads. Each time you can respond to a source with a question, you are doing the work of *analysis*. You might also pause after you read and respond to a few sources in order to highlight or mark the questions you found most compelling.

Cheat Sheets and Spreadsheets

Some people are logical and linear thinkers. Others are more visual or more associative in their thinking styles. Each brain is different, and each person has his or her own thinking habits and ways of processing and organizing information. If you find yourself stymied by a research or writing project, or if you are stuck with a source that does not make sense to you, it might help to draw a picture or make a chart. Since these exercises happen behind the scenes in your early drafts, no one has to know that pictures are the scaffolding for your writing.

The list of possible ways to organize your research is endless. You can even create wall-sized bubble charts, taping up large pieces of paper for diagrams and adding sticky notes right onto the chart as you develop questions and ideas and find more sources. A huge chart can give some visually-minded people the conceptual space to explore the topic and remind them of the room that is also available for questions and exploration.

Other visual and physical organizational methods can help cut down research anxiety by prompting you to make physical "outlines" and helping you to organize sources as you work. Although it might sound like simple paper-shuffling, you are actually pre-writing by grouping and analyzing the content of your sources. Two related practices are *labeling* and *stacking*.

Labeling is a simple habit you can get into as you read. When you review your notes, you can make big visible labels on the pages of notes that connect to each of these sub-topics. You can use the right-hand column of your research notebook for these labels, too. You can use stars, exclamation points or other symbols to mark the quotes or points you know immediately that you want to mention or wrestle with in your paper. You can write additional words in the right-hand column of your notebook to mark surprising sub-themes that you want to pursue in your project. For example, you might start your research on big jungle cats and realize that a central question is the effect of human development at the edges of the cats' habitats. You might tag this sub-topic as *humans*, and if you notice other tags like this, it might be a visual clue to look into this as a possible focus for your project.

If you have piles of articles you have printed or copied, it can also be helpful to label the actual articles at the top of the first page and stack the articles in different piles or put them in different folders on your computer desktop. For example, if you are writing about *Jungle Animals: Big Cats*, you would have different folders that might say *Types of Big Cats, Conservation, Extinctions*, and *Ecology of*. Even the accumulation of many articles in one folder can indicate to you that you have more interest or more potential in a certain sub-topic and prompt you to focus on this area.

The Gray Matter: What is a Fact out of Context?

As discussed at the beginning of this chapter, many students write papers by cutting and pasting quotes from sources. After filling in the transitions between these quotes, the writer has created a very smart-sounding garland of the most esteemed authorities on a topic. Assuming these quotes have all their verbs, nouns, and phrases in the right places, they must be important and intelligent, right?

Reverence for the printed word often leads a reader to assume that if information is published, it must be correct, verified, or insightful – despite the fact that print is cheap these days and a blog can reach millions of readers. Even if an article is published in a reputable journal or major newspaper, there is no guarantee that the author's research or quote is *fact*. Although editors and publishers try to verify what is printed in their publications, the reader must ultimately make his or her own decision about an author's general reliability and whether the information presented is relevant for a particular research topic. To go back to the analogy of baking a cake, no decent recipe includes a general term such as *spices* on the ingredient list. You should know the background of the ingredients in your paper – including being aware of whether that's gravel or sugar or salt you are adding to the mix. If you decide to throw basil instead of nutmeg into your cookies, you're responsible for the reaction of your guests.

Awareness of your ingredients also includes an understanding of the source's argument and its bias or orientation. If you quote a source, you should be able to view that source with a degree of *skepticism* – a healthy distance that offers a perspective on the author's connection to his or her subject matter, how they benefit from holding certain views, what parts of their opinions or research are controversial, who they are and why that matters. If you cannot explain these things about an author's context, you don't have any business quoting them.

Several websites exist to help you evaluate the truth claims in popular media coverage and in conversations: Politifact (http://www.politifact.com/truth-o-meter/), sponsored by the *St. Petersburg Times* in Florida, deals mainly with political issues in current events in the United States. FactCheck (http://www.factcheck.org/), sponsored by the Annenberg Public Policy Center of the University of Pennsylvania, addresses and also includes lesson plans and a special web site for students (http://www.factchecked.org/). Snopes (http://www.snopes.com), run by Barbara and David Mikkelson, addresses email rumors, anecdotes, and urban legends.

Similarly, many of your readers will not trust <u>you</u> if you don't present this healthy skepticism and background information about the so-called authorities you present. This background – often called *attribution* – does not have to take up a lot of space in your paper, but your audience will be in the dark without it. A fact out of context is like one of your internal organs dropped on the sidewalk:

it is really not very much use unless it is connected to something and unless it is easy to see who it belongs to.

Experiment 9.3: The Author in the Story

Length: *Flexible (Short, Long, or Take-home)*

Timer: *4 minutes*

Discuss: *Optional*

Step 1. Select four or five quotes from your sources or from newspaper articles and write or type each of them on a separate slip of paper.

Step 2. Exchange these with a partner. When you receive your partner's quotes, your job is to make up fake attributions and identities for the authors of these quotes. Imagine an identity for the person who made each statement – and don't worry about whether the identity is correct. What might be this person's opinions, political perspective, background, experience, occupation, and training?

Step 3. Read your attributions aloud and then share the real identities of your authors. How often were your peers right and wrong about the perspectives and backgrounds of the authors?

Step 4. Look at one of your sources to find how quickly and subtly the information about the author's identity and connection to the subject is presented. Using a highlighter, mark the words and phrases that tell the reader about an author's point of view presented in the text.

Conclusion to Chapter 9

The practical containers for research are often overlooked as being obvious, yet an awareness of these tools and ideas can be very helpful in launching a research process. Specifically, the choice to set up your physical research space and your note-taking procedure can have a huge influence on the outcome of your project (much in the same way that a round Bundt cake pan will produce a very different cake than will a square pan). If you are interested in engaging with your sources in a way that produces and provokes your own reactions, you can set up your research process to make space for and even encourage reflection.

Collecting your brainstorms, notes, charts and diagrams, and freewrites on a topic in a central place in your notebook has a deeper function that addresses one root of research anxiety. Many writers feel as though they are not doing valuable work when they think about their topic. A particularly practical and goal-oriented writer might feel frustrated to be wasting so much time making connections and brainstorming strange reactions to a topic (or in trying to connect the topic to the platypus or to croquet). But simply gathering this material together will reveal additional connections at the same time that it shows significant movement and progress. While it might feel good to turn on a computer, fire up the word processor, and start typing a sentence that will spring ready-made into the final draft of a paper, true analysis and writing do not happen that way, any more than a cake can be made from a chicken, a stalk of wheat, and a cane of raw sugar. So look back and give yourself a pat on the back – whether you knew it or not, you were making significant progress toward finding a topic that would capture your interest and that could sustain focused inquiry. In the next chapter, you will move on to the RELAX phase of research in order to gather information in a loose way that allows for and invites continued questioning and association.

10 Noodling as a Research Method

The first stage is preparation, where you immerse yourself in the problem.... [Y]ou let your imagination roam free, open yourself to anything that is even vaguely relevant.... The idea is to gather a broad range of data so that unusual and unlikely elements can begin to juxtapose themselves.
> – Daniel Goleman, Paul Kaufman, and Michael Ray,
> *The Creative Spirit*
> (Goleman, Kaufman, and Ray, 1992: 18)

Introduction to Chapter 10

Research presents a problem of scale. There is so much information available, but an individual's capacity to absorb and process it is extremely limited. Working with two eyes, two ears, two hands, and a small amount of time and energy, the researcher confronts his or her personal limits long before the ocean of information runs dry. In other words, the information always wins. The key for navigating this sea of research is to be prepared, to learn about the currents, the submerged reefs and rocks, and to combine this readiness with the ability to explore, to change course, and adapt to the unforeseen storm.

A Wet Suit for Deep-Sea Diving

You might begin your search for information about your topic by entering a few keywords as a search term in an online database. The search engine informs you, "Your search matches 7,435 documents." When you are confronted with information overload, how do you make the right choices and find the sources most appropriate to your topic?

The secret answer is: You don't.

Now, realistically, you probably do want to try a few more search terms and get that search query of 7,435 down to a more reasonable number. But let's face it: even 200 articles that exactly match your topic are too many to digest in a few hours. You might laboriously open and skim all of them, or you might read each title to check for clues to its relevance. But the real way many researchers proceed is at random.

This might seem to go against everything you have heard about research. Most guides either emphasize that your process has to be systematic and all-encompassing, or they completely skip over the actual process researchers use to wade through a sea of possible sources.

Different researchers may approach the task in different ways. Let's look at the styles of two imaginary researchers, Anna and Howard. When starting a new research quest, Anna might enter the topic into her favorite search engine and happen to find an interesting page. Or she might get a list of seven great sources from the online library catalogue. But when she goes to the library, she wanders aimlessly in the wrong section and happens to find a fascinating book on a completely different topic, so she scraps her research idea and chooses this one instead. She might take home seven books on this topic and skim through the bibliographies, where she discovers a perfect source that was not listed on any library or Internet searches. Howard, on the other hand, might open a book and flip through the pages at random until something interesting seems to leap out, maybe from a photo caption on page 74 that he happened to notice in a five-second jog through the book. Or he will find a book at a garage sale or a magazine in the doctor's office that strangely has complete relevance to his research topic.

This is not to imply that tried-and-true, systematic research methods are useless. But it is also important to acknowledge the associative and right-brained research activity I will call *noodling*. The word *noodling* is sometimes defined as "to act aimlessly or fool around." The image also evokes a slippery, looping, and spaghetti-like research route. The term also refers to the sport of catching fish with one's bare hands – an appropriate image for fishing in the information ocean!

Noodling Online

The point of noodling is to give yourself a window of time – at least an hour – and to suspend all judgment about your activity during that time period. You will be researching, but in a manner that might feel slow. Rather than throwing yourself into a pond of information to thrash around and scare the fish away, you will just look in order to study whatever attracts your attention. To noodle, get a stack of manila folders and your research notebook. Choose a location, maybe the shelves of a library or a computer. If you are online, you will use a free search engine such as Google, Yahoo, or Ask.com.

Experiment 10.1: On-line and Aimless

Length: *Long or Take-home*
Timer: *One hour*
Discuss: *Optional*

Step 1. Devote a reasonable amount of time – such as an hour – to this exercise. In your research notebook, start a page titled *search terms*. Using an Internet search engine, type in a few words related to your topic idea. As you complete searches, record the search term you used in your notebook; this is so you can keep track of what you have already looked for and retrieve successful searches later.

Step 2. Skim the list of links provided by the search engine in response to your query, and click on the links which seem interesting or relevant. Don't read an entire page unless it captures your attention. If you sort through three or four pages of page listings and nothing grabs your attention, try to look further down the list.

Step 3. Every time you find an interesting article, copy and paste it into a word processing program and save the file. Copy and paste the URL (the web address of the page, which is whatever is in the top bar of the web window that starts with *http://...*) along with the text. This will give you the exact location of the page in case you decide to use it in your research project.

Step 4. If you find an interesting page, follow the links that seem interesting; *don't worry about whether they directly connect to your topic*. If you click through to a link that seems interesting enough to read, repeat Step 3. When you reach a dead end, go to the next step.

Step 5. Return to the search engine and type in another search term related to your research idea, or related to an idea triggered by a page you just read. Be sure to keep track of your search terms, and also be sure to cut and paste interesting pages and URLs as you go.

Step 6. After your allotted time is finished, sit back and congratulate yourself. You just engaged in pure process-driven research! By allowing your curiosity to follow its own lead, you probably ended up reading about topics you could not have located initially – because you did not know they existed. Look back over your search terms and the articles you cut and pasted. Highlight or mark any terms or pieces of information that particularly sparked your curiosity.

Free Databases to Noodle

To relax into a specific pool of the information ocean, you can noodle in a database – which might be described as a hot spring or a tidal pool, a particularly active and productive area for research. A database is simply any collection of data (i.e. information) that has been sorted and organized in a way that makes it accessible to users. Some databases cost money to use, but many useful online databases are free.

Search Terms

If you have used a search engine before, you know that some types of databases work by entering in just the terms you are looking for, like this: *Chocolate pecan*. Many databases allow you to put quotes around a phrase if you're looking for that specific phrase only: "Chocolate pecan." Other databases require you to use what are called *Boolean operators*: words or symbols like *AND* (+) or *OR* (–) to provide more exact information about what you would like the search engine to include and exclude. The easiest way to navigate the database's rules is to look on the help page of each database.

To begin, you can also enter a search term like "(your topic) database" or "(your topic) research" or even "(your topic) library." Often these terms will help a search engine focus your search toward reliable information. You will also discover that there are free, online databases devoted to everything from diabetes to greyhound breeding.

Browse through the online sources presented in the next sections and type in a few search terms. Noodling is the best method for becoming familiar with these online resources.

Wikis

Many free databases are *wikis*, or online portals that allow registered users to add and edit information in a database. The power of a wiki comes from its ability to track who edits and to establish a constant conversation about the accuracy of the information it presents; the disadvantage of a wiki is that the information presented is often not verified. Many wikis provide links to external and verified sources, so they can be a helpful starting place for research.

Digital Research Tools (http://digitalresearchtools.pbwiki.com/): A vast collection of how-to digital and online research resources, including pages of links to help with everything from visualizing data to writing a paper to managing scholarly references.

Wikipedia (http://www.wikipedia.org): Many scholars and teachers recognize the amazing power of *Wikipedia* – available in multiple languages – and even use it themselves. As a database that can be corrected and compiled by anyone who wants to sign up, it's handy, easy, and growing all the time. *Wikipedia* is an excellent resource for finding legitimate sources, as most entries in the database provide links to the sources used to document and support the entries. Teachers often advise students not to use *Wikipedia* because they want students to understand that too much *Wikipedia* is like too much encyclopedia or too much chocolate. A little goes a long way toward giving you a burst of research energy, but it does not provide adequate sources or variety for a balanced research diet. Using Wikipedia as the sole source in your research project lets your teacher know that you let a potentially unreliable stranger do your research for you.

WikiHow (http://www.wikihow.com): A collection that tells you how to do just about anything: "How to Celebrate the Year of the Potato," "How to Survive a Riptide," "How to Run Up a Wall and Flip," and "How to Catch Leeches for Bait." Most entries offer links to related topics. Follow the links and you are bound to end up with research ideas.

Databases of Published Works

Director of Open Access Journals (http://www.doaj.org/): This free database allows you to look in a library of scholarly journals that offer their content free online. The site also provides a "subject tree" to help you choose which journals to search.

ERIC (http://www.eric.ed.gov): The Education Resources Information Center, sponsored by the U.S. Dept. of Education, is an excellent free database that contains reliable and published articles (some full-text and some only as abstracts) on any education-related topic, from standardized testing, to attitudes toward tattoos in schools, to "The Broccoli Syndrome."

Google Scholar (http://scholar.google.com): Unlike the random mix of sites in a normal search engine search, *Google Scholar*'s links are usually peer-reviewed. Therefore, you have scholars familiar with each source who are vouching for its reliability.

OAIster (http://www.oaister.org): Created by the Open Archives Initiative, this is a catalog of digital resources – including images, audio, movies, digital documents, and digitized texts – that usually are not available to search engines because they exist within databases. Each listing includes descriptions about the copyright issues associated with the corresponding entry.

WorldCat (http:// www.worldcat.org/): A searchable network of library catalogs around the world, including much digital and free material.

Government and Organizational Databases

EDGAR (http://freeedgar.com/): A great free resource on publicly traded companies (those that sell stock to shareholders) using publicly available data from the U.S. Securities and Exchange Commission.

NERD Database (http://www.newenergychoices.org/nerd.php): The National Energy Resources Database, in addition to creating the best acronym ever, offers a free range of material and research on conventional and renewable energy.

PubMed Central (http://www.pubmedcentral.nih.gov/): The U.S. National Institute of Health offers a free database of life sciences research.

UNICEF Evaluation and Research Database (http://www.unicef.org/evaldatabase/index.html): Reports and data from around the world on the United Nations Children's Fund.

U.S. Census Bureau (http://www.census.gov/): Lots of data on the U.S. population – including economic and demographic profiles of communities – organized by census year. Similar resources are available for other areas of the world, including the searchable databases published by the Office of National Statistics in the United Kingdom (http://www.statistics.gov.uk/hub/index.html) and the Australian Bureau of Statistics (http://www.abs.gov.au/).

WHO Global InfoBase (http://www.who.int/infobase): An online portal created by the World Health Organization to provide information on diseases and health conditions around the world.

Restricted Databases to Noodle

Other online databases require a steep fee for use, but students can often access these for free through their university libraries. A growing number of public libraries subscribe to one or more of these excellent on-line collections. To locate your local list of databases, look on your library's web page or ask a librarian for help. You may be asked to enter an access code, such as a password or the bar code on your library card.

Once you have signed in to access these databases, you may be surprised to see the range of topics and collections – everything from scholarly databases to collections of artwork, local history collections, and collections in very specific subject areas. In addition, you will see some of the services offered for accessing large amounts of data, including *EBSCO*, *LexisNexis*, and the *Oxford English Dictionary* (described below), among others. The large databases often allow you to email yourself individual entries so you don't have to print or cut and paste what you want to keep for future reference.

EBSCO: This service allows you to search multiple databases at one time. It delivers a wide range of citations for scholarly and popular articles. Some of these entries take the researcher to the full text of an article. You can search its entire collection or select which databases or subjects to focus on. One *EBSCO* database, *Academic Search Complete*, is a huge database of scholarly articles from many disciplines.

Lexis-Nexis Academic: The granddaddy of all pay-to-play research databases, this may also be listed in your library as *Academic Search Premier*. *Lexis-Nexis* offers access to newspapers, magazines, journals, newsletters, and many other kinds of written material from around the world, around your state, or your town – from a decade or more ago up until yesterday. There is so much content in this database that a researcher will need to carry out multiple searches with specific terms to find the most appropriate material, but a few extra minutes in searching will almost certainly produce useful articles. *Lexis-Nexis* also has separate databases for such data as public opinion polls, reference material, and quotations.

Oxford English Dictionary: Why pay to use a dictionary? Well, the OED is no ordinary dictionary; the physical copy of this dictionary might very well weigh more than you do. You can use the OED to find out not only what a word means, but the word's origin, what other words it is related to in various languages, when it was first used, and all other manner of fascinating information. Your library probably has a copy, but the online version is even easier to use and provides quick links to histories and related words.

Experiment 10.2: Database Wandering

Length: *Flexible (Short, Long, or Take-home)*
Timer: *4 minutes*
Discuss: *Optional*

Databases might seem very scholarly and intimidating, but they are also a fun toy for exercising pure curiosity. For example, I regularly use search engines and databases to research phrases or word combinations like "Palestine peanut butter" because I want to see what would come up. As you do the experiment below, keep track of your search terms by making another list as in Experiment 1.

Step 1. Choose a database from the list above. Using the database's search function, type in a key word related to your topic.

Step 2. Scan through the titles of the articles that match your search. Click on something that seems interesting and skim it. The article you read does not (necessarily) have to be something you would like to research or write about, just something that catches your eye.

Step 3. Choose a word or phrase from this article and do a new search. If your first search came up with hundreds of hits, you might search on your second search term along with your first. For example, if you typed in "pets" and came up with an interesting article about dog owners having lower blood pressure, you would redo your search with the terms "dog" and "blood pressure." If you found an article that looks interesting but is unrelated to your first search term, start over and do a search on a new keyword or two based on the new topic.

Step 4. For a truly strange search, choose an article from this second search, then choose a search term from within it, and do yet another search to see if something comes up.

Associative Reading

The big question is: Where does this get you? It may get you nowhere directly, but that is part of the point of the activity. These noodling search activities let you see how much information is available for specific and surprising queries. Reading in this associative way also requires you to stop thinking about your topic as a bucket to be filled up with facts. Instead, you engage with what has already been written on the topics that might overlap with yours.

After playing a bit in the database of your choice, you might want to do a multi-word search on a topic you care about to see if any articles are available. Remember to vary your search terms – for example, from "thinking" to "cognition" to "thought" to "brain" – if one search term seems to limit your results.

Blogs: How Low Can You Go?

A *blog* (short for *web log*) is simply an on-line diary. Some blogs look as well-formatted and as complex as a newspaper's website, while others are clearly the ramblings of a single lonely soul. Because a blog is a format for presenting information, there is nothing inherently reliable or unreliable about a blog. However, a general rule is that a blog is unreliable for purposes of gathering research facts unless the blog writer presents sources or unless the researcher presents quotes from bloggers as individual opinions. Using a blog as a source in a research project can be problematic because bloggers may not provide references or links to support their assertions and often present very subjective or uninformed viewpoints.

On the other hand, blogs can be helpful starting points for research. Because they provide a first-person perspective on a wide range of topics, you can see the complex viewpoints of someone who is very invested in a topic. As mentioned in Chapter 5, people who are deeply connected to and invested in a topic might have a special perspective on that topic which includes contradictions, solutions, and thoughtful reflection. *Blog rolls* – the list of links often included in the left- or right-hand column of a blog – can provide wonderful connections to other online resources. Although a personal anecdote or story from a blog does not prove the existence of a larger trend, such blog entries can provide real-world anecdotes to flesh out an abstract thesis. If you find several blogs discussing a similar problem or issue, you might compare and contrast them, adding in other types of sources to see whether the blogs and the academic sources come to similar or different conclusions. For example, if you are interested in researching the experiences of mothers with infants who return to finish their college degrees, you could look at a few academic articles and check for blogs on the same topic.

You may cite a blog entry in a research project if you provide your readers with some context for your use of the blog by stating in the body of your writing project – not just in the notes or source list – that the source quoted is a blog. This will allow the reader to view the quote in much the same way as a personal interview. For example, you might write, "One working mother, who wrote a blog entry entitled 'Textbooks and Teething,' had this to say about returning to school:…."

There are several easy ways to locate blogs. The first is to enter a search term along with the word *blog* into an Internet search engine. The second strategy is to choose a popular blogging platform such as Blogger (http://www.blogger.com), Moveable Type (http://www.movabletype.com), WordPress (http://wordpress.org), MySpace (http://www.myspace.com), or LiveJournal (http://www.livejournal.com/) and then search within that collection of blogs for your topic. In addition, Lexis-Nexis allows you to search blogs within its database – an important indication of the increasing relevance of blogs for research.

Blogs can also be an amazing source of first-hand knowledge, no less important than having a great conversation on the bus. (These conversations, by the way, also take place on listservs, which are email group conversations, and the same caveats and opportunities exist for quoting these emails.) The added benefit of using blogs for research context is that you can have access to conversations with people around the world. A blogger volunteers his or her perspective and announces that he or she is ready and willing to talk. Many students and researchers also join these conversations by emailing bloggers about blog entries and then conducting email interviews with the blogger to ask more focused and specific questions. A blog search can lead you from a general idea to specific events, places, and people. Whenever you get more grounded in reality and detail, you are bound to introduce more complexity, more questions, and more interesting avenues for research. The result is likely to be a more in-depth and wide-ranging process and thus a better research project in the long run.

Experiment 10.3: Bunches of Blogs

Length: *Long or Take-home*

Timer: *None*

Discuss: *Optional*

Step 1. Enter a topic along with the word *blog* in a search engine. Explore a few of these links. If you click on a blog but do not find any mention of your topic on the page, you might have to search within that blog (a feature offered by most blog providers) or to perform a *Find* on your page (often accomplished by holding down the *Control* and *F* keys at the same time and then typing in your search term).

Step 2. Now examine the *blog roll* – the list of links many bloggers provide as a *sidebar* (a column running down the left- or right-hand side of the screen). Explore a few of these links, which may lead you to other blogs or other sources of information. Occasionally, a blogger references a useful piece of reliable news or research material that a search engine for some reason did not capture. At other times, these blog links will lead you to pages that no longer exist or to blogs that have not been updated in years. No matter – just retrace your steps and follow a different random path.

Step 3. Bookmark or cut and paste the web addresses of interesting blogs or entries as you go, or keep multiple windows open in your web browser. Continue clicking on the chain of blogs, from one to the next, and keep on going. You may discover whole communities devoted to informal commentary on your research topic. You may have to follow a few dead ends before you stumble onto some interesting material.

Old-Fashioned Search Engines

It may be difficult to imagine a research project today without the Internet. Similarly, a researcher in the pre-Internet era could not fathom beginning a research project without using a huge set of bound indexes such as *The Reader's Guide to Periodical Literature*. Every generation has its improvement on research methods, but older research technologies will still often produce relevant and necessary results. Walking around in the real world and observing with your senses is the oldest form of basic research, much more elemental than the sorted Internet and the bound index. You already know how to walk around, but you may not be used to walking around while wearing an invisible researcher's hat. For an example of wandering real-world research, please see Conversation 4 with author Joe Mackall. In two different research projects, Mackall set out to explore neighborhoods he knew well – the place he grew up and the area in Ohio where he currently lives. This real-world research was essential, even though Mackall covered ground that was familiar. Both journeys gave him new views and generated questions about his past and his surroundings that led to two books.

Experiment 10.4: Rubber to the Road

Length: *Take-home*
Timer: *None*
Discuss: *Yes*

Step 1. Get a small notebook, a few pens, and maybe a digital camera. With your topic in mind, look through the local phone book or at a map of your city or town to see what physical resources might be available. At first, this seems counter-intuitive, because you might assume that a worthwhile source would have a web page. As you will discover, this is often not the case.

Step 2. Make a list of any locations that might have a connection to your topic. For example, if your topic is tornados, you might ask where on your college campus you could visit to learn about tornadoes. Who in town might have supplies or equipment that would help you get tornado-ready? Don't censor your list or yourself by mentally eliminating places you might not be willing to visit. Instead, list all possibilities you can brainstorm.

Step 3. Check your brainstormed list by using the Internet. Search for the name of your area along with your topic to see if anything comes up online that could provide you with a specific local destination. Maybe there is a store or a museum devoted to your topic; add these locations to your list. The Internet is often a quick way to find contact information, maps, and addresses for these locations.

Step 4. Circle one place you are willing to visit and devote an hour of your time to this off-line research project. Don't worry about talking to anyone or preparing a list of questions. Just go there. During your visit, be sure to watch your mind. Record any questions or observations that occur to you, whether they have a direct or indirect connection to your topic.

Step 5. At your destination, list everything you observe, even if you are not able to locate the material or information connected to your topic.

Step 6. After you return home, review your notes and highlight or circle anything that provides a connection to your topic. Now brainstorm a list of questions and observations produced by your visit, including any specific ways to focus your topic that might not have occurred to you.

Using Real-World Research Material

Sometimes the act of research can seem like wandering in the dark, even when you are sitting in a comfortable chair at your desk.

Real-world, three-dimensional research in particular can feel like blundering far off the beaten path; you may be frustrated at first by the lack of specific information produced. These real-world methods offer a way to re-see the world and to open your mind to new and truly interesting research ideas instead of packaged and pre-made quotes to be dropped into a paper due tomorrow. In addition, this type of research usually produces results that are interesting to you and to readers and that actually connect to reality in a fresh and creative way.

The Gray Matter: Giving Credit Where Credit is Due

Noodling will produce a pile of information that looks suspiciously like a plate of spaghetti. The looping and associative research methods require extra attention to the sources of information and to keeping track of where you found them. If you pull one noodle, the whole plate of spaghetti shifts and slides in response, so if you fail to keep track of your noodle, you might not be able to find it again later – even using the same search engine and the same search terms.

Seeing the Internet as an ocean can help explain, metaphorically, why a piece of information might be visible one afternoon and then slip out of view a day or two later. Like the ocean, the Internet is pushed and shaped constantly by a myriad of natural and man-made forces, and its sheer size presents a challenge if the goal is to locate a single drop of water or a certain fish. *Google*, for example, delivers its search results by using a system called *PageRank* to analyze the number of links to a website and to assign a value to each of those pages. Since the Web and its many links are constantly being altered by programmers, other users, and programs that create automatic content, the information on the Internet is constantly pulsating, growing, and changing. Therefore, a search that responds to the links to sort content in a list can easily change search results from one hour to the next. If you forget to keep track of the actual Web address for each interesting page, your finds might slip through your net. You will spend more time re-locating your information than analyzing or branching out into new topics. For that reason it is important to develop the habit of copying and pasting source and page information into a separate document as you research.

Sorting the Information

Depending on your inclinations, you might want to try one of the following methods:

1. Cut and paste every piece of text that looks remotely interesting into a massive document, along with the source web pages. Don't worry about rephrasing or writing summaries. You can go back and take notes later from this raw material. Because you still have the exact wording from each of your sources, you can use this document to double-check and make sure you are not plagiarizing.
2. Email yourself a batch of articles from a database.
3. Cut and paste a list of interesting web addresses into an email, and use those web addresses later to take notes and to write citations.
4. Use a free and handy bookmarking service like the online link collector *Diigo* (http://www.diigo.com), which allows you to organize and keep track of web links in many different categories. Another web collection source, which even makes bibliographies, is *Zotero* (http://www.zotero.org). Both services require registration and allow you to share links with other registered users.

Crediting Your Sources

Plagiarism is wrong, of course, because it is stealing others' work and ideas. A plagiarist these days also has a self-interested reason for concern: in a matter of seconds, an instructor can determine with a basic Internet search whether a student is taking credit for other people's intellectual work. Aside from the moral argument and the self-interested argument, plagiarism produces non-information. Rather than analyzing facts and viewpoints, the plagiarist throws sentences together and repeats the words of others, usually without building an argument and often without telling the reader where the information came from. The reader is then left with no way to interpret or make sense of the information.

The real underlying problem with plagiarism and bad sourcing – whether or not the person means to do anything wrong or to steal – is that the cut-and-paster takes real information and strips it of its context and connection to the real world. In other words, presenting a quote without its source and without reflection on the source's meaning is a little like taking your family album, cutting the noses out of everyone's pictures, and presenting a series of noses as portraits of your relatives. A friend viewing this album would understand that something was missing. Worse yet, your friend would see that a real album had been destroyed in order to make this strange album of noses. In other words, plagiarized text is worse than no text at all because it doesn't make sense. Instead of information, you have infor-mess-ion.

Experiment 10.5: Infor-mess-ion

Length: *Short*
Timer: *None*
Discuss: *Yes*

Step 1. Choose an in-depth article on any topic from a newspaper or magazine. Print or cut out a copy of the article.

Step 2. With a permanent marker, go through the article and heavily black out any words that refer to sources. In journalism, these sources are called *attributions* and include any clues about who said what, such as "said the mayor" or "according to local weather reports." In scholarly work, attributions and sources include any reference to an author's name, a scientific study, or the context for research.

Step 3. Reread the article. You might share these aloud with your classmates. The results usually sound like nonsense or rumor. Keep this article in your binder to remind you that without a connection to reality, your writing and your reader's sanity both suffer.

Conclusion to Chapter 10

Research can be hilarious, surprising, and even relevant to your life. The key to finding such topics is to start with a broad net and to realize how many oceans of research are available. A researcher in a hurry will often miss the relevant and interesting writing on a topic because of bad research habits that lead to shallow or stagnant pools of information.

The best research looks not at facts by themselves but at a "family tree" of facts, including the complicated paths and people that produced the facts, debated them, and offered varied perspectives on each fact. For that reason, the Internet with its network of links offers a valuable resource for following the history of a fact. Each source citation you provide helps a reader understand the true meaning and origin of the facts and viewpoints you offer in your research.

Conversation 4 with Joe Mackall: Places, People, and Paper

Joe Mackall is the author of *Plain Secrets: An Outsider Among the Amish* (Mackall, 2008) and *Last Street Before Cleveland* (Mackall, 2006). This conversation took place via email.

How did the research process start for you in either or both books, and how did this beginning feel? Had you started focusing/obsessing/collecting about your subject matter before you identified this as research?

Mackall: These books are so drastically different from one another that the "research process" for each would read like the processes of two wildly different writers. I'm not the most logical or organized guy in the world, so I have to trust my intuition and my subconscious probably more than is healthy for an adult human being. For example, I had not planned to write the book that turned out to be *The Last Street Before Cleveland*; I wanted to write in a more documentary style about the neighborhood I grew up in and the kids with whom I shared that neighborhood. I wanted to learn why so many of these working-class, Catholic guys had so much trouble with alcohol, drugs, jobs, and women.

It all began, at least on the subconscious level, when I was haunted by the death of a boyhood friend. He was found in his car, dead from an accidental overdose. His death was heard as a whisper, if anything. For nearly five years, I thought about this guy at least a couple of times a day. When I couldn't shake his ghost, I knew I had to write about him, and about my old neighborhood. So I began talking to old friends of ours, visiting the places we used to hang out, telling and listening to old stories about our youth. All this was research. I also read a lot of books about the early life of the suburbs in America and about the psychology and sociology of working-class guys around my age. Soon I visited this friend's grave, which led me to his parents and siblings. I went to the place he was found dead. Pretty soon I had a book emerging, although it turned out to be a book different than the one I had intended to write, which is something research can do.

I like the research best that doesn't ostensibly resemble research. One of the first things I did with *Last Street* was meet two old friends – one I hadn't seen in about eight years and another I hadn't seen for two decades – for coffee at McDonald's in the old neighborhood one bitterly cold January morning. I was looking forward to seeing these guys and we had a great time telling stories and laughing our asses off at inappropriate things, but in the back of my mind I knew something my friends didn't know: I was doing research.

The research I did for *Plain Secrets* was much different. I spent a few years reading all I could on the Amish. I had also spent years becoming friends with my subjects. None of this was official research. Reading about the Amish was valuable, educational, and fun. Getting to know a family of Amish was great on all kinds of levels, mainly on the level of just relating to human beings who are different than you are. Once I had my subjects' permission to write a book, I hung around their house and farm all the time. The head of the house, Samuel Shetler, and I had an agreement, and it went something like this: I'm going to be around all the time, I told him. If you're sick of me on any given day, just tell me to go. He never did tell me to leave, which tells you what a nice and patient man he is. Who really would want me following them around day after day asking thousands of annoying questions? Nobody I know.

I generally follow the three Ps of research, which for me are *place*, *paper*, and *people*. I need to go to as many places as possible. For *Last Street*, I went to the place my friend died, where he was buried, the church we used to attend, our old houses, where we played baseball and football, where we drank, where we smoked pot. I visited these places in all four seasons and at different times of the day. When I'm writing about the past in particular, place is the perfect portal. Under the umbrella of paper, I include books, newspapers, public records, and the Internet. People are just that, people. The three Ps can get a nonfiction writer a long way in the research process.

What for you makes a topic worthwhile to serve as the focal point for such a research project?

Mackall: I chose *Last Street* because I was afraid I'd burst – which would be ugly as hell – if I didn't write that book. Other topics would have sold more books. I wish I would have written about my dogs, for instance. But I have to write what I have to write. Since I figure I'll be spending a couple of years at least researching and writing a book, I have to be obsessed. I can't merely be connected to the book intellectually. I have to be passionate about it. If I have the passion, I know it's a good topic for me. All I can do is write what I have to write and then see what happens.

One winter night a few years ago just before Christmas, I stopped by my Amish friend's place just to say hello. He and his wife were in their barn milking cows. Several kerosene lanterns hung around the barn, casting a soothing, soft yellow glow. We talked and laughed easily that night; and after I took my leave I said to myself, "You are an effing idiot if you don't write a book about these people." Soon after that, I asked their permission to write what became *Plain Secrets*. I don't know if it was because of the barn light, or the conversation, or our laughter, or the proximity of Christmas – but on that night I knew *Plain Secrets* would be my next book.

What for you personally is the most challenging part of conducting research? What is the most enjoyable?

Mackall: I love nearly all aspects of research. For one, it's a great way to put off writing without feeling too guilty. That I love. I love just digging and digging until I get at what I believe is as close to the "truth" as I'm liable to get. I love finding out that what I first saw as merely a tree is, specifically, an ash tree. In other words, I love almost nothing more than learning things I didn't know before. Because I know so very little about so very many things, my learning curve is huge, which is why research is always a kick.

I guess the least enjoyable aspect of research is being uncertain when it's over. I mean, my Amish friends are still living their lives, even though *Plain Secrets* has been out for over a year. Since the book came out, they've built a new school, had some family conflicts and God knows what else. I've decided to work by the credo that although research probably never ends, stories do. I told my story of my Amish friends. Oh, and I also hate microfilm. I become nauseous and have to quit. That's usually a good time to start writing.

11 Conversations

But on second thought, someone who didn't know how to ask wouldn't know how to listen.

— Gloria Naylor, *Mama Day*
(Naylor, 1989: 10)

Introduction to Chapter 11

When a large or small challenge arises, most people will pick up the phone or find a friend. You might dash off an email or send a text message to share the details or ask for advice. What you reach for in each of these different forms is connection through conversation. A good conversation lifts the spirit, allows you to see things from a new point of view, and makes you laugh or cry as you talk with and listen to friends in a free-flowing exchange. When you speak and a friend responds in a certain way, you feel heard; your friend gets it, understands, and an emotional connection is made. This activity and the human need for it are close to the core of life as a social being.

An interview might seem very different from a relaxed conversation with a friend. Instead of an open-ended give and take, one's responses are recorded for analysis. If you have ever had to request and conduct an interview, you might have noted that it creates anxiety. It doesn't feel polite to ask a near-stranger about a personal experience or a professional challenge.

Interview Anxiety

The stereotypical reporter character in a movie is a tough guy or gal on a tight deadline who barks question as the editor yells in the background. The reporter dashes from one source to the next, peppering innocent bystanders for details and information while scribbling madly in a notebook.

The pressures of real-world interviewing are not always this intense, but the interview, as it is practiced by many reporters, can leave a source wondering what misquotes will show up in the next day's newspaper. Reporters often work under constraints that include limitations of time, space, editorial goals, and format. As a result of this compressed and pressurized process, the word *interview* often evokes a bit of anxiety for the person being interviewed. Most people will want to know where the interview information will be published and how they will be portrayed.

Even the terms used to describe an interview conversation partner imply a one-way process in which information is taken and mysteriously transformed into something else. Journalists call the people they interview *sources*; ethnographers call them *informants, interviewees*, or *subjects*; and essayists call them *characters*. Even these words can imply an attempt to study a person under a microscope rather than to engage in a reciprocal conversation. Other field workers are even beginning to describe these people as *co-researchers* or *research partners* to reflect how essential these participants are to the research process. Maybe you can think of your own term!

Active Listening

The interview, if done carefully and respectfully, offers an opportunity to connect with another person and to learn. In much the same way as a heartfelt conversation, an interview offers the chance to move beyond surface interactions and to be able to understand, to hear, and to ask deeper questions. The quote at the beginning of this chapter – from the novel *Mama Day* by Gloria Naylor and mentioned in Fieldworking – offers an important insight: although listening and asking questions seem to be passive activities, they are both active skills (Naylor, 1989: 10). How do we know when someone is truly listening? The cues are subtle, but we can track them down and then use them to more deeply analyze the skills that lie behind them.

Experiment 11.1: Listen and Hear

Length: *Short*

Timer: *2 minutes + 4 minutes + 4 minutes = 10 minutes*

Discuss: *Yes*

Step 1. Think about a class you might have attended in which most of the students' attention was not on the academic work at hand. Make a list of at least five specific behaviors and actions that indicated that the students' attention was distracted or elsewhere.

Step 2. Think about someone you know who is a good and sympathetic listener. Take four minutes to describe how this person acts and what this person does to convey active listening. What qualities and actions do they exhibit?

Step 3. Take four minutes to recall a person you really listened to, or a conversation in which you were deeply engaged. What did it feel like? How would you describe your thought processes at that time, your goals in the conversation, and your physical behavior?

Step 4. Share these results with your classmates to brainstorm a list of common listening behaviors and attitudes and another list of inattentive behaviors and attitudes.

Listening Behavior

As you may have noticed after completing Experiment 11.1, a person's behaviors in a conversation often reveal attitudes and beliefs about what is being said and who is speaking. Impatience or boredom will show in a rolling of the eyes, a curt interruption, a tapping of the foot, or a leaning back in one's seat and a drifting off into near-sleep. This behavior is often seen as acceptable because of the underlying value we place on "critical listening," a term used by Mary Rose O'Reilly. She writes that in many places, including academia, "We tend to pay attention only long enough to develop a counterargument; we critique the student's or the colleague's ideas; we mentally grade and pigeonhole each other" (O'Reilly, 1998: 19).

It may be surprising to see critical listening behaviors described in a negative light, as the ability to wield a snappy comeback or find the weak point in an opponent's argument is often viewed as the very definition of intelligence. Critical listening and the rhetorical skills that go along with that kind of banter and argument definitely have their place. But other types of listening allow the listener to hear and collect different types of information. If your goal is research and learning, you might actually get more accomplished if you experiment with other types of listening.

In the textbook, *FieldWorking,* Sunstein and Chiseri-Strater (2007: 244) observe that good listeners "don't interrupt or move conversations back to themselves. Good listeners use their body language to let informants understand that their words are important to them.... They encourage response with verbal acknowledgments and follow-up questions, with embellishments and examples…." In Conversation 5 with author and researcher Robin Hemley, you will see an example of how a researcher realizes and becomes more reflective about his own role in an interview conversation.

Consider an interview in which the person interviewed tells a personal story. An interviewer with good listening skills might respond with a combined comment and question such as: "I can't believe that happened. What did you do next?" An interviewer who is not as focused on listening might respond with: "That reminds me of something funny that happened to me." A good interviewer will have a list of prepared questions to ask, but will watch also for the ebb and flow of the conversation, following the interviewee's lead and asking questions that arise naturally as the discussion evolves.

The researcher who risks a bit of anxiety, takes a breath, and enters into the conversation as an active participant rather than as a critical judge will emerge with different types of knowledge. In exchange, the active listener will have to surrender a bit of certainty and control over the subject matter of the conversation. This attitude has multiple benefits. It allows you to hear and receive more complex information, and it also changes your interaction with your interviewees. Developing good listening skills can put an interviewee at ease and completely alter the kind of conversation you have.

Asking for a Formal Conversation

Newspaper stories often contain quotes from experts, usually people involved in politics or academia who study a subject on a full-time basis and have written books or articles on the subject. Strategies for finding these kinds of sources are covered in many journalism textbooks and classes, and interviews with experts often take place via phone or email.

For in-depth and open-ended research, a face-to-face conversation will limit you in some ways to people in your community and area but can also offer much more potential depth for your conversation.

Experiment 11.2: Who Knows?

Length: *Long or Take-Home*

Timer: *None*

Discuss: *Recommended*

Step 1. Choose a topic you would like to research or have already begun researching. Make a list of at least five people in your area who would know a great deal about this topic. You don't need to have their names at this point; if your subject is beekeeping in your area of the country or state, one of your entries on the list might be "Head of the Entomology Department at the nearby university." This is more of a brainstorming sketch than a to-do list.

Step 2. Next, make a list of at least five people in your town or city who might have practical experience with or knowledge about your topic. For example, if your topic is beekeeping, the manager of the produce stand selling locally produced honey might be fascinating to talk to.

Step 3. Think about people who might not consider themselves experts on your topic but who might be affected by your topic in some way. With beekeeping as our example, you might list someone at a local poison control center or hospital to learn about the number of fatal bee stings among people with severe allergies.

Step 4. Finally, make a list of at least five people who may not consider themselves experts on your topic but who would have interest areas or hobbies that might overlap with your topic in some way. Maybe a local gardener with a fantastic wildflower garden is concerned about how the decrease in local honey bees is affecting her garden. Maybe a local chef who uses honey in recipes might have opinions about which honey works best in his recipes and why. A local doctor might be able to comment on whether eating local honey helps in curing pollen allergies.

Step 5. If you have particular trouble with any of these steps, share your list with a group of classmates, and see what other ideas your fellow researchers have for you.

Seeking Sources

Many reporters use news archives to generate sources. If you use a database service like Lexis-Nexis, you can do a keyword search on your topic and limit the search results to those articles that were published in your local newspaper. Read those articles and see if you can retrace the reporter's steps to find these sources. Sometimes a scattershot and conversational approach works best. Talk about your topic with strangers on the bus. You may have been lucky enough to run into someone with stories to tell, an expert's perspective, or a unique set of experiences. In any case, the first task is to find some real-live people to talk to. Bring your topic up to anyone. The woman working at the corner coffee shop will surprise you by telling you her aunt is a beekeeper who loves to talk about the subject. Post a message on Facebook or another social networking website to let your friends know that you're looking for unlikely experts on your topic.

It might seem strange to interview close friends or family members, particularly about subjects you have discussed with them before. Listening to a family member tell a familiar story around the dinner table is one thing, but sitting down together in a serious and focused interview setting to record the details gives you the opportunity to ask follow-up questions, to pay attention, and to let your source reveal more than a dinner-table anecdote.

An interview is a request for help without compensation. It can be difficult to ask someone to give freely of their time, and many interviewers feel anxiety at the thought of imposing on someone. If you fit this description, you can remind yourself that you are more than an inconvenience. In requesting an interview, you are offering this person a chance to share personal stories and insights. Amid the daily rush of responsibilities and packed schedules, many people don't have the time required for a deep conversation with even close family members or friends. An person being interviewed gets the opportunity to be listened to, to tell his or her story, and to make a contribution to your education.

Invitation to an Interview

Asking for an interview is not something most people do every day, so it might be helpful for you to write out a script to use for your interview request. Start with maximum politeness and flexibility to let the person know you are interested in accommodating their schedule and would be grateful for their time. For example, you might say, "I was wondering if I might be able to interview you sometime during the next few weeks for a school project on beekeeping."

Give information about your availability and the time you think it will take to do the interview, so the person knows this will not be a major time commitment: "I could stop by the produce stand if that is easiest for you, and I think we would need no more than a half hour." For the sake of respect, you want to make sure to plan your interviews well in advance of any project deadlines. It's very frustrating for a potential source – who you are asking to help you out without compensation – to hear about your looming deadlines and your lack of planning.

One of the first things people want to know when you ask them for an interview is, "What will you use this information for?" You can jot down a few easy-to-say sentences to provide this information. If the interview is for a school project, be sure to say so. If it seems unlikely that the interview will be published, be sure to explain this, as it will probably put your potential interview subject at ease to know their words will not appear in print. Be sure to tell the person if an interview transcript will be shared with classmates. Your instructor may or may not require you to sign a *release form*, which is an all-purpose document with the interview participant's contact information, a record of their consent, and their advance permission to use the results (in case you write a fantastic interview that ends up in print). After explaining the use of the project, you can then give a bit more information about why you want to talk to this person. For example, you might say, "I would like to talk with you about the types of honey you sell at the produce stand and your relationship with local beekeepers."

Some people are simply too busy or too shy to consent to an interview. This never means that your project is at a dead end or that your ideas are lacking. Whether the potential interview subject agrees to an interview, always end your conversation with the question, "Do you know of someone else you can recommend I talk to about this topic?" Using the extensive personal contacts of people in your community is the true hallmark of an experienced researcher. In fact, there is even an official social research methods term for this practice: *snowball sampling*. The group of interviewees starts with a central person and then builds and branches out to that person's contacts, friends of friends, and so on, like a snowball picking up snow as it rolls. The advantage to this method is that the personal introduction will go a long way in getting a second, third, and fourth interview.

Brainstorming the List of Questions

Congratulations! You've landed an interview and scheduled a time and a place to meet. Now you will begin a two-step preparation for your interview: background research and question brainstorming.

Doing your work on these steps will make your interview much more worthwhile for you and your interviewee.

First, pull together everything you can find about your interviewee and your research topic, using basic tools such as an Internet search engine and an online search of a local newspaper. Enter the person's name into a search engine and you might quickly learn, for example, that he or she received the Honeybee Protector Award in 2003 – the perfect launch pad for a series of questions about this award. A basic understanding of your interviewee's history and accomplishments conveys your respect for the person.

Then you will want to take a good amount of focused time to think about your questions; this step often determines whether the interview is useful or not. Some reporters bring in only a handful of questions to an interview or say that they work best asking whatever comes to mind during the conversation, but brainstorming a list of at least twenty questions in advance has many benefits. Brainstorming helps you to become comfortable with asking questions and to identify what you really want to know. You certainly don't have to ask all twenty questions; you might ask more or less, or veer off your question list to talk about another topic that comes up.

In *FieldWorking* Sunstein and Chiseri-Strater (2007) describe two categories of questions: *open* and *closed.* A closed question can usually be answered with a word or phrase, such as: "Did you enjoy your vacation?" or "What is your favorite flavor of ice cream?" Closed questions can be helpful for gathering information, but Sunstein and Chiseri-Strater (2007: 239) caution that closed questions "can shut down further talk. Closed questions can start an awkward volley of single questions and abbreviated answers."

Other types of questions are technically "closed" but can serve as a bridge between basic information and surprising revelations. These are the questions you might want to know but might be tempted to avoid because they might seem too basic or even silly. For example, "Don't you get stung a lot as a beekeeper?" or "Do you feel a sort of affection for your bees? Or are you scared by them?" These are the closed questions that come from a child's perspective of honest curiosity, and they open the way to stories and even laughter. Both of those responses are desirable because they are signs of a comfortable and engaged conversational interview.

Open questions ask the person being interviewed to explain his or her memories, motivations, doubts, questions, stories, and goals. Examples of open-ended questions are: "What first got you interested in beekeeping?" or "Have you ever experienced significant difficulties with your small business?" or "Do you think beekeepers will become a more important part of the local economy? Why?" Sunstein and Chiseri-Strater (2007: 239) advise: "Because there is no single answer to open-ended questions, you will need to listen, respond, and follow the informant's lead. Because there is no single answer, you can allow yourself to engage in a lively, authentic response."

Authentic Conversation

Educator Mary Rose O'Reilly describes true listening as a "deep, openhearted, unjudging reception of the other" (O'Reilly, 1998: 19). In the context of an interview – or any conversation – *judgment* is different from *analysis* or *reaction*. Real engagement with another person's statements and ideas in a true conversation requires that you analyze and watch your own responses in the conversation. It might be helpful to look more closely at O'Reilly's descriptive key words to develop a list of interview goals.

A *deep* interview experience allows the conversation to head in the direction of larger social and life issues if the interviewee seems open to exploring those themes. The interviewer is deeply committed to hearing whatever the interviewee has to say, without attempting to cut off or manipulate the conversation in order to get the quotes he or she originally hoped to collect. Rather than attempting to rephrase an interviewee's statement in your language, you might ask further questions until you're clear on what is being said. Rather than moving with relief from a complex topic to a simple one and an easy answer, you might push yourself and the person you are interviewing to explore the complications.

The word *openhearted* does not mean "mushy" or irrational. In the context of an interview, an openhearted researcher acknowledges the value and place of a basic human emotion: *empathy*, the ability to imaginatively step out of one's shoes and imagine the world from another person's perspective. Neuroscientists like Marco Iacoboni are learning all the time about the hard-wiring of the human brain for empathy and identification – and the survival and social benefits this skill creates (Iacoboni, 2008: 6). When you are able to practice and develop the skill of empathy, you can more easily wonder what it felt like to act or think in a certain way and to ask about a person's motivation, emotions, and experiences.

An *unjudging* interviewer is merely someone who is willing to wait and follow the train of an interviewee's thoughts, engaging with the interview content rather than reacting and commenting internally. As you listen to another person's statements in an interview, it is very tempting to listen critically by formulating internal comments and disagreements. Sometimes this behavior is useful, because you can catch what seem like contradictions or omissions in a person's statements and ask them to explain or explore these. But judgment of a person – whether they are intelligent or foolish, wrong or right, admirable or despicable – usually produces an interview without any complexity. Instead of truly listening to the person and using the opportunity to see their complex worldview, you are producing a simplistic version based more on your own prejudices than on the person.

Experiment 11.3: Twenty Questions

Length: *Long or Take-home*
Timer: *5 minutes + review time*
Discuss: *Optional*

The goal of this experiment is to generate at least ten closed questions and ten open questions based on a real or imagined person to interview. It might be especially helpful if you have a particular person in mind for a real research project. You can start by dividing a piece of paper into two columns and numbering the rows in each column from 1-10. Label one column "open questions" and the other "closed questions."

Step 1. Take 5 minutes to brainstorm as many basic questions as you can, letting the questions on your list trigger still more questions. As you think of a question, determine whether it is an open or closed question and then add it to either the *open* or *closed* column.

Step 2. When you reach a dead end, take a step back to look over your list and try a completely different approach. If you have focused on one element of your story (such as how a person becomes a beekeeper), shift gears to focus on another element (maybe the average day of a beekeeper, whether beekeepers get together for statewide meetings, how friends react to a beekeeper, what safety gear is needed).

Step 3. Look over your list and make sure your questions are all grouped in the correct category. Imagine a possible answer to a question, and if your question could be answered in a few words, move it to the *closed* column. If you're having trouble coming up with *open* questions, consider questions that ask about the future, the dreams, goals, family stories, missteps and challenges, the views of this person toward his or her subject matter. For example, questions that begin with phrases like "Do you ever.../ Did you ever.../ Have you ever.../ Would you ever...." are great ways to get a person to open up.

Step 4. The last phase in preparing your list of questions for a real interview is to group them by category or subject. This way, you can be sure to ask all questions on a particular subject before moving into the next theme. Sometimes, too, a person being interviewed will answer a question before you even ask it, in which case you can cross it off your list.

Interview Process and Technology

An audio recorder often creates anxiety during an interview. Some people associate audio recording with movies about espionage and police interrogations, and they worry their words will be used against them at some point in the future – even if the interview topic is completely innocuous. Others become self-conscious about how they will sound on the recording and begin to choose their words so carefully that they can't speak. For these reasons, some potential interviewees might not agree to an audio recording, and you must obtain their permission in order to record. But in most cases, an audio backup is an essential tool for an interviewer.

A small tape recorder or digital voice recorder is unobtrusive and silent. Knowing you have an audio recording to review later may help you relax and focus on the person you are interviewing rather than on frantically scribbling down notes. You can jot down key phrases as the person speaks to trigger further questions. The recording will provide many surprising details and turns of phrase that you will likely miss if you only record with shorthand. If you decide not to use an audio recorder and want to have some sense of accuracy of your quotes, you will have to ask your interviewee to pause frequently and to repeat his or her quotes. This sets up an unnatural slowness to the conversation. Another possibility is to do a phone interview in which you type as the person speaks, or to bring a laptop to the interview and try to capture the interviewee's words (if you can type at an efficient pace). But this, too, can be a challenge, and some people find clacking keys to be distracting.

When you review the recording of your interview, you also get the opportunity to hear yourself along with the person you interviewed. As you write your transcript, you will notice whenever your own excitement or laughter cuts short a sentence or point the interviewee was trying to make. In a normal non-recorded conversation, conversation partners constantly step all over the paths of each other's sentences in a verbal dance of interruption and layering. However, when you're doing an interview, it can take extra practice to pause after a person finishes a sentence to make sure that they are finished. Sometimes a silent nod to show the person you are still listening is all the prompt a person needs to continue with a story or bring up a new perspective.

Beyond the Quotes

Another benefit of using a voice recorder is that it frees you to notice non-verbal communication and reactions. In an interview, you can rely on your recorder to catch dialogue while you jot down gestures, clothing, posture, facial expression, and details to capture setting. Powerful and complex emotions and insights can be communicated nonverbally, and although these observations won't be useful for every type of research project, adding them to your interview transcript or research transcript can help to capture an interviewee's personality on the page.

Another part of your attention should be turned to yourself during an interview. Using the skills you learned about in earlier chapters, note the moments in any interview that you find particularly compelling. Mark these moments in your notebook with an exclamation point, star, or other symbol. Also make notes during the interview about your own reactions: when were you confused or troubled? Mark those points with a question mark. Remember that if something is vaguely unsettling or confusing but you can't articulate it during the interview, you can always contact the person you interviewed later for a few follow-up questions. Your reactions to comments and statements during the interview can point out areas for further exploration and research.

Experiment 11.4: Practice Interview

Length: *Long or Take-home*

Timer: *None*

Discuss: *Yes*

Step 1. Choose a classmate to interview. The interviewee will choose the theme of the interview; the only restriction is that it must be about a meaningful and challenging event in that person's life.

Step 2. Ask the person several questions about the event and its impact on the person's life.

Step 3. Write up a short narrative (one or two paragraphs) with quotes that illustrate the main points of this story. Include a third paragraph of a few sentences in which you attempt to distill or summarize the main importance or impact of this event or challenge on your interviewee.

Step 4. Switch roles and repeat Steps 1–3.

Step 5. Share the narratives with each other and write a reaction. How close did the summary come to capturing your feelings about the event or challenge? What was left out? What insights does this give you about the role of the interviewee and the interviewer?

The Gray Matter: Being Trustworthy with the Stories of Others

Reporters quote experts in news articles partly because an expert source knows what is expected of him or her. These expert sources know that an interview is not the same thing as a new friendship, and that the quotes might very well appear in any format or order. The relationship is cordial but distant, and is in some ways bounded by the interviewee's professional identity.

A person who has never been interviewed might have a completely different and much more personal reaction to this experience. During the interview, a person might share things he or she has never reflected upon. Being listened to can be quite intimate and can cause the person to see him or herself and his or her experiences in a new light. Ethnographer Mary Hamilton, in an article entitled "Histories and Horoscopes: The Ethnographer as Fortune-Teller" (Hamilton, 1998: 349), explains that people make sense of the interview process and product in different ways. Some see it as a kind of ghostwriting, in which an interviewer helps shape a narrative in collaboration with an interviewee. Others see it as a new sort of friendship, or a counseling session in which difficulties and doubts can be worked out. Still others view it as a chance to impress a certain viewpoint on a stranger or to correct a common misconception. Most interviewees have a combination of these and other associations. Being aware of these possible views and undercurrents in an interview is helpful, because you can redirect the interviewee in the event that he or she seems to veer off track. If your subject shares something highly personal, it might be appropriate to provide an opportunity to retract any statements that he or she might not want in your record.

Hamilton describes the awkwardness many of the sources in her study felt when they saw a description of themselves written by someone else. Seeing a transcript of one's own spoken words – in context or out of context – can force a person to wrestle with the implications or meanings of one's own statements. The quotes might not capture the essence of the matter or might create the sense that, in Hamilton's words, "You recognize yourself, yet you do not" (Hamilton, 1998: 351). As she observes, "It was common among the people we interviewed to view the research process as *imposing* order or pattern on their lives rather than as a more or less accurate reflection of facts..." (Hamilton, 1998: 352). An interviewee in Hamilton's study described the interview process as similar to visiting a fortune-teller in that the interviewer picks details and quotes to analyze; in the end, even though the pieces are technically accurate, they may not produce a portrait that the interviewee recognizes. There will always be a gap between another person's view of you and the contradictory, complex, and deep experience of your own existence. As the interviewer, it's important to keep in mind that a person might consent to an interview and then later express confusion, dismay, or other negative reactions after reading the text. Getting an accurate portrait of a person on paper involves as much deep listening and intuition as it does copying down quotes.

An interviewee sometimes gets the chance to see his or her words in some form in print, either before or after the work is published. While journalists often refuse to share their notes with sources or to show a source an article before it is published, researchers in other fields are sometimes more flexible with their notes and may show interviewees drafts or transcripts, even allowing them to suggest revisions, cuts, or retractions. Researchers in various social science fields, mindful of the power imbalances and stress that result from having one's life studied, can try to counteract the interviewee's anxiety by letting the person review the transcript.

Questions for Thought or Discussion

1. What would you say to a person who agreed to be interviewed but was then unhappy with the types of quotes you selected from your transcript for the paper?
2. If you were being interviewed, what would you do if you felt an interviewer had missed the point of your statement?
3. How might you integrate or address the challenges of doing an interview into a research project?
4. How might a challenging interview process make for a more interesting or useful research project?

Conclusion to Chapter 11

An interview is a wonderful opportunity to enliven and deepen your research with live communication. Many students who have not engaged in an interview process imagine it as another phase of information-gathering, but the complex process of conducting and negotiating an interview reveals it to be much more than picking and collecting facts. A good interview is not judged by the content or quotes it produces, but by the questions asked and by the extent to which the interviewer is present, focused, and listening to the responses given. One of the most exciting elements of an interview is the opportunity to discover complications and complexities that arise out of your interviewer participant's experiences. An interview's surprises may lead you to frame your research quest in a new way, and this openness to new perspectives is a research skill to be explored in greater detail in Chapter 12.

Conversation 5 with Robin Hemley: Interviewing

Robin Hemley has published seven books of nonfiction and fiction. His book, *Invented Eden, The Elusive, Disputed History of the Tasaday* (Hemley, 2007) deals with a purported anthropological hoax in the Philippines. He is the author of the memoir, *Nola: A Memoir of Faith, Art and Madness* (Hemley, 1998); a book on the craft of writing, *Turning Life Into Fiction* (Hemley, 2006); a novel, *The Last Studebaker* (Hemley, 1993); two collections of short stories; and the memoir *Do-Over* (Hemley, 2009). This conversation took place via telephone and email. The author photo is courtesy of Peter Parson.

How did you get obsessed with the case of the Tasaday tribe in the Philippines?

Hemley: I became obsessed partly because the sides were so obsessed and squared off. I felt part of some big drama. So it was kind of exciting. It became a puzzle: what really happened? I'd fly off to Switzerland to interview the journalist. It was exciting to go to the rain forest, or to talk to various anthropologists. With the Tasaday case, I knew every useless fact. I became that person at the party that no one wants to talk to.

How did your views change through the course of the research?

Hemley: I [began] with the side that believes it's a hoax. I built that into the architecture of the story. My opinions about the story changed depending on who I talked to.

You talked to almost everyone available who had been involved with the Tasaday case. How did you start the interview process? What advice do you have about interviewing?

Hemley: In the first interviews, I seemed to do all the talking, and playing them back was painful. I tried to tell them what to say. Another nonfiction writer said that the best thing you can do is the "village idiot" approach, like you're sitting at the master's feet. Your sources will just completely open up. You obviously want to know enough so you don't insult them.

[Interviewing is] about gaining people's trust. Once I got one person who could vouch for me, then other doors opened. For instance, I did an Internet search [at the beginning of the research process on the Tasaday book] and I came across an anthropology professor who'd been at the first conference in 1986 in Manila. He lived right across the state from me. He didn't seem to have any vested interest in the question, so I emailed him.

If you're doing something controversial, interview the person who is considered in the middle first. Basically, if I had spoken to someone on the *hoax* side, then the *authenticity* side would think, "See, he's getting an earful from them." This way, I had someone who both sides thought was neutral. They both wanted to talk to me. Both sides would ask me what I thought about the case, and I would say, "How can I take sides when I haven't done my research?" I would keep mum and let them talk and give as many non-committal answers as possible.

Then if you've been researching it for two years, you have the right to seem like less of an idiot. As you go on, you can cite important dates and facts. If you're really involved in something, you go from village idiot to being an expert. Now I could confidently have a conversation with any anthropologist about the Tasaday and hold my ground.

What is your research process? What's your organizational system for keeping track of all the research you collect?

Hemley: I am not the most methodical person. I'll research in my own quirky way. I'll read here and there, do primary interviews, I'll visit a place where whatever it was happened. I'll read in a very scattered way. I won't read everything that's written. My ideal process is to have a cross-referenced filing system. My real system is digging madly through a box of papers.

What led you to the research project? What were your larger goals?

Hemley: I look for something that's anti-intuitive. If something seems immediately a hoax but more pressure reveals it to be more complex, then it makes for more interest. I wanted to complicated people's views about authenticity. I wanted to present a story that is inherently ambiguous. That was my goal, to question our desire to understand. Also, my own romantic notions of innocence were at stake. Usually, I think that if something withstands a couple months' scrutiny and I don't get bored with it, that's a good topic.

Section IV
Open Minds Invite Surprises

12 Twists and Turns in the Research Story

With writing and with teaching, as well as with love, we don't know how the sentence will begin and, rarely ever, how it will end.
　　　　　　　　　　　　　　　　　– Nancy Sommers, *I Stand Here Writing*
　　　　　　　　　　　　　　　　　　　　　　　　　　(Sommers, 1993: 428)

Introduction to Chapter 12

A research project might begin and end within a few weeks, and when you are done it might be out of your life forever. Some topics, however, might have such a personal resonance or evoke such deep interest that you find yourself haunted, touched, or changed by the act of research. Maybe you begin researching a topic – tornadoes, for example. As soon as you become immersed, the topic also seems to crop up in your non-research life. You meet someone at the Laundromat whose house was destroyed by a tornado. Then the following week three tornadoes sweep across the areas where you live. You flip through a magazine in a doctor's office and find the perfect tornado article. What is going on?

In the search for a true research obsession, you are opening yourself up to change. It's like opening a window – there's no telling what will fly in and make itself at home. In a way, the openness of curiosity creates vulnerability, and this vulnerability begins a story with an unpredictable ending.

Filter and Focus

At the level of your personal psychology, we might say that in a situation like the tornado project, your subconscious mind has become fixated on the research project along with your conscious intellect. In a sense, your brain is honing in on your research subject and using it as a filter to collect anything that triggers a connection to that subject. Although you're probably not consciously drawing these events toward you, you are changing your interaction with the world in subtle ways as a result of the questions you carry around in your brain.

Your subconscious mind works hard to integrate new information and priorities into the fabric of your life. As you focus on a new subject, your brain generates these possible connections, trying them on for size to see what useful associations can be generated. In the tornado example, a strong interest in tornados will result in a level of awareness about the connections between tornados and whatever you are seeing. The movie *The Wizard of Oz*, the local weather forecast, and the twisted tree on the corner all become connections to your topic that evoke still more research ideas and further sharpen your tornado *vision*. Conversation 6 with author Jill Christman provides an example of a research project that seemed to haunt the author and to demand investigation.

These ideas, associations, and reactions might easily be dismissed during a normal research process as *noise* or random thoughts. But such images – often occurring out of the blue – are valuable signposts that can be saved and used later to help tell the story of your search, to explain your topic to others, and to develop further questions. To take advantage of these potential connections, we will practice a few strategies for collecting these loose thoughts.

First, choose a strategy for making space in your research notes for these journal entries, the random associations and thoughts that seem unrelated to your project. You might simply jot words, phrases, and observations in the margins along with dates, or you might insert pages of freewrites that are connected to specific research entries. You can also use the left column of a divided research page to note your observations and the right column to react. If you include your journal entries with the rest of your research-related notes, you might want to use a mark along the margin or a highlighter to separate your random notes from your research-related material.

Experiment 12.1: Take Notes on the Rest of Your Life

Length: *Take-home*
Timer: *None*
Discuss: *Optional*

Step 1. If you are currently involved in a research project, use your research notebook to record events that seem unrelated to your research but that draw your attention, using one of the strategies described above for marking these notes consistently.

Step 2. Over the course of a week or more, record any thoughts, topics, pieces of conversation, and news items that come up in your life and that strike your interest. Mark these with a highlighter or use a separate page in your notebook, as described above.

Step 3. If a strange coincidence occurs in which your subject matter emerges from your life in a surprising way, note that in your records. Also note if you are researching a particular subject and seemingly unrelated events or topics catch your attention. You don't need to connect everything

to your research topic; in fact, contradiction and juxtaposi-
tions will also be very helpful to observe.

Step 4. It may seem counter-intuitive, but you don't have to
plan on including this information in your final research
project. It will be there if you need to refer to it, or it might
offer a tangent or connection to explore. But for now, you
can keep up this practice in order to get a little bit more
background information about your primary piece of lab
equipment: your brain.

Rough Roads and Smooth Sailing

Paying attention to your thoughts can change the course of your
research, as you explored in Chapter 5. But as you move further
into a research project and challenges arise, the pattern of your
reactions can help generate solutions – even if these reactions seem
to indicate only that you are stuck or frustrated.

Anxiety over learning, research, and writing are common experiences, even for professional researchers. Canadian anthropologist Petra Rethman lived with a group of reindeer herders in the
Kamchatka Peninsula in Siberia, and she struggled as most field
researchers do with the gaps between her culture and the experience
of living with the herders. She describes her research difficulties
with surprising honesty: "There were many moments when I hated
fieldwork.... But the difficulties lay within me...in what I had
brought to the situation" (Rethman, 2007: 50).

Her scholarly article presents detailed information about the
community of reindeer herders alongside personal and universal
emotions such as fear, including her own "[p]anic at not asking
enough questions, at not being inquisitive enough, not getting
enough data" (Rethman, 2007: 51). These two strands connect
when viewed together. Her fear of failure and anxiety teaches her
valuable lessons about the mindset of the reindeer herders and
their approaches to learning. While she observed the herders, they

observed her as well and noted her stiffness and distance. They took action, calling her attention to this set of behaviors and confronting her about the effect of this viewpoint. In effect, they taught her how to relax and how to be with them in a way that allowed her to see them accurately.

Rethman struggled to understand the life of the reindeer herders. But her ultimate confusion and reorientation emerged from an area beyond her notes and her ability to do fieldwork. To gather the material she wanted, she had to take a step back and rework her *epistemology* – the process by which she created knowledge. She learned that her attitudes, behaviors, beliefs, and ways of interacting with her subjects all influenced the kind of knowledge she could absorb and create.

Experiment 12.2: Know Your Equipment

Length: *Short*

Timer: *5 minutes + 5 minutes=10 minutes*

Discuss: *Optional*

Step 1. Chapter 9 described the process of noting your emotional reactions to your research. Now that you have begun to do this a bit, look through your research notebook to locate these types of comments and reactions, which you marked with a circle or a star to make them more visible in your notes.

Step 2. Choose five reactions that seem most emphatic or strong, including any piece of information that deeply confused, troubled, excited, or annoyed you. On a blank piece of paper in your notebook, jot down a word or phrase to summarize each of these pieces of information. For example, your list might include phrases like "Men better at math?" or "Coffee as an addictive substance!"

Step 3. Using this list as a reference point, write for five minutes about any common themes that connect these emotional reactions. Is there a topic, an activity, or a question that seems to elicit a certain kind of reaction? What might this mean? Why do you think a certain type of source tended to be annoying? What about a certain challenge in your research provokes your interest or excitement?

Step 4. For five minutes, try to forget that this list was created by you. Look back at the list as if you were using it to describe the particular brain that created it. You might imagine that you are writing an owner's manual for this brain as a piece of lab equipment. Certain cars tend to want to turn left; a particular thermometer might always give a reading one degree higher than another. If an alien or ghost were able to inhabit this brain and use it, what would be its particular quirks and tendencies? For example, you might note, "This brain tends to like questions of controversy in history," or "This brain is easily annoyed by authors who sound pompous in their writing." What patterns and reactions does this brain tend to focus on? What results does it record with greater and less detail? What emotions best fit its observational abilities?

The Changeable Brain

Seeing your brain as a piece of lab equipment raises an important question. How reliable are the results generated by such a unique – distracted, emotional, interested, judgmental – brain? It would seem impossible to calibrate a brain to produce reliable results, particularly as an emotional attachment to one's subject changes the lab equipment itself! Some anthropologists have worried about "going native" – a process in which a researcher begins to take on the behaviors and value systems of the culture or field being studied.

Yet Rethman's experience in the Kamchatka Peninsula indicates that, sometimes, reactions to and even entanglements with subject matter can be more of a help than a hindrance to the research process. These connections and attachments can create knowledge and frameworks for knowledge creation. In the book *Extraordinary Anthropology*, anthropologists Jean-Guy Goulet and Bruce Granville Miller talk about the value of "letting go" of some of our artificially imposed distance from our subjects in order to "draw upon unanticipated abilities to experience the real" (Goulet and Miller, 2007: 6). In this sense, you might seem to almost grow an ability to see into a subject as you approach it with openness. As you learn, you watch for unanticipated patterns or types of knowledge that might not even make sense at first or are beyond the realm of your expectations.

Seeing Chromosomes

Barbara McClintock, a geneticist who worked with corn plants (Keller, 1983), developed a brilliant ability to look at a corn plant and visualize the corn chromosomes. While other geneticists of the 1950s were envisioning genes as immobile "beads on a string," McClintock worked quietly on a model that she could envision clearly based on her close observation. Her study of corn characteristics and attention to the patterns in corn plant growth led her to develop an internal framework of knowledge for the ways in which genes express themselves in corn plants. In effect, her level of understanding about the corn plants produced a sort of massive internal database in which she was able to intuit and rapidly calculate, or see, the ways that genes would express themselves. She "saw" the movement of individual chromosomes and thus anticipated by decades the current thinking on cutting-edge developments in the field of genetics. McClintock describes her relationship with the corn plant in words we might usually reserve for close friends:

> I start with the seedling, and I don't want to leave it. I don't feel I really know the story if I don't watch the plant all the way along. So I know every plant in the field. I know them intimately, and I find it a great pleasure to know them. (Keller, 1983: 102)

McClintock faced scorn from her colleagues, whose models and metaphors did not allow them to see what was obvious to her. McClintock kept going with her research because she developed a deep attachment to and appreciation for her subject as the result of her close study. As she described in an interview, "I was part of the system.... I even was able to see the internal parts of the chromosomes – actually everything was there. It surprised me because I actually felt as if I were right down there and these were my friends" (Keller, 1983: 103).

Becoming friends with a corn plant might sound like a strange side-effect of careful research, but to understand it, you might think of your best friend in the world. Don't you often have an intuitive sense of how this person will react in a given situation? To know this, you have formed an internal model or metaphor of this person based on your own day-to-day close observation of his or her behavior. Rather than starting with a general principle of human behavior to understand your friend, you got to know your friend through spending time with this person in all sorts of situations. That experience is what leads you to know him or her.

If you gather experience and observations first, and then attempt to figure out the general principles that can be used to describe those moments of observation, you are using *inductive* reasoning. McClintock found her way to her cutting-edge discoveries based on this principle. She became frustrated with her colleagues, who were starting with the principles they believed in and then looked for material and evidence to back up those principles. While *inductive* reasoning is "bottom-up" in drawing conclusions from the evidence, *deductive* reasoning is "top-down" and uses generally accepted or previously proven rules and laws as well as familiar models and patterns to predict the outcomes or meanings of new situations. We use both methods of reasoning constantly in our daily lives, but the challenge is in gathering – and even seeing – data and information that seems to contradict our expectations and theories.

Scientific experiments are designed to be objective in an attempt to remove biases from the results. However, as McClintock's career path shows, our goal of objectivity is often unattainable, because even scientists have blind spots and expectations, which can affect the questions asked, the subjects pursued, and the experiments planned. McClintock's attachment to her subject matter – her emotional investment in it – allowed her to develop new abilities to see it. McClintock got better at seeing the corn plants – even down to their genetic structures – the longer and more passionately she studied them.

She sometimes could not even find words to describe how she accurately predicted the corn plants' genetic structures and behavior. This insight, or ability to seemingly intuit structures and answers, is a common experience among scientists who have made groundbreaking discoveries:

> [A]lmost all great scientists – those who learn to cultivate insight – learn also to respect its mysterious workings. It is here that their rationality finds its own limits. In defying rational explanation, the process of creative insight inspires awe in those who experience it. They come to know, trust, and value it. (Keller, 1983: 103)

This insight, however, is far from magic; it grows out of deep study of one's material. McClintock believed that "…the closer her focus, the greater her attention to individual detail, to the unique characteristics of a single plant, of a single kernel, of a single chromosome, the more she could learn about the general principles by which the maize plant as a whole was organized, the better her 'feeling for the organism'" (Keller, 1983: 101).

Experiment 12.3: More than a Feeling

Length: *Long*

Timer: *3 minutes + 3 minutes + 2 minutes + 3 minutes + 3 minutes = 14 minutes*

Discuss: *Optional*

Step 1. For three minutes, make a list of activities you have a feeling or instinct for – those you can perform without much or any conscious decision-making or analysis (for example, driving a car).

Step 2. Choose one of these activities and write for three minutes on what it was like for you to acquire this skill or body of knowledge. How long did it take? What methods worked best in making this skill more automatic?

Step 3. Choose another one of these activities (or the same one you wrote about in Step 2) that is most enjoyable to you. Write for two minutes about what makes that activity enjoyable.

Step 4. Using the same activity you wrote about in Step 3, write for three minutes about how your enjoyment of the subject might affect your ability to research it. For example, would your enjoyment make you more or less likely to want to see negative effects of this activity? Would your enjoyment of it make you less aware of difficulties others might have with learning or completing this activity?

Step 5. Now consider a current research project or one that you may start. Write for three minutes about your current state of relationship to it: your feelings about it, your anxieties, your interest level, your pleasure or discomfort in researching it. Do you think these viewpoints might affect how you research and what you find out?

Feeling, Physics, and the Playground

Most scientists have documented some form of an *observer effect*, in which the process of observing something affects what is observed. To imagine this, picture children running around a playground, maybe making up nonsense songs and taunting each other in a good-natured way. Now add a stern-looking adult with a clipboard to this scene. The children notice him and wonder what he's scribbling about them on his clipboard. They might act nervous, or exaggerate their arguments to attract the attention of the adult stranger, or abruptly stop their antics – but in any case, their behavior has changed.

Researchers traditionally correct for this observer effect by making sure the subject doesn't know he or she is observed or by minimizing the effect this observer might have on the scene. In the playground example, a researcher might stand where he can see the children but they cannot see him, or he might appear every day until the children are accustomed to him and ignore him. As interpreted with a framework of classical objectivity, this researcher could produce objective results if these observer effects are corrected for or taken into account. A framework of classical objectivity, however, does not ask whether the person with the clipboard is changed in the process of doing the research or whether the subjects themselves are changed by this research process.

Quantum physicists, in attempting to make sense of the universe at a sub-molecular level, have stumbled upon much more central challenges to our notion of objective reality. As an important example, Einstein's relativity theories boil down to one consistent finding: What a researcher will see depends on where he or she stands. You might stand at one point in the universe and see a beam of light as a certain kind of phenomenon moving at a certain speed. But another location will produce different – though also technically correct – results. Atoms and subatomic particles seem to behave differently depending on how they are measured.

How does this happen? To study something, the researcher has to see it as an object. To define the object – to focus in on it, to put a frame around it – physicist Fritjof Capra explains, the researcher must "cut through some of the interconnections – conceptually, as well as physically with ... instruments of observation – and in doing so ... isolate certain patterns and interpret them as objects" (Capra, 2000: 331). What this means is that the acts of measuring and studying require the researcher to cut off areas of potential knowledge by choosing questions to ask and questions to ignore.

Quantum physics challenges our notion of separate pieces of concrete and immovable reality. In the quantum view, space and time are inextricably connected – almost interchangeable; matter is energy, and space is curved. These far-out ideas might be mere curiosities if they did not produce results that consistently predict the actions of atoms and other pieces of our physical world.

Quantum physics has helped to reveal that the world, at the sub-molecular level, is more of an interconnected process than a box of separate objects or pieces. The idea of the building blocks of the universe – smaller and smaller pieces to be fit together and broken apart – does not seem to hold up at the sub-molecular level, because these pieces flit in and out of existence, and connect and communicate in a constant dance of energy and motion. The detour into the land of quantum physics is important for research, because it demonstrates that questions of *epistemology* – how we know what we know – are not merely esoteric or "touchy-feely." They indicate that the researcher's ability to see connections with a research subject is inevitably shaped by the research process itself.

Moving beyond a traditional concept of objectivity does not mean that research and knowledge creation are impossible. Several disciplines have developed similarly advanced theories of knowledge based on known perspectives. In the social sciences, researchers check with each other to see if the results are similar. Alan Wallace writes, "In the final analysis, *all* scientific observations boil down to multiple individuals' firsthand experiences, and when those experiences are similar – or *intersubjective* – they are regarded as third-person scientific observations" (Wallace, 2007: 79). Basically, the notion of intersubjectivity (also introduced in Chapter 1) allows researchers to come up with concepts of shared reality as they check with other people who have experienced something similar in order to see if all or many can agree on what is observed. Many quantum physicists work with their own version of this orientation, in which theories are built not based on the idea of absolute truth but based on the areas in which the theories agree and overlap. Thus, using the connections between theories, a *net* of overlapping theories is created.

The Gray Matter: Nothing to Know?

Placing these caveats and conditions onto the notion of classical objectivity might leave you wondering why anyone bothers to research, if nothing can be known for sure. Is there any point? For many researchers, the point of these caveats is not to make research more hopeless or more intimidating. Instead, this insight might actually make research easier. By knowing that you are directly connected – through your questions and your interest – to your subject matter, you might be able to understand your results much more quickly. If you choose a topic that is very connected to you, these connections can help you understand what is happening if the research goes well or badly, and in general to understand your results more deeply than someone who is unconnected to your topic.

Questions for Thought or Discussion

1. What subject matter might be overwhelming or infuriating for you to study?
2. Can you imagine a research project that would change your life? What would it be?

3. Is it better or worse for people to study things they already know well?
4. How could a particular life experience affect the outcome of a research project in positive ways? In negative ways? In ways with mixed consequences and results?

Conclusion to Chapter 12

Becoming aware of your changing, shifting, and subjective relationship to your subject matter might feel quite unsettling, but the ability to see this shifting ground is a dependable and useful research skill. As you have honed your ability to see how you connect to your research subject, you become more aware of the subject itself, almost as if you are looking at it through a camera lens and gaining the knowledge of how to use various settings and to focus to achieve a crisp image. The RELAX and REFLECT phases of the research process go hand in hand here as you settle your mind so that you can see deeply without distraction or preconceptions.

If you followed these steps repeatedly, your relationship to your research subject has changed significantly since the beginning of your research journey. You have learned how to use your specific view of your subject – including the points at which your subject overlaps with your life or the areas in which your subject is most difficult or pleasant for you – to generate questions and further areas for research.

As you have gotten to know your subject in this way, you have also gotten to know yourself a bit better in the process. You have probably begun to formulate a portrait of yourself as a researcher, along with your particular likes, dislikes, and quirks. Just as an explorer knows his or her weak points – fear of snakes, a tendency to underestimate time constraints, difficulty reading maps – that explorer can also guess that these tendencies will generate excitement and challenges. The next section of this guide will take you down into the inevitable difficulties of the research quest. As you will explore in the next chapter, your knowledge about your tendencies as a researcher can help you diagnose and solve research problems, adding to your awareness and preventing future roadblocks in the process.

Conversation 6 with Jill Christman: The Research Journey

Jill Christman is the author of *Darkroom: A Family Exposure* (Christman, 2002). This conversation took place via telephone and email. Author photo courtesy of Tim Berg.

What is your current book project, and what sparked your interest in the topic?

Christman: My current book project began in the Human Ecology archives at Cornell University, researching the *practice apartments* (the capstone element of the curriculum for home economics students 1919-late 1950s in which the "girls" would live an apartment together and share domestic tasks, such as cooking and laundry, and including the care of an infant whom they would "borrow" from an orphanage, or more disturbingly for me, from an economically disadvantaged family, and "raise by the book").

Michael Martone (a writer and professor of creative writing at the University of Alabama) mentioned these babies (for some reason I can't remember!) during a fiction workshop one day when I was a grad student. It seemed too weird to be true. Practice babies? From orphanages? I didn't look into it, but I couldn't get it out of my head. Every once in a while I'd ask someone, "Have you ever heard about practice babies?" but no one ever had, so I figured Martone had made it up. After all, he'd mentioned these babies in a <u>fiction</u> workshop, right? And if we'd been using babies like living dolls in our colleges and universities, wouldn't we all know about it?

Years passed. The mysterious babies wouldn't leave me. They were like a tickle at the back of my neck, and that's something I'm learning to pay attention to as a writer – those things that won't leave me. Those things that pop into my brain at 3 a.m. So one day I sat down and wrote to a research librarian at Cornell University. These librarians know how to find things out. They are waiting for us to ask. They want to help us. They are information specialists, for heavensakes! What writer doesn't need an ally like that? Every time I have ever asked a research librarian for help, I have been glad – for example, last year I was working on an essay about my mother's insistence that we modern-day parents are just too safety conscious, why, when we were babies, a mother could just <u>hold</u> her baby in her arms on the way home from the hospital, etcetera, and I needed to know whether we have indeed made our children safer with all our helmets and booster seats, so I asked a research librarian, and she got me the facts. So there, Mom. (But of course, that wasn't the end of the story: research and facts, used well in creative nonfiction, provide a jumping off point, not a place to stand and feel self-righteous, because of course, self-righteousness, even when it comes to car seats, is the enemy of truth-seeking.) <u>Anyway</u>, I couldn't stop thinking about these babies, so I sent of my email to the librarian at Cornell, thinking he was going to laugh in my virtual face, but also knowing that I had to take a stab or I'd wonder forever. (I'm reminded here of the etymology of the word *essay* – *essai* from the Old French: "to take a stab, to try") You know where this story is going, of course. Turns out there had been practice apartments at Cornell, and in 1919 they brought in their first "borrowed baby."

The research librarians lead you to the archives of the practice apartment program at Cornell University, where you later went to conduct research. What did you find? What surprised you?

Christman: The baby books were surprising and disappointing. I realize now that I had all these preconceived notions of what I wanted to find, you know? I wanted to find stories of students falling in love with the babies, students who couldn't bear to leave when their six weeks were up, students who wanted to talk about how it felt to hold little Joanie when she got colicky in the night, and on and on. In reality, these were students enrolled in a course. Their job was to measure cod liver oil and take their infant charges out on the porch for a specific amount of time (every day! Even in the middle of an Ithaca winter! Now that was a little surprising. . .). The baby books were mostly charts and measurements, entries about rickets, and how much physical improvement the babies were showing. The photographs were the best part. The first picture might show an underweight baby. By the end, there's a chubby, rosy-cheeked one-year-old. After having been "raised by the book," the babies coming out of the practice apartments were much in demand. Most were adopted quickly. So, ultimately, they were better off. I did find a letter from a mother who wanted to come visit her baby, and my heart was breaking when I read that. But for the most part, I came out of the archives with the feeling that the program was good for these babies. That's a great thing about research, right? You might go into a project thinking you're going to find something particular, but you don't – you find something else. The trick maybe – and isn't this the challenge in all writing? – is to remain open to these changes. To let the unexpected surprise us and nudge us down the next path towards some kind of truth.

I had wanted to find real stories about these babies and their temporary "mothers," but I reached a wall. For example, when I interviewed a woman who had been a student "mother," I was expecting stories of attachment or something, but she wasn't even sure she remembered the name of the baby she'd cared for in the practice apartment. Why would she? I realized later. She was a college student. It was over fifty years ago! Now she was a grand-mother who'd raised many children of her own – why would she want to talk about that long-ago baby who didn't even belong to her? She told me that many of the "girls" in the program resented the inclusion of the babies because it was a lot of work. On the nights you were in charge of the baby, you couldn't go out on dates. It wasn't the story I'd anticipated hearing, but it made sense: These women didn't need practice babies. They wanted their own.

How did research change your thinking about and your relationship to your topic?

Christman: I went into my investigation of borrowed babies feeling pretty judgmental. And, as my life would have it, I was five months pregnant with my own first baby at the time, and very, very emotional on the subject of babies. I sat there with my white cotton gloves pulled up over my swollen hands, turning the crinkling pages in the baby books, reading about orange juice and cod liver oil and naps out in the freezing cold and thinking – sheesh – how am I going to take care of <u>this</u> baby? <u>My</u> baby?

When I got into it, I lost a little of that judgment, as we all do, I think, when we get deep enough into any subject, right? The more I thought about the borrowed babies at Cornell – and, in fact, at land grant institutions all over the country, including the one where I teach and where my own children attend, yes, the modern-day equivalent – the more morally ambiguous it became in my mind. Here were programs training women to be good homemakers and mothers, but they were in college, right? They were being taught by women, women who were earning respect in academia. And the babies themselves. Some of them were in really rough shape when the program took them in, and a year later, they were thriving. In the beginning, it was pre-attachment theory. Nobody thought there was anything wrong with being cared for by seven or eight mothers – the more the merrier, right? We know – or we <u>think</u> we know – now that this is not the case, but before attachment theory came along in the forties, nobody was worrying about a baby being passed from one caregiver to another.

Ultimately, the book I'm writing changed. At some point I realized that I was not the person to write the story of borrowed babies in practice apartments. I didn't have the time or the resources. So I failed to write the book I had imagined, but in the meantime, my own first baby was born. And in the first year of her life I realized that the work I had done in the archives at Cornell thinking about babycare and babies, all the ways in which the world comes in to issue instructions on how we should care for our babies, wasn't wasted. (I don't think research ever is, right? How could it be a bad thing, ever, as a writer to know more about any subject?) I didn't have any answers, but at the intersection of my research and my life, I came up with a question I wanted to pursue: What does it mean to mother? We want to know what is good for our babies, but the idea of what is good is always changing. And since then I have added what seems to me a central question of parenting: how do we deal with the fear of being a parent? All that worry? Since my initial conception then, the book has morphed considerably, away from what I'd initially thought would be a kind of oral history and toward memoir that thinks about issues of caretaking, motherhood, fear/worry, etcetera, rooted in these unanswerable questions. For me, research can be a launching pad for so many things in writing, and I try to remember that it's not so much the definitive answer I'm looking for – is there such a thing? – but better and more complicated questions.

What counts as good research for you? How do you decide what to research?

Christman: I think one thing I'm always trying to teach my students is to keep their antennae up, to pay attention to those things that bug you, disgust you, thrill you, or make the hair on the back of your neck stand up. And then go after that thing. When I assign a research-based essay to my students, I tell them this. Find out everything you can. Enter into a subject – any subject – where you have something to learn, where you have questions, where there is the lingering of something unresolved for you, where you are puzzled/curious/enraged/hopeful (or?). Whatever you choose as your subject, I tell them, have at least a working idea of why you're interested in this something or someplace or someone – <u>why</u> have you chosen this place/issue/environment/person? Then put yourself there and pay attention. Stay alert for those "moments of being." Remember that you are a writer all the time. Take notes. Immerse. Engage. Absorb. Synthesize. As you put together the pieces, stay open-minded. What you see might change your mind. Let that happen if it happens. Enter into your research and writing with a willingness to ask big questions, I remind them: What <u>is</u> this piece of the world? What does it mean to the rest of us?

If you don't allow the research to tell you something, to change your mind, to alter your questions, then that's the worst kind of research. In my own development as a writer, it has been critical to realize that <u>what I don't know</u> is often the most exciting thing. We have to let go of the idea that we write what we know. We have to write what we don't know, toward what we don't know. Now I get excited when I don't know something. If we always wrote what we already knew, how boring would that be? There's something wonderful in not knowing.

13 The Research Road Map

[E]vidence suggests that people often fail to solve problems not because the problems are insoluble but because they give up prematurely.

– Daniel Goleman, Paul Kaufman, and Michael Ray,
The Creative Spirit
(Goleman, Kaufman, and Ray, 1992: 19)

Introduction to Chapter 13

It's easy to write a convincing paragraph or two when you have done a little bit of research. All the facts add up, and you can confidently say that soybeans are the fuel of the future, Franklin Delano Roosevelt was the best president ever, or the painter Salvador Dali was a Surrealist. It feels good to be one hundred percent certain. In this Research Fantasy World, your confidence and expertise grow as you accumulate note cards and page numbers, you achieve a sense of clear confidence in your subject matter, and high grades appear on your papers.

On the other hand, if you feel like tearing your hair out over a research project, you have moved past Research Fantasy World into Research Reality. In this version of research, you will often feel stranded at a point of utter confusion. Although it may not seem like a joyful moment, take a second to cheer, or to strike a silent victory stance if you're in the library. If you are facing what seems like an immovable research roadblock, you have just encountered a necessary building block for a good research project.

Research Roadblocks

The faults and flaws of a research project often appear global and catastrophic at first, and you may be tempted to diagnose the problem as unsolvable: "I can't do this; the assignment is impossible." Gaining specific focus about your research dilemma will help you move beyond this initial reaction. You will need this diagnosis to understand how to solve the problem and turn it into a solution that fits. Here are some of the difficulties in which you may be stuck:

1. Red-Hot Debates: Two authorities have completely opposing views on a subject, and there seems to be no way to bring their perspectives together. Or the debate over the topic is so emotionally charged that all sources resort to name-calling or moral arguments without much support for their views.
2. Huge Questions: You have three hundred quotes from various sources and no way to focus. Your subject is massive and almost too complicated to write about in the time or space you have left.
3. Confusion: Maybe you have phrased your research question and written your whole paper in a way that reveals you have misunderstood the subject. Or you realize you don't know what your sources are talking about. Maybe the heroic/evil person you were writing about turns out to be complicated and not so perfect/evil, or you've discovered some other complicating factor in a formerly clearcut thesis.
4. No Available Sources: Researchers and sources have not published anything definitive on your topic.
5. Not Enough Time: You have a huge third point of view to consider and you have half an hour to write your conclusion,

print out the paper, and turn it in. Or you have devoted a lot
of time to learning about something that you realize is less
interesting than a related topic you have just discovered.

Experiment 13.1: Choose Your Own Misadventure

Length: *Short*

Timer: *4 minutes + 4 minutes = 8 minutes*

Discuss: *Recommended*

Step 1. Have you faced any of the challenges listed above – or a
different one – in a research assignment or task? Write for
four minutes about what happened. Consider your research
process, the time you took to research, the time you took to
formulate the question, and what the experience of reaching the roadblock was like. If you have never experienced
a research roadblock or can't think of a specific example,
write about the roadblocks from the list above that seem
most alarming or frustrating to you.

Step 2. Consider and write for four minutes about any blind
spots that might have led you to that particular roadblock.
For example, did a desire to write an easy paper lead you
to pick a topic that seemed deceptively simple at first? Did
a strong attachment to a particular topic lead you to put off
or avoid looking into a counter-argument? If you have never
experienced a research roadblock, write about the types
of blind spots or assumptions that might lead a person to
whatever roadblock you wrote about in Step 1.

Roadblocks as Stepping Stones

As an added challenge, the research roadblock usually appears in a
hurricane of fear and frustration over practical concerns: "What's

going to happen when I miss this deadline or turn in something awful? I'm exhausted, and I hate this class/project/job/area of study. I'm bad at this; I have some sort of genetic inability to understand 19th-Century Art History." And so on. These fears and concerns can be pretty overwhelming, so it is important to see through them and to realize that you have some concrete choices to make about your research.

Making a few decisions can lighten the load and the fear, but when facing this situation it is often tempting to try a last-ditch solution (which rarely works) to get out of your predicament: an all-nighter of frantically stringing quotes together while drinking too much coffee, channeling the last paragraphs from some sleepy, semi-comatose state and kept awake (just!) with delirium and adrenaline. In desperation, some students might even cheat, buy a term paper, or string quotes together from other sources and claim these words as their own; all of these approaches are plagiarism and should therefore be avoided like the plague. More productively, you might beg your instructor for help/an extension/ mercy/a different assignment. Or, fearing catastrophe, you might drop the class, the job, the assignment, or take the F.

There are other options that lead through research failure to success. As Ken Macrorie writes in his book, *The I-Search Paper*, "A search that failed can be as exciting and valuable as one that succeeded" (Macrorie, 1988: 64). Opportunities to create value from failure emerge from the research roadblocks, as you will see below.

Confusion

By far, the most common variety of research roadblock involves the vague but painful sense that the question is wrong, that you're not understanding the answers, or that you're not even entirely sure what you're studying. The beginning researcher might be tempted to blame this on lack of intelligence or difficulty with the subject matter. But this problem – in all its manifestations – is what researchers confront every day.

The path toward a solution is to get more specific about what you don't understand. To do this, look at your notes sentence by sentence, or your paper line by line. If you'd like, you can use a highlighter to mark any specific points where you lose the thread of your argument or your research. Now write for two or three minutes, brainstorming as many possible specific questions as you can think of. The goal here is to hone in on what exactly you are unclear about.

The reason for this practice is that in generating questions, you may begin to see that you have discovered a valuable new entry-point for research. Maybe you are asking an excellent question that has confused others, or maybe your question contains an insight or a connection that other researchers have not pointed out.

Once you have generated your list of questions, write for two or three more minutes on whether the answers can be obtained by further research. Even if these are the kinds of questions you're not sure how to answer, save all of this writing, as it might very well be incorporated into your final paper.

Huge Questions

One common research predicament is that the question asked is simply too large to be answered with the time and resources available to the researcher. Ideally, the researcher could have identified a narrow-enough question early on; this is also why your instructors might repeat "focus, focus, focus" like a mantra. Sometimes, however, you just can't tell that you've asked a huge question until you start trying to answer it.

To address this, write for three or four minutes on the different manageable research questions that are contained within your large topic. You might also write about what led you to choose this large topic, what you initially thought the research project would look like, and what specifically led you to see that the question was huge. Again, whatever you generate here will probably find its way into your research paper.

Red-Hot Debates

Many writers look for a fierce war of words to help them choose their research topics, believing that if a debate is polarized and if there are clearly laid-out "camps" of opinion, it will mean more material and more interest for the reader. Choosing this kind of topic presents two challenges. First, a researcher will have greater difficulty finding sources that address the complexity of the argument. Many sources will instead choose a "camp" and build a case for that position. A question that inspires passionate responses is not a bad question, but these questions require more effort and care on the part of the researcher.

The second challenge of a red-hot debate emerges as you write up your research and analyze your sources. In a polarized battle of words, both sides will launch rhetorical attacks that are very convincing, and it will be much easier to simply go along with the side that you encounter first or the side that has the strongest rhetoric. A large collection of sources discussing the positions in a heated debate will inspire quite a bit of rhetoric, making it difficult for the researcher to sort through the research and to separate the various positions.

You might also choose a topic with no idea that there's a war brewing under the surface. Before you know it, you discover that all of your sources are sniping back and forth at one another. Even if you didn't plan on getting into the middle of the conflict, your choice of topic forces you to address the conflict as part of your research.

Rather than starting out by choosing a side, write for three or four minutes on the elements of each position that seem convincing, confusing, or troubling. What are the central questions that seem to divide the sides in the debate? What kinds of support does each side offer? Describe the debate as fully as you can, including asking yourself whether there might be a middle position or more sides to the issue than what you have encountered so far in your research.

No Available Sources

Given the massive number of research tools available online for research – especially to students enrolled in universities – the roadblock of no available sources must first be separated from the beginning research challenge of not knowing where to look for information. If you have combed the various databases and diligently tried a variety of search terms, you may truly have reached a subject that few authors have addressed. This is an unexpected breakthrough: you reach the edge of what has been written about, or you find that other researchers have posed questions to which there are no clear answers.

This feels, at first, like a research failure. Beginning researchers often assume that a good research project results in clear answers or a definite position. But most professional research projects discuss and include what is unknown as well as what has been discovered. A good conclusion thoroughly addresses areas for further research, unanswered questions, and open dilemmas. To see whether you might be able to write about an interesting gap in the research for your paper, write for a few minutes about the specific reasons why researchers have not yet come up with clear answers on your question. For example, maybe a certain experiment is needed but the technology has not yet been invented. Maybe studies that address the effects of a law are inconclusive. Or maybe public opinion on a topic is changing, so it's not clear what the debate will look like in the future. If you can't name a specific limitation, chances are that someone has actually done the research but you haven't found the source. If, however, your research points to the limits of knowledge, you've found a good topic to discuss in your paper. What kinds of studies might help generate more useful knowledge to address this question?

Not Enough Time

At a practical level, time limitations are the common thread that unites all research. When you procrastinate until midnight on the day a paper is due, you might think you have little connection to a full-time researcher writing up research findings, but both of you are facing the same fundamental problem: the research has to end in order for findings to be shared and analyzed, but the questions will always lead to more questions. In this sense, the subject matter is always open to further consideration and investigation. Both you and the professional researcher have to choose your goals and limitations, and also to plan for a point at which to stop.

The difference, of course, is that the time element becomes more and more central to research the more experience a researcher gains. A devoted researcher will be willing to devote much more time to a complex project addressing bigger questions with more complex methods. As a researcher's expertise grows, so does the ability to judge how long a particular project will take. Whether or not the researcher meets a time deadline determines whether or not the researcher will get a degree, a job, or a career. However, even experienced researchers sometimes find their neatly planned timelines dissolving in chaos. What seemed like a slight detour becomes a messy knot to unsnarl. Sources take longer to read and analyze than expected. A simple question reveals a tangent that redirects an entire project.

Time problems become a legitimate item for discussion in a research project when you have encountered an unexpected difficulty that is somehow connected to the subject matter, not just the result of your lack of planning. Discussing your procrastination does not contribute to the research – and will probably only annoy your reader. But sharing the ways in which the subject matter itself presented unexpected problems is actually a contribution to the reader's understanding of the subject.

Experiment 13.2: The Adventure of Finding Your Material

Length: *Short*

Timer: *3 minutes + 2 minutes + 3 minutes = 8 minutes*

Discuss: *Optional*

Ken Macrorie writes that the quest for the real story is a central part of the story itself (Macrorie, 1988). To understand this idea, think about an adventure movie you enjoyed watching. You will analyze its elements to see how the expectation and the unknown create interest for the audience. You will use some of your findings from analyzing these story elements in the next section.

Step 1. Take three minutes and write down the plot of your chosen movie as a list of events and actions.

Step 2. In two minutes, describe the opening scenes in the movie. What first draws the audience into the plot of the movie? What is the question to be resolved?

Step 3. Write for three minutes about one or more later scenes in the movie that expand on and change the question. What unexpected twists and turns crop up? What about these twists and turns creates interest for the viewer?

Research Drama

A story with twists and turns creates suspense. At a basic level, humans are drawn to stories; anything that has a story-like structure is described as *narrative*. From the earliest bedtime tales, children enjoy and learn from stories that capture emotions and engage their sense of mystery and exploration. Adults identify with the universal experience of failing, wondering, and doubting as a character searches for answers or solutions.

As you have seen in previous chapters of this book, questions are the foundation for knowledge. Doubts and concerns – and even mistakes and confusions – are manifestations of thought that are a legitimate part of the research process. Your questions are the exact area where you intersect with your subject. Robert Davis and Mark Shadle sketch out an alternative vision of research in which the unknown is welcomed: "Knowledge plays leapfrog with mystery; meanings are made to move beyond, and writing traces this movement. Research becomes seeking as a mode of being" (Davis and Shadle, 2000: 422).

Your research project will benefit by including your own reflection and thought rather than merely a set of quotes and statements from sources. As you write, you explore your findings, reveal the surprises contained in your research, and analyze the gaps between expectations and results. This drama of known and unknown involves the reader and yourself in a process of knowledge creation. Understanding that there is always more to know doesn't mean that the conclusion of your research is vague. Instead, you will use your questions and surprises to focus in on what you have discovered. Including your questions helps the reader put your research in context.

The true story of your research process includes much more than your findings and conclusions. Your research journey began as you located a topic and generated questions about it. You thought carefully as you read, noodled, considered sources, and followed your questions. The thoughts and analysis of each step form the story of your research journey, and as you go back to retrace your steps and tell that tale, you also unfold a series of ideas that explain your topic to your reader. Explaining how your research changed and how you adapted to the challenges you discovered gives the reader a sense of the analytic process you went through as you evaluated each piece of information. The story of your research is exciting, but it is also a very clear guide for a reader who wants to understand the complexity of a topic based on the experience of someone who has already explored it.

Experiment 13.3: Research Flow Chart

Length: *Long or Take-home*
Timer: *None*
Discuss: *Optional*

Sometimes a visual map of the twists and turns in a research project can help reveal the story of the research. Use this exercise when you have finished your research and are considering how to write up your findings.

Step 1. Draw a bubble or circle and write your initial question inside it.

Step 2. Look back at your research notebook and think about the first set of sources you found to address this question. Draw a line from your center question to another bubble containing your first source.

Step 3. Look at the right-hand column in your research notebook beside the notes you took from this source. Circle any questions you raised as you took notes. Write each of these questions as a separate bubble connected to the source.

Step 4. Did one of these questions shape or change your research? Did it influence which source you chose to look at second? If so, draw a bubble connected to the question and leading off in the direction of your second source.

Step 5. Continue with the flow chart to see how your research unfolded. Then write the story of this research quest, explaining to the reader how your questions changed and developed as you researched.

The Gray Matter: Navigating Research with the Moral Compass

Some moments of research create a rush of hope as all of the facts seem to line up and clearly indicate that your theory is correct. Then you might read one last source that brings up an uncomfortable fact, a contradictory study, or a complexity you hadn't considered. That sinking feeling is like watching a balloon deflate and splutter away into the corner. And for a split second, you might confront research temptation: wouldn't it be great if you could just un-know or un-find that last fact?

Questions for Thought or Discussion

1. Is it unethical to bluff your way through a topic by pretending to know more than you do, or by using vague language to distract the reader from the gaps in your knowledge?
2. How does acknowledging your biases affect your readers?
3. Why is it tempting to leave out a source that contradicts your main idea?
4. What academic practices and standards may influence or create the desire to leave out any contradictory information or gaps in our knowledge?

Conclusion to Chapter 13

Telling the story of your research – including the roadblocks and turning points – marks the beginning of the end of your research project. As you tell a story, you create an interpretation and begin to make theories about why and how your research quest developed and concluded. This research story is also the beginning of writing your project in a form that your reader can understand, and you will explore the most useful containers and packages for a research project, along with the useful methods for creating these containers, in Chapter 14. Then, in Chapter 15, you will return to the story sketches you created in order to expand and share the scenes in your research drama and to help readers connect to the tale.

14 Finding Your Way

[A] very conscious and complete letting go is pivotal – letting go
of the subject, feelings, the process, and what we have created.
This provides a fresh space for whatever it is that you are going
to do next.

– John Daido Loori, *The Zen of Creativity*
(Loori, 2005: 93)

Introduction to Chapter 14

So far, the research bucket has been bottomless, and your task has
been to gather as much interesting information as possible and to
follow the questions that lead to still more questions. At a certain
point, however, the mountain of material will overrun any container.
A researcher who becomes invested in a topic and pursues its complexity might have to pull away from the chase as the deadline for
a written project or presentation draws near.

How do you know when to stop researching? Experienced researchers often notice that at a certain point, their sources begin to
sound repetitive, each echoing themes that previous sources have
brought up. For many researchers, however, a deadline or due date
is the "dead end" sign at the end of most research projects. But
as you speed toward the deadline, you might feel as though the

wheels of your research vehicle are spinning and slipping as you attempt to stay on the road. You might have the feeling that the subject is too big to ever cover in a comprehensive way, or that you are missing the path as you switch gears from researching to reflecting and writing about what you have learned.

Putting on the research brakes can feel like pure panic, but this process happens to a greater or lesser degree in every research project. You can also think of this shift as a momentary pause to check the map and see if you're headed in the right direction – or if you've already reached your destination. A map of your research-in-progress can indicate possible organizational structures and connections that already exist within and among the sources you've gathered. First, you can use the quick methods below to see when you have left major gaps or whether you are heading exactly in the right direction.

Containers, Walls, and Buckets

Outlines are supposed to be aids for writing, but the rigid terraced structure can also stop the free flow of thoughts. Some writers like to compose an outline immediately before they write a draft as a way to organize research. However, rougher outlining methods can be helpful at an earlier stage in your writing. To see if your research already has a hidden structure, take a break from research-gathering to group and sort your sources.

1. Labeled Folders: If you have physical copies of articles and sources, stack the sources in piles according to rough subtopics. For example, if you are researching methods of preserving coral reefs, you might label one folder *Construction of Barriers* and another folder *Water Temperature Concerns*. Label a file folder for each subtopic. If a source addresses two subjects, print two copies and put one in each folder.

2. Cut and Paste Text: Many researchers type their quotes into a word processing file, along with the information about the source from which the quote was taken. As you type information from each source, carefully indicate with quotation marks which sentences are direct quotes. If you take notes this way, you can brainstorm a list of your subtopics at the top or bottom of your document, or using a separate file, and then move the quotes to fit under these categories as if you are completing a puzzle. If a quote fits in multiple categories, copy it multiple times.

3. Print, Tag, and Shuffle: Another method that often works with a large project is to take notes – by hand or by computer – from various sources, always carefully indicating the direct quotes with quotation marks. Next, print out your files if you are using a computer, or make a photocopy of each page if you are using a research notebook. Write phrases that indicate themes or subtopics in the margin next to each quote. (For those who use blogs and other internet organizational services, this is also called *tagging*.)

   Now get out the scissors. Cut up each quote along with its label and then make piles on a desk or the floor. Organize the piles and quotes so that related ideas are near each other, in the same way that you used a bubble chart to connect ideas in Chapter 7. What you will have is a stack of quotes by subtopic that you can arrange to see patterns, repetitions, and connections. You might also see that you have too much material on one topic, or that you are missing a connection between two themes.

   For some researchers, a workspace this large is essential, and the window of a computer screen is unnecessarily constraining. If you think and organize ideas in a visual manner, this method might be especially helpful because it allows you to see connections and organizational possibilities in front of you all at once.

The Simplicity of Scaffolding

Focusing and paring down a huge stack of sources and quotes can challenge any researcher. Every source has something to offer and represents minutes or hours spent in the search, and most sources sound authoritative, polished, and important. A composed and completed argument, presented in print and published, has the weight of careful consideration and rhetoric. The quotes from these sources sound impressive, and it may be tempting to step off the stage entirely, presenting quotes to readers who must draw their own conclusions. But research is not a gift basket or a fruit salad. Instead of throwing in every piece of information and every possible ingredient, you will want to choose the elements of your argument carefully to make an attractive finished product. At some point, you must let go of the great insight that won't fit or the tangent that refuses to be contained by your paper.

Letting go and cutting are processes that both run counter to social and cultural messages you may have absorbed. John Daido Loori, a photographer and longtime practitioner of Zen meditation, writes, "Simplicity does not come easily to us in the West...We tend to accumulate things, thinking that if something is good, we should have more of it" (Loori, 2005: 154). Zen can be said to approach life with the philosophy of "less is more." Practitioners of Zen Buddhism focus on simplicity in life because, as Loori writes, "To be simple means to make a choice about what's important, and to let go of all the rest. When we are able to do this, our vision expands, our heads clear" (Loori, 2005: 154).

To visualize the mental clutter of too much information, you might recall the uncomfortable feeling of being trapped in a conversation with someone who insisted on giving you too much irrelevant detail about their latest home repair, their vacation, or their weekend escapades. In conversation and in writing, the invisible act of clearing away the unnecessary is vital to success. Loori describes this process of clearing and honing with a Japanese proverb: "A thousand-pound bow and arrow won't hit a mouse"

(Loori, 2005: 199). You can easily have too much information, which can weigh your project down so much that it fails to hit the mark. Half of the artistry and analysis in composing research – or any piece of original work in any discipline – is deciding what to leave out. As in previous chapters, you will use your instincts and your sense of interest and curiosity as a guide to help choose what to cut and what to use.

Experiment 14.1: Winnowing

Length: *Long*

Timer: *5 minutes + 5 x 1 minute + 4 minutes = 14 minutes*

Discuss: *None*

Step 1. Without looking at your notes, take five minutes to freewrite in order to summarize the information you have discovered about your topic. What themes and questions do your sources address?

Step 2. Look back at the freewrite and circle five words or phrases that are most interesting to you. Write for one minute on each of these words or phrases to describe why each is interesting.

Step 3. Think about what you don't yet know about your topic and what still interests you and sparks your curiosity. List a few interesting words or phrases to describe this unknown area.

Step 4. Write for four minutes on those words or phrases that you don't know much about. What specifically interests you? How do these questions or phrases connect to what you have found out so far?

Step 5. Look back at your first list of four to five interesting words and phrases. Copy them onto an index card or blank sheet of paper and use them for Experiment 14.2.

Experiment 14.2: Interest Ranking

Length: *Long or Take-home*
Timer: *None*
Discuss: *None*

Step 1. Use the four or five words or phrases you circled in Step 2 of Experiment 14.1 to rank each article. To rank them, mark each of your sources with one point for each of those words or phrases. In the example of the research project on multiple sclerosis, two words might be *cure* and *virus*, so an article discussing both of these issues would get two points.

Step 2. Look at the sources that received low scores, and consider dropping them from your source list. You might see these as background material, or you might decide that they need to be removed from your source list.

Step 3. If one source receives a much higher score than the rest, this might be a signal to do a bit more research. You might have just scratched the surface of something you are very interested in, and you probably need a few more sources that take this perspective in order to confirm or expand upon what interests you most.

Rock Climbing

Research in its true sense requires that we strike out into the unknown and become willing to adapt in response to what we discover. The researcher balances between knowledge and mystery, exploring the central questions while also being open to curiosity and the unexplored. Striking that balance – giving your readers knowledge while also acknowledging the questions and gaps – is the art of truly informative research.

One way to sabotage a research project is to try to go too far afield from your central question while still hanging onto it. For the reader, this can cause an experience that feels like trying to climb up a mountain while maintaining a firm grasp on the ground; one's arms and legs are likely to get pulled out of their sockets. When you feel torn between two topics, try Experiment 14.3 to evaluate whether the original question or thesis needs to be abandoned or returned to.

Experiment 14.3: Distance from the Center

Length: *Long or Take-home*

Timer: *None*

Discuss:. *None*

For this exercise, use a modified bubble chart to see whether you have generated some fascinating tangents that don't belong in your research project, or whether your project needs to be reframed to follow the direction most interesting to you.

Step 1. Write out your initial question and circle it, making it a central bubble in a bubble chart, as you did in Chapter 7.
Step 2. Write a short list of the major questions addressed by each source.
Step 3. Draw bubbles from the center to plot out the ways in which each source connects to the central question, along with a tag (such as the author's name) to help you identify the source.
Step 4. Examine your bubble chart. Are certain sources tending in a direction that is too many steps removed from the center?
Step 5. If a source seems to address several peripheral concerns but shows up near the center in one question, you know that this is the topic to use from this source. Consider

paring away the sources which address questions related
or repeated by other sources.

Behind the Scenes

This behind-the-scenes planning may seem to take valuable time
away from writing your paper. After all, bubble charts and interest rankings are rarely required for a final draft. Yet this energy is
never wasted. You probably won't need to do bubble charts and
other formal planning exercises for every research project. Instead,
you will gradually internalize the ability to select the sources that
most closely relate to your central question. You will also build
research muscles as you learn to recognize when you are stopping
too quickly or failing to follow the thread of your own interest.

Your bubble chart from Experiment 14.3 might have shown you
that you have a thought-provoking question not addressed by any
of your current sources. This is the time to make a difficult decision
that can feel risky: the choice to search for some very specific information. In fact, most students turn away just when the research is
getting interesting, because they feel like they have enough sources
to meet a minimum required for an assignment. After learning just
enough to discover a true focus that inspires interest, the beginning
researcher may turn away from the most fascinating element of
their findings. One more focused and quick search might uncover
exactly the sources to tie the project together.

Your research will engage and serve your readers if you present
your own path of discovery and thought processes, including the
descriptions of your questions as they evolve and change. For example, your freewrite about unanswered questions might lead you
to a focus or an analysis that is the perfect conclusion to a paper.
You might find yourself writing, "Coral reefs have been protected
in several ways, but the question raised by all of these methods is
who will pay for these solutions in the future." You are raising a
question that focuses your research and probably that also echoes

a question lingering in your reader's mind. Whether you find a source to address this question or not, you are bringing the reader along with you as your expertise develops.

Experiment 14.4: Plunging into the Unknown

Length: *Long or Take-home*
Timer: *None*
Discuss: *None*

Step 1. Hone your keywords for your last research effort to the specific *interest* words or phrases you have used for Experiments 14.1-14.3. Use a search engine or research database and a few alternate phrasings to look for sources that address these topics.

Step 2. Reject any new sources that don't directly address your open interest. You might find that this directed and specific source search gives you a great way to end your paper by turning up either evidence of unanswered questions or new research!

Focus and Cut

The purpose of an outline or any scaffolding for research or writing is not simply to build a structure for containing every piece of material. If you are a brick layer, you are constantly scraping off extra mortar with your trowel as you lay each line of bricks. You discard the cracked bricks and check your work constantly, making sure your lines are straight so your bricks can support those that are to come. With writing and researching, you also evaluate as you go, discarding any quotes or points that lead away from your topic and the questions you are most interested in exploring. (You can save the extra quotes for a different research project!)

After sorting your sources for a project – on multiple sclerosis, for example – you might see that most of your sources address the possible causes of the disease. You have to choose: either switch gears and focus on the range of treatments, or focus your thesis and devote your paper to the causes. You might cut a section on treatments or mention those questions in your conclusion. Cutting creates space for the reader to see your points and gives you room to explore.

The Gray Matter: The Challenge of Giving Credit

If you have completed a research project, you know that reading and absorbing information changes the way you see your subject. Even with a rigorous note-taking system, it can be difficult to figure out what sources have shaped your opinions – especially if you don't copy down any direct quotes from the source. As mentioned in Chapter 13, a major temptation and problem with research is the danger of leaving out sources. Paradoxically, you can improve your project but cutting and focusing, yet when you cut tangents, you are also cutting out a history of your research and learning on a topic. So you may need to acknowledge your debt to sources that helped you develop your understanding but that don't directly figure into your final product. As your research changes, you can use some simple techniques to acknowledge the sources you've read – even if they have become less relevant to your focused research.

Background Paragraphs

One concrete way to do this is to add in a paragraph that describes the first direction you took with your project. Without needing to give any direct quotes, you can still mention the sources you used to get a background understanding of the subject. For example, you might write, "Smith (1995), Adelman (2004), and Younkins

(2007) are the three most widely known authors who explore important solutions to the coral reef problem, though I will focus on the solutions presented by Price (2008) because her work takes global warming into account."

You can also include a sentence that explains what most authors or researchers are interested in, and follow that with your own departure into the unknown. This gives the reader a sense of where you've been and why you decided to turn in a new direction, while still giving credit for how you found your way along the path. For example, you might write, "Harris (2002) provides many widely adopted solutions for coral reef preservation off the coast of Australia. However, this work does not address the question of cost of these solutions."

Keep in mind, too, that a question is a form of analysis, so if a source raises a point – even if you don't explore it in your paper in detail – you should cite it, i.e. "Harris (2002) raises the important question of how tourism will affect the coral reefs."

Footnotes and Endnotes for Your Comments

Most students use footnotes and endnotes only for source citations, but if you turn to a nonfiction book in the library, you will see extensive notes that do much more. The note is a great opportunity to let your readers know about interesting research, tangents, and places to look for more information, and to offer your own comments on this information. These notes are considered optional, so the interested reader can pursue them while the general reader can also skip them and still understand your argument. Used judiciously, they can offer your reader glimpses into the complexity of your sources. Because the skill of writing a useful footnote or endnote is covered in advanced nonfiction research courses, ask your instructor whether this format is acceptable for presenting your research.

The Disagreeing Source

Another major dilemma confronted by researchers is how to address a source that says the opposite of everything you believe or that contradicts your argument. As mentioned above, it might be easiest to simply leave it out, but it will make your research project more complex – and ultimately more interesting and useful – if you mention it and give some detail about the argument. You can also wrestle with the source's argument on the page and consider what sorts of evidence the source uses. Finally, you can give the reader helpful context by explaining whether the disagreeing source expresses a widely held belief or one that is controversial and rare.

Questions for Thought or Discussion

1. Why are students tempted to include long quotes in their research projects?
2. When you read an article with a number of long quotes, what effect does it have on you? How does this decision affect your opinion of the writer and/or of the topic? How does the use of extensive direct quoting affect your understanding of the subject?
3. Find examples of research that cite groups of sources without providing direct quotes from each one.

Conclusion to Chapter 14

Organizing and analyzing your sources for a research project is an important *writing* step, and laying out your sources according to the types of arguments they make can help you see how your paper needs to be written. These visual and cut-and-paste strategies allow you to compose your argument in a logical way that keeps you focused on the questions that interest you, and avoid the common problem of writing a dull and unfocused paper using exciting research. Focus and interest often come as the result of <u>letting go</u> of sources by mentioning them briefly or recognizing that they take you and your reader too far away from your research question. Once you have made your cut-and-paste files or charts or stacks, you will write up your work of analysis in the form of a research paper, which is merely the record of your thoughts about this process.

15 Writing the Story's Journey

A tangerine has sections. If you can eat just one section, you can probably eat the entire tangerine. But if you can't eat just one section, you cannot eat the tangerine.
— Thich Nhat Hanh, *The Miracle of Mindfulness*
(Hanh, 1976: 6)

Introduction to Chapter 15

You've researched, chosen the best sources, and reflected on what you learned. Now you stare at the white space of a computer screen or notebook. If you had been using a traditional research process, you might face a mess of quotes without any sense of structure or meaning. But since you have been reflecting on your sources and organizing them as you researched, your first task is to transfer your reflections to the page and begin to arrange them. Then you expand and look for patterns as you tell the story of your research quest.

Many writers freeze up when they begin at the beginning. The introduction is an important welcome to the reader, but the opening sentences must contain a sure sense of what is to come in the paper, which is difficult to write if you don't have a paper yet. You can imagine your project as a house under construction. The door needs to be framed and hung and the walls need to go up before the welcome mat is laid on the front porch. You will see some strategies for writing your introduction at the end of this chapter. For now, you can jump right into the main supports for your project – the outline of your search. Like eating the sections of a tangerine, there is no rule stating that you have to start with one particular piece. If you start with any piece that seems most appealing, you can more easily move onto the next.

A good place to start is to tell the *story of your research*. You can simply describe your initial interest in the topic, and then track the course of the research as it unfolded. This is the method described in Ken Macrorie's book on the I-Search paper (Macrorie, 1988). Instead of starting with your findings and your final position, start by describing what you wanted to know and what led you into this question, as described in Chapter 13. As you tell the story of your research, even the pitfalls and wrong turns may end up conveying helpful information to the reader.

Students often feel that the opening lines of their research projects have to sum up their work in the broadest possible sense. The disadvantage to this approach is that it carries the writing off into abstraction. To counteract that tendency, you can brainstorm concrete details for a research paper that is vivid and captures the reader's imagination. Rather than starting with an abstract argument based on ethical principles or numerical evidence, begin by writing concrete and sensory details from life experience.

Senses and Experiences as Research Hooks

Academic writing, in its worst forms, can sound as though it was written by a particularly unimaginative robot. Because such writing often wrestles with abstract ideas and concepts, getting the ideas right is task number one. Abstraction is obviously vital to human society and thought, but raw abstraction on the page can put up a barrier that prevents a reader from actually engaging with your research or thought process. The attempt to communicate concepts in a vibrant and involving way is often neglected. For example, a research paper about coral reefs could start with a list of general concerns about saving reef formations around the world. Or it could be started with the portrait of a single vibrant reef off the coast of Australia, colored by the symbiotic algae that cover the calcium structure, sheltering fish of every color, bathed by bathwater-warm ocean, providing a source of nutrients to plants and fish that would otherwise have no source of food or shelter in a rough and shallow ocean environment.

Images and concrete details are more than pretty window-dressing for abstract concepts and logical arguments. Images and concrete details can also play a vital role in organizing and thinking about abstract concepts. Depending on the way you are neurologically "wired," your ability to grasp and organize abstract concepts can vary tremendously. Many people wrongly assume that abstraction equals intelligence. But we are visual creatures, and abstract thought often uses concrete *hooks* such as visual images. Your instructors and other public speakers often use stories, analogies, and examples to communicate. Establishing a true grasp of a new idea is much easier when it can be seen in practice or associated with a story, object, or image. If you become more willing to use concrete details in your academic writing, you might be surprised at how much more easily the writing flows from your fingers and how much easier it is to communicate and organize your thoughts.

Experiment 15.1: The Five Senses

Length: *Short*
Timer: *5 minutes + 3 minutes + 4 minutes = 12 minutes*
Discuss: *Optional*

Step 1. Take five minutes to list the sensory information that comes to mind when you think about your topic. For example, the topic of multiple sclerosis brings to mind the physical feelings that people with the disease experience in their bodies. If you are writing about space exploration, you might list the feeling of walking in zero gravity or the taste and texture of food eaten by astronauts.

Step 2. Now take three minutes to list the objects (not people) that come to mind when you think about your topic; these might be anything from a device used in a laboratory, a virus that causes a disease, a planet, or a country.

Step 3. Look over your lists and circle three or four of your objects, senses, and images that seem particularly vivid or important. Consider including these as paragraphs in your draft. You might start by expanding on each of these for four minutes to brainstorm ideas for using this concrete detail to help your reader better understand your topic.

Research has to connect with the reader in order to communicate information in a way that the reader can understand. Readers grasp the value of your research when they see – and smell, touch, taste, and feel – its causes, effects, and impact on the world. As you will explore in the next section, asking the reader to connect to or empathize with a person or group of people can also help a reader to better understand your topic.

Experiment 15.2: Characters in Your Story

Length: *Short*

Timer: *None*

Discuss: *Optional*

Step 1. List the names of people who seem particularly important in your research. These might include researchers or academics playing a central role in a discovery, or a person whose life story was central to your topic.

Step 2. Now list a few other people or groups of people who might not be named specifically in your research but who are affected by your research in some way. For the example of the research project on multiple sclerosis, the group of people with the disease and the group of children who might inherit a genetic predisposition are both important.

Step 3. Now consider your own role. How central are you in this story? Is there anything about your personal history or experiences that led you to choose this topic? How did your life experience change the way you interacted with the topic, conducted research about the topic, or the decisions you made during your research process?

Step 4. Circle or underline the name of a person or group of people who seem to be most important to this story; you will use this person in Experiment 15.3.

What's a Scene?

In Chapter 13, we imagined and analyzed a scene from a movie to understand how vivid action captures our interest and imagination. Action can play an important role both in organizing your paper and in creating interest for your reader.

To think about research as narrative, imagine your research story as composed of a series of scenes. A scene is merely a package that contains characters and their actions in a particular moment in time and at a particular place. Authors who plan and write movies or novels plot out their long works in scenes to understand how one action leads to the next. Telling the story of your research can play an important role in illustrating and explaining abstract concepts you introduce. A story or scene can pull in readers and give them tools for retaining and understanding the ideas you share.

Experiment 15.3: Scene and Heard

Length: *Short or Long*
Timer: *5 minutes*
Discuss: *None*

Step 1. List any concrete events, conversations, or real-life moments that happened to you during the course of your research.

Step 2. List any concrete events, conversations, or real-life moments that are central to your research project. For example, did a conversation between two people spark an important event connected to your topic? Did a discovery in a lab or a tragic death play a central role?

Step 3. Now look back at the list of people you generated in Experiment 15.2. Choose the person whose name you circled as most central to the story of your research. Describe the person's engagement with the topic from beginning to end, as if it were a movie, using a list of actions and events.

Step 4. Circle any moments that seem particular dramatic, or that show something important about your research topic. Write one of those moments as if it were a scene from a movie. For example, what happened between two researchers that led to a disagreement? How did an inventor react after making a significant discovery? How do families react when dealing with a new illness?

Plotting the Framework

Hopefully you are beginning to get a list of possible paragraphs and points to explore in your written research project. The exercises above will produce many thoughts that will not end up in your final paper, but these might indicate a range of approaches you could take to explore your research and share it with readers.

As you begin the process of choosing how to communicate with your reader, it is often helpful to make a list of the options you have uncovered for structuring your paper. Consider a balance between abstract ideas and concrete examples to give your readers a variety of ways to grasp your points. You might also make a list of possible subtopics, then write each on a scrap of paper and shuffle them around like a jigsaw puzzle. For example, if you consider the topic of multiple sclerosis as an example, your research might include these significant points: Aunt Sally; her struggle with multiple sclerosis; what's happened in her life; changes in diagnosis; changes in treatment; looking forward to the future of treatment of MS; and unanswered questions.

Your first thought might be to present Aunt Sally's story as a brief example to show one point in your paper, but you could also start with a vivid description of the way life has changed for her since her diagnosis, including the symptoms and how she manages. Each paragraph could include elements of her story as a way to connect to the experiences of millions of people with multiple sclerosis and to serve as a concrete bridge between your reader and the abstract research about the disease.

One challenge as you structure your project is to keep listening to your own interest and your own questions. In the research example about MS, eight sources might explain similar concerns about treatment of multiple sclerosis and conclude that more money is needed for research. When you read enough authoritatively written material on a topic, it can be difficult to step back and get distance from these sources to consider your own views and questions. As you put your ideas on paper, this is an important time to refocus on what interested you in this topic and your central concerns and questions about it. A bit of distance between you and your sources helps to preserve your interest and reactions, which contain your insight and analysis about your topic.

Experiment 15.4: Refocusing on the Heart of the Story

Length: *Short*

Timer: *2 minutes + 4 minutes = 6 minutes*

Discuss: *Optional*

Step 1. For two minutes, sit and think about your topic. What has frustrated you in this research process? What has amazed and interested you? What questions are nagging, and what can't you seem to understand? What has surprised you?

Step 2. Take four minutes to write about your reactions. More than likely, these paragraphs will generate useful ideas for your introduction and conclusion. Don't try to address everything from your freewrite in your paper; use these ideas to help locate the strongest theme and make that the center of your introduction and conclusion.

The Last Step: The Introduction

You might imagine your introduction as a literal chance for a reader to get to know you. When you introduce one friend to another, you give both friends' names and usually say something brief about each person, kind of a *hook* for each friend to begin to understand the other. You might say, for example, "This is Joey, the guy I told you about with the pet ferret," or "This is Ida from my Spanish class."

When you introduce and later sum up your findings, you do much more than give an overview of facts and sources. You become a guide for the reader through the complex terrain of your subject, and your own reactions to the subject provide a trail for the reader to follow. Instead of telling the reader what to think, imagine your research story as an example of how the terrain was explored. The reader may agree and choose to follow your path, or decide on another, but you have made a contribution by giving an important example of how one person engaged with the subject. Your specific encounter with a topic is a concrete example of how the research topic connects with the real world – through you. Personal examples give the reader a way to connect with the topic.

When writers talk about *audience*, all they really mean is the person they are writing or speaking to. If you are speaking to one friend, you know the possible hooks that will make your introduction meaningful to that friend based on what that friend cares about. When you're writing more generally, it can seem as though there's no possible hook to connect your specific topic with a general group of readers.

For a larger audience or less defined audience – such as readers of a research project – you might imagine a reader who has the least possible interest in your subject, just as a way of making sure you're providing a *hook* for almost any reader. Try this short exercise as a way to brainstorm an introduction with a hook to catch readers' interest.

Experiment 15.5: Letter to a Beekeeper

Length: *Short*

Timer: *5 minutes*

Discuss: *Optional*

Step 1. Imagine a few people who might have the least possible interest in or knowledge about your research subject. If you are researching literary theory, maybe you'd choose your Uncle Frank or a tax accountant. If you are telling the story of health insurance reform, maybe you would start by writing a letter to your younger sister's friend Jan.

Step 2. Take five minutes to write a letter to this person, starting with "Dear Uncle Frank," "Dear Beekeeper," or whatever person you choose. Then try to explain exactly why your research subject might be of interest to this person. What's the main point? What lessons could the person learn? How does that person's life overlap in some way with your subject matter? For example, if you wrote a letter to Jan about health insurance, you might have asked Jan what happens when she gets sick and then asked her to imagine the total cost of a doctor's visit in the United States and then in another country such as Finland.

Step 3. You might initially have found the connection to be a stretch, but hopefully you came up with a few good ways to show the subject's relevance to this person's life. Underline the more general approaches that might apply to a broad range of readers instead of just to beekeepers or your Uncle Frank, and consider launching your research project with a direct appeal to the reader. For example, you might use the approach from your letter to Jan to generate an opening sentence that grabs reader interest, such as, "When you visit the doctor in the United States, the total cost for these services can be as high as $300 or more. In Finland, this same doctor's visit would cost less than one quarter of the price" (Those are made-up statistics, but you get the point).

The Gray Matter: Known and Unknown

The traditional five-paragraph essay presents a research topic as a neat little puzzle with five pieces: introduction, three pieces of evidence, and conclusion. That approach is a helpful framework to use in order to learn how to do research and connect information to a topic, but a simple tool can be abandoned or altered as you grow and become a stronger writer and thinker. Just like you grow out of your shoes as a child, you need to move on to other options that give you more room to think and express yourself. As your world and your research about the world becomes more complicated, it is essential to acknowledge that any topic worth writing about cannot be addressed in only five paragraphs.

Any topic worth writing about has unanswered questions, and there's no need to adopt a fake-scholarly tone of the expert when the subject is muddy or confusing and evidence exists to support multiple perspectives. This mode of argument – almost a one-sided sales pitch rather than a careful consideration – has in some ways become the default mode of expression in many parts of society. It is easy to slip into broad rhetoric and over-confident argument without even realizing it.

Questions for Thought or Discussion

1. What are the dangers of pretending to know more than you do? What are the benefits?
2. Why don't people like to acknowledge gaps in their own knowledge?
3. Which situations – or workplaces, cultures, careers, or subcultures – might encourage this bluffing about not-knowing? What might be the causes?

Try This

After you've finished a draft of your paper, search for the loose threads. Try to answer these questions: What are you leaving out of your paper? What topics were beyond you? What couldn't you understand? What are you still unsure about?

Conclusion to Chapter 15

There is no written commandment that academic or researched writing has to be as abstract as possible. Images, color, senses, scenes, and characters can all make the reading of your work a more pleasurable experience. These concrete details do much more than decorate your work or make it more palatable. They get the job done more effectively and efficiently, allowing you to communicate clearly with a wide range of readers and allowing your reader to understand and retain your arguments and the information you found during your research. As you tell the story of your research, remember to think about the real-world moments that made that research possible.

Each of the lists you made in this chapter and in previous chapters have been more than prewriting for a paper. You have actually been writing rough drafts. They might be messy or sketchy or incomplete, but in using the tools of REFLECTION, you have compiled a substantial record of your own engagement with your subject matter. That is a research paper. So every step between now and the end is just a matter of revision, which is the subject of the final chapter.

16 Revision: Seeing Again

Most processes engaged in by live organisms are cyclic, developmental processes that run through time and end up different from how they began. The fact is that most people find they improve their ability to think carefully and discriminatingly if they allow themselves to be sloppy and relinquish control at other times.
— Peter Elbow, *Writing Without Teachers*
(Elbow, 1973: 34)

Introduction to Chapter 16

Facing a messy or confusing draft can be quite discouraging. You might look at the disconnected pieces and feel a sense of defeat, or you might worry that these threads will never connect to form a finished piece of writing. As you mature as a writer, however, you will recognize this feeling as a necessary and unavoidable step between the beginning and end of any project. The familiarity of the feeling might make it less daunting each time you experience it. This is the same type of feeling that long-distance runners experience about midway through a race, and they recognize it as a pattern.

The saying, "A lotus grows from the mud," implies that beautiful finished projects must emerge from murky places, from darkness and chaos. For many writers there is simply no way to write a finished piece without a confusing, contradictory first draft. These same writers encounter failure when they skimp and try to finish a project in one draft. Many writers who skip revision assume they cannot write well. In truth, they have not given themselves a chance to move from draft to revision to polished writing.

The technology of word processing allows us for constant revision, and in some ways the idea of a draft is outmoded because many writers constantly redraft as they write by cutting, pasting, typing, and erasing. If this is your writing process, you might make the argument that it is unnecessary to print out a draft in order to revise. The true sense of the word *revision* is to see something from a new angle. To gain this perspective and new angle, you need to take a break, step back from your essay, clear your head, and then return to see your text with fresh eyes.

Experiment 16.1: A Refreshing Pause

Length: *Take-home*
Timer: *None*
Discuss: *Optional*

This is probably the easiest assignment you'll ever have.

Step 1. If possible, tell yourself that your paper is actually due 24 hours (or any other substantial amount of time, as long as it is 8 hours or more) before the due date set for your class. Your instructor can also build this into an assignment by setting a due date and then giving the entire class a planned extension, or by requiring a final draft on a certain date and a post-final revision a day or two later.

Step 2. Finish your paper or project, then leave it alone and do nothing. Go have fun, sleep, work on other homework, or watch a movie. You don't have to consciously think about your draft, but because you've been working on it recently, a certain portion of your mental energy will probably continue to mull over the problems in your assignment. All you have to do is pay attention to any insights that crop up.

Step 3. Take notes on anything that occurs to you. You might get a sinking but productive feeling that your supposedly finished project needs a bit more attention.

Step 4. With a clear head, look back at your draft and read it over from beginning to end. Mark any places that seem confusing, and clarify. Add extra evidence, transitions, and emphasis for your strongest points. Congratulations – you've just completed a basic revision.

From a Word to a Conversation

Revision requires a re-seeing of your material, but truly complex writing requires more than one parting glance. Like an oil painting or a fantastic meal, any accomplished piece of writing is created with several – even hundreds – of steps that are usually not visible in the finished product. As with any art form, the artist or writer tries a bit of spice or a hint of blue on the canvas and then steps back to survey the effect.

This process might look from the outside like a calculated series of steps driven by genius. But any writer, chef, or other artist will tell you that their process of creation includes a series of mistakes and happy accidents – driven by skill and experience, of course, but also by chance and adaptation. Complex works are always conversations between creators and themselves: a move, a step back to adjust, a reassessment, another move, a look at the accumulated effect, another adjustment. The brilliance of a finished artistic work expresses – often – much more than could be created by any human at one moment. As you layer your inspiration and mistakes, as you assess and adjust, you can slowly create lovely structures the way a sea creature builds a fragile and perfect spiral shell.

To add to the draft work in a systematic way, most practiced artists and writers develop a conscious or subconscious routine to reassess and address their own weak points. In the research text *FieldWorking,* Sunstein and Chiseri-Strater (2007: 432) describe the process as "thickening" a draft by asking questions like "What's going on here?" and "Where's the story?" Both of those questions invite the writer to step back and think about patterns and connections. At this stage in your draft, you might consider looking at your draft and try to pose questions from an imagined reader who sincerely wants to understand your points. You might try to refocus by answering big questions in a few sentences that connect your topic to larger concerns, such as:

1. Do the different sides in this debate disagree over values or ideals? How do fundamental differences shape the way this research topic has been investigated or portrayed?
2. How do practical concerns – misunderstandings, financial ties, or conflicts of interest – shape this topic?
3. How might this research topic shed light on a larger social, political, or cultural issue?

Experiment 16.2: Re-seeing Your Revision Process

Length: *Short*

Timer: *4 minutes + 3 minutes = 7 minutes*

Discuss: *Yes*

Step 1. Write for four minutes about your strengths and areas for improvement in the revision process. If you are having trouble identifying these, you might first try to describe what you do after the first draft is done, and then reflect on how this works for you. Do you procrastinate and then not allow enough – or any – time for substantial revision? Do you fool yourself into thinking that because it's typed,

it must be a finished paper? Or do you sometimes reorder
your paragraphs and work on transitions?

Step 2. Look back at your freewrite, and locate one area or task
in revision that is most problematic. Write for three minutes
about why this task is problematic or challenging for you.
What about this step in the process is difficult? How would
you describe your feeling when looking at a finished paper,
and what do you think causes those reactions?

Clearly Unclear

One of the ironic side effects of good research is that it reveals to
the researcher the many unknowns and questions about a topic. A
beginning researcher will often have a sense of certainty about a
topic that seems simple, and a researcher with years in the topic
will see his or her questions grow exponentially as knowledge
expands.

The stereotype of academic writing – with the confident style of
words like *obviously* and *clearly* as confident-sounding transitions
– can set up a revision roadblock. When the writer starts out with
an overly confident or *opposing argument* tone, it can be difficult
to go back to the project to discover where to edit and where to
raise questions. You can end up tricking yourself into believing
there are no places for questioning, no areas to explore or expand.
Editing your paper in a way that sounds like you – the way you
talk – can loosen and clarify a revision. Talking to your readers in
a voice you recognize as a version of your own can also help to
restore your excitement for and connection to a project and give
you a last burst of energy to get the project finished.

Tone and Voice

Tone and *voice* are two terms adapted from the world of music
and sound. They point to the fact that speech and sound are the

parents of text, and text is only an approximation of conversation. Since these words are analogies taken from the world of sound, they are sometimes confusing and can further muddy the water when describing writing. Tone is something akin to mood, to the music of speech, the cues that communicate with raw sound how you feel. Voice is the expression – what you say and the way in which you say it.

If you think about your own speech during the course of a day, you'll quickly see that you have several, maybe even hundreds, of different tones and voices. Quite simply, you adjust your voice based on each situation. The tone and voice you use for discussing a friend's mother's funeral is not the same tone and voice you use when laughing with friends at a party. As social creatures, we learn early how to modulate our voices depending on social cues from other people and cultural cues from the environment and past experience. Writing is more of a leap because it is more difficult to address an audience if that audience is, at least for the time being, imaginary. Your research project does not have to – and probably should not – sound exactly the way you talk to a friend. Using that speaking voice as a guide can help you locate areas where you're trying so hard to sound authoritative that you may be losing control of your own writing.

Experiment 16.3: Letter to a Beekeeper, Part II

Length: *Short*
Timer: *None*
Discuss: *Optional*

Step 1. Look back at your responses to Experiment 15.5. How would you describe the voice you used in this letter? Some questions to think about: Is the vocabulary simple or complex? Do the sentences sound official or casual, direct or wordy?

Step 2. Look at the draft of your paper. How would you describe the voice you used? How much or little does it sound like your speaking voice?

Step 3. If there is an area of your project you are having particular difficult with, try to rewrite that section as simply as possible, using your speaking voice. This does not have to be language that will go in your final paper, but it can help you see where you are tripping over your own language or covering up interesting points with needlessly complicated words.

Experiment 16.4: Questions to Observations

Length: *Long or Take-home*
Timer: *None*
Discuss: *Optional*

Step 1. Look back at your draft and mark any places where you are not sure about something: a question of fact, a dilemma about a source, or a point of contention within your research subject area.

Step 2. Write down your specific question for each of these areas; include the source of the problem in each question. Be as specific as possible. Most students automatically blame themselves and their own supposed lack of intelligence for not understanding a subject, but the causes of questions are much more varied and interesting than that. Look back at your responses to the Experiments in Chapter 13 if you need help gathering ideas.

Step 3. Rewrite each question as a statement. For example, if your question revolves around which of the two sources to believe, you might rewrite it as a statement of fact about the disagreement, such as "This debate is polarized, and two scholars present very different positions about it. Each side has its merits, and each position cites different research to support its argument."

Step 4. You might consider grouping these statements into a paragraph near your conclusion, or adding some of them to the paragraphs that are most relevant throughout your paper. While you don't need to add all of these, you should definitely consider pointing out the most important areas in which gaps in your knowledge, gaps in sources, or other research challenges have shaped the final research product.

Seeking Uncertainty

Including your sources of confusion or questions might feel wrong, as if you are merely admitting a weak spot in your research, but this work is actually a form of analysis in which you group the sources available and share your views on similarities and differences among your sources.

Every act of seeking in the world is a balancing act between certainty and uncertainty. Scholars and researchers, writers and artists all know that a new project is only worth doing if it is a leap into the unknown. Wrestling with the unknown – studying it, analyzing it, seeing it in new ways – is the only way to generate knowledge. Although certainty and confidence of tone and organization are positive attributes, they must be balanced with the willingness to admit what is unclear, ambiguous, or confusing. Being open about your confusions and questions allows you to see them, to focus on them, and to seek the answers. Research is truly about loving the question.

The Gray Matter: Integrity Check

One of the most important elements of revision is an integrity check. Just as you review a heated conversation or mull over an important letter before you send it, looking back at any written document gives you a chance to make sure you can stand behind what you say. As you review your final paper, you might use this *integrity checklist* below to make sure you have accounted for the areas of ambiguity in your project.

Integrity Checklist

- Do you introduce an idea that is not yours? If so, add a citation.
- Have you cited all direct quotes?
- Have you fairly represented the sources' own views on the subject?
- Have you left out sources that contradicted your position? If so, add at least a paragraph acknowledging and commenting on the contradictions, along with a citation.
- Have you overstated your own confidence in your research? Why?
- Have you written a conclusion that sounds exactly like your introduction? If so, consider closing your paper by mulling over the questions that your research revealed.

Questions for Thought or Discussion

1. Is there a connection between over-confidence and falsification of research?
2. What character traits are associated with people who ask questions? Is questioning often rewarded or seen as problematic?
3. How might changing tone in research change your views about the research product and its result?

Conclusion to the "Backwards" Research Guide

Revision is much more than fixing errors and grammar in spelling. Instead, you can see revision as a constant process you have been using since you started your research. Each attempt to see your topic in a new way has been a kind of revision. Your written work should reflect the difficult and open-ended nature of this search, telling the complete story of your relationship with this topic. Almost no writer is skilled enough to tell a complex story perfectly when they sit down to type. The conversation you began with yourself in Chapter 1 required many attempts to review and become aware of your own thinking process, because writing is a *reflective* act that asks the writer to evaluate his or her own statements and then to use those statements to build bridges to other statements and to questions. If you don't look back constantly, you have little to work with in order to move forward toward a finished project.

You have produced a substantial body of work if you have completed all or most of the experiments and activities in this book. You have hopefully produced *a research project* that connects to your life in some central way. In addition, you have gained *a record of your interests* and a thick *collection of research ideas* that puts you ahead of the game in any future research-related assignment. Unlike most of the students in your classes, you have a beginning list of interests and topics that can be turned into research projects in relatively short order, regardless of the specific topic you are assigned. In addition, you have accumulated *experience and skill in the practices of reflective research writing,* so that your writing process has become more visible and less mysterious to you, which will make future writing projects less intimidating. Finally, you have probably *learned quite a few things about yourself and your own research and writing process,* which will help you to diagnose future research challenges and turn them into foundations for research opportunity.

I hope that the most substantial shift you have experienced in completing this guide is the one that's least measurable. If you have

come to see the search for knowledge as a chaotic, messy, sometimes enjoyable, and open-ended process, if you have come to see it
as an adventure that anyone can embark upon, then you have gained
a sense of yourself as a creator of knowledge and a participant in
a global conversation about the questions and solutions that face
our world. And that would be a very good thing indeed.

Appendix A. Experiments in this Book: Short

Many of these exercises can be adapted for longer in-class or take-home assignments work. The exercises marked with an asterisk are also listed in as either long in-class assignments or take-home assignments.

Experiment 1.1: Your Research Stories*
Experiment 1.2: Just Sit*
Experiment 2.1: Sit with a Word
Experiment 2.4: Five Objects (with take-home preparation)
Experiment 4.1: Questions and Questioners
Experiment 5.1: You Are Here*
Experiment 5.6: Real-World Research, Part II
Experiment 6.4: Reading Between the Lines and Beyond the Screen
Experiment 7.1: Geek, Nerd, Freak*
Experiment 7.3: Six Degrees*
Experiment 7.4: Double-Bubble Chart
Experiment 8.2: The Power of Not-Knowing
Experiment 8.3: Questions to Consider
Experiment 8.4: Question Launch Pads*
Experiment 9.1: Taking Notes*
Experiment 9.2: Fishing Net*

Experiment 9.3:   The Author in the Story*
Experiment 10.2:   Database Wandering*
Experiment 10.5:   Infor-mess-ion
Experiment 11.1:   Listen and Hear
Experiment 12.2:   Know Your Equipment
Experiment 13.1:   Choose Your Own Misadventure
Experiment 13.2:   The Adventure of Finding Your Material
Experiment 15.1:   The Five Senses
Experiment 15.2:   Characters in Your Story
Experiment 15.3:   Scene and Heard*
Experiment 15.4:   Refocusing on the Heart of the Story
Experiment 15.5:   Letter to a Beekeeper
Experiment 16.2:   Re-seeing Your Revision Process
Experiment 16.3:   Letter to a Beekeeper, Part II

Appendix B. Experiments in this Book: Long

Many of these exercises can be adapted for shorter in-class or take-home assignments work. The exercises marked with an asterisk are also listed as either short in-class assignments or take-home assignments.

Experiment 1.1: Your Research Stories*
Experiment 1.2: Just Sit*
Experiment 2.2: Hunter/Gatherer Profile*
Experiment 2.5: Room for Improvement*
Experiment 3.1: Activities and Questions*
Experiment 3.2: Catalogue the Unseen Skills*
Experiment 3.3: Choices, Choices, Choices*
Experiment 4.2: Questions without Answers*
Experiment 5.2: Take Three*
Experiment 5.4: The National Association of Yo-Yo Aficionados*
Experiment 5.5: Real-World Research*
Experiment 6.1: Reading the Newspaper with Scissors*
Experiment 6.2: Don't Know Much About History, Biology, the Economy
Experiment 6.5: Comparing Two Frames*
Experiment 7.2: Outward Bubbles*

Experiment 7.3:   Six Degrees*
Experiment 7.4:   Double-Bubble Chart*
Experiment 8.1:   I Don't Know
Experiment 8.2:   The Power of Not-Knowing*
Experiment 8.4:   Question Launch Pads*
Experiment 8.5:   Research Sampler*
Experiment 9.1:   Taking Notes*
Experiment 9.2:   Fishing Net*
Experiment 9.3:   The Author in the Story*
Experiment 10.1: On-line and Aimless*
Experiment 10.2: Database Wandering*
Experiment 10.3: Bunches of Blogs*
Experiment 11.2: Who Knows?*
Experiment 11.3: Twenty Questions*
Experiment 11.4: Practice Interview*
Experiment 12.3: More than a Feeling
Experiment 13.3: Research Flow Chart*
Experiment 14.1: Winnowing
Experiment 14.2: Interest Ranking*
Experiment 14.3: Distance from the Center*
Experiment 14.4: Plunging into the Unknown*
Experiment 15.3: Scene and Heard*
Experiment 16.4: Questions to Observations*

Appendix C. Experiments in this Book: Take-Home

Many of these exercises can be adapted for in-class work. The exercises marked with an asterisk are also listed in as either short or long in-class assignments.

Experiment 1.1:   Your Research Stories*
Experiment 1.2:   Just Sit*
Experiment 2.2:   Hunter/Gatherer Profile*
Experiment 2.3:   Interview Your Friends
Experiment 2.5:   Room for Improvement*
Experiment 3.1:   Activities and Questions*
Experiment 3.2:   Catalogue the Unseen Skills*
Experiment 3.3:   Choices, Choices, Choices*
Experiment 4.2:   Questions without Answers*
Experiment 4.3:   Two Hundred Questions
Experiment 5.1:   You Are Here*
Experiment 5.2:   Take Three*
Experiment 5.3:   Obsession Notebook
Experiment 5.4:   The National Association of Yo-Yo
                  Aficionados*
Experiment 5.5:   Real-World Research*
Experiment 6.1:   Reading the Newspaper with Scissors*
Experiment 6.3:   Research in Motion

Experiment 6.5:   Comparing Two Frames*
Experiment 7.1:   Geek, Nerd, Freak*
Experiment 7.2:   Outward Bubbles*
Experiment 7.3:   Six Degrees*
Experiment 7.4:   Double-Bubble Chart*
Experiment 8.2:   The Power of Not-Knowing*
Experiment 8.3:   Questions to Consider
Experiment 8.4:   Question Launch Pads*
Experiment 8.5:   Research Sampler*
Experiment 9.1:   Taking Notes*
Experiment 9.2:   Fishing Net*
Experiment 9.3:   The Author in the Story*
Experiment 10.1:   On-line and Aimless*
Experiment 10.2:   Database Wandering*
Experiment 10.3:   Bunches of Blogs*
Experiment 10.4:   Rubber to the Road
Experiment 11.2:   Who Knows?*
Experiment 11.3:   Twenty Questions*
Experiment 11.4:   Practice Interview*
Experiment 12.1:   Take Notes on the Rest of Your Life
Experiment 13.3:   Research Flow Chart*
Experiment 14.2:   Interest Ranking*
Experiment 14.3:   Distance from the Center*
Experiment 14.4:   Plunging into the Unknown*
Experiment 16.1:   A Refreshing Pause
Experiment 16.4:   Questions to Observations*

Appendix D. Recommended Reading

Narrative Nonfiction

Below are a few among many excellent works of research-based nonfiction with a creative, personal, or narrative twist. Reading some of these may show you how often interviews, outside sources, and first-hand experience translate into gripping writing!

Adiele, Faith (2005) *Meeting Faith: The Forest Journals of a Black Buddhist Nun*. New York: W. W. Norton & Co.

Almond, Steve (2004) *Candyfreak: A Journey Through the Chocolate Underbelly of America*. New York: Harcourt, Inc.

Christman, Jill (2002) *Darkroom: A Family Exposure*. Athens: University of Georgia Press.

Ehrenreich, Barbara (2008) *Nickel and Dimed: On (Not) Getting by in America*. New York: Holt.

Fadiman, Anne (1998) *The Spirit Catches You and You Fall Down*. New York: Farrar, Straus and Giroux.

Gourevitch, Philip (1999) *We Wish to Inform You That Tomorrow We Will Be Killed With Our Families: Stories from Rwanda*. New York: Picador.

Hemley, Robin (2007) *Invented Eden: The Elusive, Disputed History of the Tasaday*. Lincoln: Bison Books, University of Nebraska Press.

Hersey, John (1968) *Hiroshima*. New York: Bantam.

Kidder, Tracy (1990) *Among Schoolchildren*. New York: Harper Perennial.

Kidder, Tracy (2009) *Mountains Beyond Mountains: The Quest of Dr. Paul Farmer, a Man Who Would Cure the World*. New York: Random House.

Kingsolver, Barbara, Camille Kingsolver and Stephen L. Hopp (2008) *Animal, Vegetable, Miracle: A Year of Food Life*. New York: Harper Perennial.

Larkin, Emma (2006) *Finding George Orwell in Burma*. New York: Penguin.

Lowry, Beverly (2002) *Crossed Over: A Murder, A Memoir*. New York: Vintage.

Mackall, Joe (2006) *The Last Street Before Cleveland: An Accidental Pilgrimage*. Lincoln: University of Nebraska Press.

Mackall, Joe (2008) *Plain Secrets: An Outsider Among the Amish*. Boston: Beacon Press.

Martin, Lee (2003) *Turning Bones*. Lincoln: University of Nebraska Press.

Mendelsohn, David (2007) *The Lost: The Search for Six of Six Million*. New York: Harper Perennial.

Ray, Janisse (1999) *Ecology of a Cracker Childhood*. Minneapolis: Milkweed Editions.

Roorbach, Bill (2006) *Temple Stream: A Rural Odyssey*. New York: Dial Press.

Schwartz, Mimi (2008) *Good Neighbors, Bad Times, Echoes of My Father's German Village*. Lincoln: University of Nebraska Press.

X, Malcolm (1964) *The Autobiography of Malcolm X, as Told to Alex Haley*. New York: Ballantine Books.

Sullivan, Robert (1999) *The Meadowlands: Wilderness Adventures on the Edge of a City*. New York: Anchor.

Guides to Research, Writing, and Inspiration

Franklin, John (1994) *Writing for Story: Craft Secrets of Dramatic Nonfiction*. New York: Plume.

Gerard, Philip (2004) *Creative Nonfiction: Researching and Crafting Stories of Real Life*. Long Grove, Illinois: Waveland Press.

Goldberg, Natalie (2006) *Writing Down the Bones: Freeing the Writer Within*. Boston: Shambhala Books.

Lamott, Anne (1994) *Bird by Bird: Some Instructions on Writing and Life*. New York: Doubleday.

Loori, John Daido (2005) *The Zen of Creativity: Cultivating Your Artistic Life*. New York: Ballantine Books.

Macrorie, Ken (1988) *The I-Search Paper, Revised Edition of Search Writing*. Portsmouth, New Hampshire: Heinemann.

Marius, Richard (1998) *A Writer's Companion*. New York: McGraw-Hill.

Roorbach, Bill (2008) *Writing Life Stories*: *How to Make Memories into Memoirs, Ideas into Essays, and Life into Literature* (2nd edition). New York: Writers Digest Books.

Sunstein, Bonnie Stone and Chiseri-Strater, Elizabeth (2007) *FieldWorking: Reading and Writing Research* (3rd edition). New York: Bedford/St. Martin's.

Appendix E. Source Citations Using MLA Style

The style for citing sources in your research paper will vary depending on the class or the place where your work will be published. These styles evolve constantly as editors try to make them easier or more consistent. "MLA style" is merely the style used by the Modern Language Association, a professional group of writers and teachers who work in the humanities in the United States. Other styles are set by the American Psychological Association (APA) and other groups. The *MLA Handbook for Writers of Research Papers* (7th edition) is noteworthy because you no longer need to give web addresses for your sources, though you will notice that all source citations now include the format (print, web, etc.) of the source. (You might also notice that the works cited page in this book uses a slightly different style, one determined by the publisher.)

The important thing to note about citations is that they ask you for more information than is usually displayed directly on a page you find through a search engine. You need to do a little sleuthing through a web site to find these pieces of information:

1. Publisher – usually the group that puts out the page. If no publisher is listed, use *N.p.*
2. Author – which may be unlisted or may be an organization or individual.
3. Publication – which may be the same as the general web site or it may be the same as the publisher.

4. Article title – this may be the heading at the top of the page.
5. Date – the most reliable web site publication will include this or will include a date in the form of a "last updated on…" tag. You also need to provide the date on which you found the information on the web, which is called the *date of access*.
6. Page number – for online publications that don't provide page numbers, add *n. pag.* where the page number would go to indicate this.

These pieces of information are important – they help a reader figure out whether your information is reliable and whether or not your research can be trusted.

Book
Almond, Steve. *Candy Freak: A Journey Through the Chocolate Underbelly of America*. New York: Harcourt, Inc., 2004. Print.

Scholarly Publication (Journal)
Sommers, Nancy. "I Stand Here Writing." *College English* 55.4 (1993): 420-428. Print.

Online Periodical
Holland, Norman N. "Style, Identity, Free Association, and the Brain." *PSYART: An Online Journal for the Psychological Study of the Arts*, Article 060821 (2005): n. pag. Web. 17 Jan. 2008.

Online Database Scholarly Journal Article
Give the database name in italics.
Davis, Robert and Mark Shadle. "Building a Mystery": Alternative Research Writing and the Academic Art of Seeking." *College Composition and Communication* 53.1 (2000): 417-46. *JSTOR*. Web. 2 July 2009.

Online-only Publication
Brady, Richard. "Learning to Stop; Stopping to Learn: Embarking on the Contemplative Learning Path." *Mindfulness in Education Network*. Mindfulness in Education Network, 2005: n.pag. Web. 22 Nov 2008.

References

Almond, Steve (2003) *My Life in Heavy Metal*. New York: Grove Press.

Almond, Steve (2004) *Candyfreak: A Journey Through the Chocolate Underbelly of America*. New York: Harcourt, Inc.

Almond, Steve (2006) *The Evil B. B. Chow and Other Stories*. Chapel Hill, North Carolina: Algonquin Books.

Almond, Steve (2008) *(Not That You Asked): Rants, Exploits, and Obsessions*. New York: Random House.

Almond, Steve (2010) *Rock and Roll Will Save Your Life: A Book by and for the Fanatics Among Us*. New York: Random House.

Almond, Steve and Baggott, Julianna (2006) *Which Brings Me to You: A Novel in Confessions*. Chapel Hill, North Carolina: Algonquin Books.

Bayles, David and Orland, Ted (1993) *Art & Fear: Observations on the Perils (and Rewards) of Artmaking*. Eugene, Oregon: Image Continuum Press.

Brady, Richard (2005) Learning to stop; stopping to learn: Embarking on the contemplative learning path. *Mindfulness in Education Network*. Retrieved on 22 November 2008 from http://www.mindfuled.org/2004/11/articles.html.

Capra, Fritjof (2000) *The Tao of Physics* (4th edition). Boston: Shambhala Publications.

Christman, Jill (2002) *Darkroom: A Family Exposure*. Athens: University of Georgia Press.

Cook, Ian (2005) Positionality/situated knowledge. In David Atkinson, Peter Jackson, David Sibley and Neil Washbourne (eds.) *Cultural Geography: A Critical Dictionary of Key Concepts* 16–24. London: IB Tauris.

Davis, Robert and Shadle, Mark (2000) "Building a mystery": Alternative research writing and the academic art of seeking. *College Composition and Communication* 53(1): 417–446.

Dickinson, Emily (1988) "The Brain is wider than the Sky…" In Richard Ellmann and Robert O'Clair (ed.) *The Norton Anthology of Modern Poetry* 632 (2nd edition). New York: W.W. Norton & Co. Reprinted from *The Poems of Emily Dickinson* (ed. T. H. Johnson). Cambridge, Massachusetts: The Belknap Press of Harvard University Press.

Didion, Joan (1968) On keeping a notebook. *Slouching Toward Bethlehem* 131–141. New York: Farrar, Straus and Giroux.

Elbow, Peter (1973) *Writing Without Teachers*. New York: Oxford University Press.

Garrison Institute (2005) A survey of programs using contemplative techniques in K–12 in educational settings: a mapping report. *Contemplation and Education*. Garrison, New York: Garrison Institute. Retrieved on 14 February 2008 from http://www.garrisoninstitute.org/programs/Mapping_Report.pdf.

Goldberg, Natalie (2006) *Writing Down the Bones: Freeing the Writer Within*. Boston: Shambhala Books.

Goleman, Daniel, Kaufman, Paul and Ray, Michael (1992) *The Creative Spirit*. New York: Dutton.

Goulet, Jean-Guy and Miller, Bruce Granville (2007) Embodied knowledge: Steps toward a radical anthropology of cross-cultural encounters. In Jean-Guy Goulet and Bruce Granville Miller (eds.) *Extraordinary Anthropology: Transformations in the Field* 1–13. Lincoln: University of Nebraska Press.

Hamilton, Mary (1998) Histories & horoscopes: The ethnographer as fortune-teller. *Anthropology & Education Quarterly* 29(3): 347–356.

Hanh, Thich Nhat (1976) *The Miracle of Mindfulness* (trans. M. Ho). Boston: Beacon Press.

Hart, Tobin (2004) Opening the contemplative mind in the classroom. *Journal of Transformative Education* 2.1. Retrieved on 14 February 2008 from http://www.mindfuled.org/files/tobin.doc.

Hemley, Robin (1993) *The Last Studebaker*. Minneapolis: Graywolf Press.

Hemley, Robin (1998) *Nola: A Memoir of Faith, Art and Madness*. Minneapolis: Graywolf Press.

Hemley, Robin (2006) *Turning Life Into Fiction* (2nd edition). Minneapolis: Graywolf Press.

Hemley, Robin (2007) *Invented Eden: The Elusive, Disputed History of the Tasaday*. Lincoln: Bison Books, University of Nebraska Press.

Hemley, Robin (2009) *Do-Over: In Which a Forty-Eight Year Old Father of Three Returns to Kindergarten, Summer Camp, the Prom, and Other Embarrassments*. New York: Little, Brown and Company.

Holland, Norman N. (2006) Style, identity, free association, and the brain. *PSYART: An Online Journal for the Psychological Study of the Arts*, Article 060821. Retrieved on 17 January 2008 from http://www.clas.ufl.edu/ipsa/journal/2006_holland01.shtml.

Iacoboni, Marco (2008) *Mirroring People: The New Science of How We Connect with Others*. New York: Farrar, Straus & Giroux.

Johnson, Samuel (1846) *The Rambler* 150. In Samuel Johnson and Arthur Murphy (eds.) *The Works of Samuel Johnson, LL. D.: With an Essay on His Life and Genius*. London: A. V. Blake. Retrieved on 24 October 2008 from http://books.google.com/books?id=o5ELAAAAIAAJ.

Keller, Evelyn Fox (1983) *A Feeling for the Organism: The Life and Work of Barbara McClintock*. San Francisco: W.H. Freeman & Co.

Koren, Leonard (2003) *Wabi-Sabi: For Artists, Designers, Poets, and Philosophers*. North Clarendon, Vermont: Tuttle Publishing.

Lamott, Anne (1994) *Bird by Bird: Some Instructions on Writing and Life*. New York: Doubleday.

Loori, John Daido (2005) *The Zen of Creativity: Cultivating Your Artistic Life*. New York: Ballantine Books.

Mackall, Joe (2006) *The Last Street Before Cleveland: An Accidental Pilgrimage*. Lincoln: University of Nebraska Press.

Mackall, Joe (2008) *Plain Secrets: An Outsider Among the Amish*. Boston: Beacon Press.

Macrorie, Ken (1988) *The I-Search Paper, Revised Edition of Search Writing*. Portsmouth, New Hampshire: Heinemann.

Mysterious "neural noise" actually primes brain for peak performance (2006) *Science Daily*. Retrieved on 1 July 2008 from http://www.sciencedaily.com/releases/2006/11/061112094812.htm.

Naylor, Gloria (1989) *Mama Day*. New York: Vintage.

Nicholson, Christie (2007) Better brains: the revolution in brain science. *Scientific American* online podcast interview with S. Begley. Retrieved on 22 November 2008 from http://www.sciam.com/podcast/episode.cfm?id=465B1677-E7F2-99DF-36E1378B1640D492.

O'Reilly, Mary Rose (1998) *Radical Presence: Teaching as Contemplative Practice*. Portsmouth, New Hampshire: Boynton/Cook.

Palmer, Parker (1998) *The Courage to Teach: Exploring the Inner Landscape of a Teacher's Life*. San Francisco: Jossey-Bass.

Perry, Bruce D., Hogan, Lea and Marlin, Sarah J. (2000) Curiosity, pleasure and play: A neurodevelopmental perspective. *HAAEYC Advocate*. Retrieved on 24 October 2008 from http://www.childtrauma.org/ctamaterials/Curiosity.asp.

Rethman, Petra (2007) On presence. In Jean-Guy Goulet and Bruce Granville Miller (eds.) *Extraordinary Anthropology: Transformations in the Field* 36–52. Lincoln: University of Nebraska Press.

Richmond, Lewis (1999) *Work as a Spiritual Practice: A Practical Buddhist Approach to Inner Growth and Satisfaction on the Job*. New York: Broadway Books.

Rilke, Rainer Maria (2001) *Letters to a Young Poet* (trans. Stephen Mitchell). New York: Modern Library.

Roorbach, Bill (ed.) (2001) *Contemporary Creative Nonfiction: The Art of Truth*. New York: Oxford University Press.

Roorbach, Bill (2002a) *Big Bend: Stories*. Berkeley: Counterpoint.

Roorbach, Bill (2002b) *The Smallest Color*. Berkeley: Counterpoint.

Roorbach, Bill (2006) *Temple Stream: A Rural Odyssey*. New York: Dial Press.

Roorbach, Bill (1998) *Writing Life Stories: How to Make Memories into Memoirs, Ideas into Essays, and Life into Literature*. Cincinnati: Story Press.

Rose, Deborah Bird (2007) Recursive epistemologies and an ethics of attention. In Jean-Guy Goulet and Bruce Granville Miller (eds.) *Extraordinary Anthropology: Transformations in the Field* 88–102. Lincoln: University of Nebraska Press.

Sommers, Nancy (1993) I stand here writing. *College English* 55(4): 420–428.

Spiro, Alison M. (2005) *Najar* or *Bhut*—evil eye or ghost affliction: Gujarati views about illness causation. *Anthropology & Medicine* 12(1): 61–73.

Sunstein, Bonnie Stone and Chiseri-Strater, Elizabeth (2007) *FieldWorking: Reading and Writing Research* (3rd edition). New York: Bedford/St. Martin's.

Suzuki, Shunryu (1973) *Zen Mind, Beginner's Mind*. Boston: Weatherhill.

Tremmel, Robert (1999) *Zen and the Practice of Teaching English*. Portsmouth, New Hampshire: Heinemann.

Vogt, Benjamin (2004) *Indelible Marks*. Columbus, Ohio: Pudding House Publications.

Vogt, Benjamin (2010) *Without Such Absence.* Georgetown, Kentucky: Finishing Line Press.

Wallace, B. Alan (2007) *Contemplative Science: Where Buddhism and Neuroscience Converge.* Columbia Series in Science and Religion. New York: Columbia University Press.

World Health Organization (2009) The world's forgotten children (poster). *Inheriting the World: The Atlas of Children's Health and the Environment.* Retrieved on 2 November 2009 from http://www.who.int/ceh/publications/en/poster1.pdf.

Subject Index

abstraction 6, 87, 296–297

analysis 13, 28, 70, 112, 120, 137, 145, 181, 187, 191, 219, 229, 254, 256, 276, 285, 287, 291, 293, 301, 314

anecdotes (in research) 151, 167, 189, 204, 225

anthropology 13, 22, 29, 72, 107, 135, 239–241, 248, 250–251

anxiety 39–42, 85, 87–88, 101, 160–161, 175

   (in choosing a topic) 39–42, 59, 87, 160

   (in interviewing) 220, 223, 226, 232, 236

   (in research process) 8–9, 59, 87–88, 187, 191, 248

   (in writing) 248

associative (reading) 203

   (research) 5, 11, 195, 209

   (thought) 5, 43, 47, 144, 187

attribution 189–190, 212

audience 33, 136, 170, 175, 189, 275, 303, 312

authority 66, 130

awareness xvi, 7, 29, 137, 150, 189–190, 246; *see also* self-awareness

   (as skill or tool) 7, 11, 35–37, 57, 83

   (benefits of) 44

     of bias 30, 144: *see also* bias

   (of possible topics or subjects) 2–3, 5, 83, 122

   (of self or thoughts) 3–5, 7, 33, 50, 107–108, 144, 162, 259

   (public) 89, 116, 119

beginner's mind 11, 160, 163–164, 172–174, 176

bias 5, 13, 28–30, 118, 136, 151, 171, 189, 253, 278

bibliography: *see* citations

blog 188, 204–206, 283

brain 3, 4, 27, 31–35, 39–43, 47–50, 55, 59, 104, 109, 111–112, 130, 144–145, 166, 187, 203, 246, 248, 250, 262

   (and neuroscience) 32–34, 230

   (as research tool) 31–35, 41, 48, 161

   (processing speeds of) 32, 42

brainstorm 2, 3, 5, 7, 9, 11, 13–17,
    41–42, 44, 47, 50, 79, 85, 92, 104,
    115, 122, 135, 139, 146–149, 153,
    160–161, 168, 172, 176, 181–183,
    191, 227–228, 271, 283, 296, 303
    (in Experiments) 42, 45–46, 56,
        77, 93, 110, 117, 149, 165,
        172, 182, 183, 208, 222, 224,
        231, 298
    (research ideas and questions) 9,
        16, 44, 85, 92, 104, 117, 122,
        135, 149, 168, 172, 181–183,
        227–227, 271, 283
broadening 149
bubble chart 146–152, 160, 174,
    187, 283, 287–288
career 2, 9, 23, 101, 166, 253, 274,
    305
categories (of research questions)
    57, 60, 72–73, 92–93, 165, 172,
    183, 228, 231, 283
citation (of sources) 30, 45, 185,
    201, 210, 212, 291, 315, 329–330
closed questions: see questions
clustering: see bubble chart
concentration 35, 44, 49, 74
conclusion (in writing) 41, 168, 268,
    273, 276, 288, 290, 296, 302, 304,
    314–315
conflict of interest 171
confusion (in research) 83, 87–88,
    129, 170, 173, 182, 186, 236, 249,
    267, 270, 276, 314
containers (for writing) 190, 279,
    281–282
contemplative xvi, 3–6, 10, 11, 13,
    15, 16–17, 35, 109, 111, 145, 150
controversial 40, 59, 89, 189, 240,
    292
controversy 40, 116, 118–119, 250

conversations (in research) xvi,
    11–12, 25, 33, 53–54, 79, 103,
    129, 144, 179–180, 186, 189, 198,
    205, 217, 219–233, 241, 247, 284,
    300, 309, 312, 314, 316–317
creative xv–xvi, 2, 5, 23, 63, 112,
    125, 166, 262, 325
    (research as) 1, 23, 69, 104,
        146, 175, 193, 209, 253, 267
critical listening: see listening
curiosity xvi, 5–10, 15–17, 24–26,
    50, 91, 104, 127, 130, 142,
    196–197, 202, 229, 246, 285–286
    (as a skill) 6, 24, 130, 133, 135
    (benefits of) 25, 174, 184
    (measurement of) 16–17
    (observation of) 6, 30
database 44, 115, 174, 194, 197–203,
    205, 210, 225, 251, 273, 289
deadlines 14, 40, 112, 220, 226, 270,
    274, 281
deductive reasoning 252
deep interview: see interview
depth 16–17, 168, 172, 224
direct quotes 65, 283, 290, 292, 315;
    see also quotes
distance (from subject) 13, 28,
    29, 47, 55, 119, 122, 135, 189,
    249, 251, 287, 301: see also
    perspective
double-column notebook (use of)
    17, 184–188, 247, 277
doubt 41, 91, 121, 142, 156–157,
    229, 235, 276
dualistic (thinking) 119, 169
efficient 2, 75–76, 99–100, 232, 306
emotion 25, 48, 230, 233, 248, 276
    (and research) 9, 12, 39, 171,
        249–250, 253
    (in writing) 276

emotional 16, 46, 74, 88, 130, 145, 219, 264, 268

empathy 46, 230

empiricism 145, 163

empirical 4, 51, 59, 145

enjoy 2, 70, 75, 90, 92, 100, 103, 152, 228, 254, 275–276
    (research) 1, 23, 126, 130, 158, 161, 218, 317

epistemology 249, 256

ethics 30, 87, 168–171

ethical 12, 30–31, 78–82, 107, 169–170, 296; *see also* unethical

ethical engagement 16–17

evidence 11, 16, 119–120, 151, 169, 175, 252, 289, 292, 296, 304–305, 309

excavation (as research metaphor) 36, 55–57, 59, 142

excitement (in research) 2, 59, 64, 66, 101, 142, 164, 233, 250, 258, 311

experience (as research) xvi, 2, 3, 5, 10, 13, 24, 26, 29–32, 49, 53–54, 69–72, 76–80, 83, 88, 90, 107, 130, 151–153, 162–163, 175, 180, 185, 224, 235, 251–258, 296, 299, 301

expertise 6, 10, 69, 130, 151, 155–158, 164, 167, 174, 267, 274, 289

failure (feelings of) 9, 86, 168, 248, 270, 273, 308

framing (as selective presentation of information) 136–37

freaks 141–143, 155; *see also* obsessions

freewrite 5, 15, 17, 31, 160, 181–183, 191, 247, 288
    (in Experiments) 51, 58, 86, 89, 122, 129, 131–132, 134–135, 137–138, 143, 151–153, 162–163, 170, 174, 182, 285, 302, 311

hook (for reader interest) 296–297, 302–303

I-Search Paper xvi, 3, 111, 270, 296

identity 32, 50, 121, 162, 190, 234

images (in writing) 246, 297–298, 305

imagination (in research) 116, 193, 296, 299

inductive reasoning 252

interest inventory 10, 51–54, 74, 160

interests (as research ideas) xvi, 2, 6, 9–11, 22, 24, 29–30, 37, 39, 48, 50–55, 59–60, 64, 71–75, 83, 92–104, 111, 114–117, 135–136, 144, 146–147, 160, 168, 182, 184, 210, 224, 229, 245–247, 261, 266, 286–289, 316

interest (for the reader) 121, 272, 275, 291, 303–304

intersubjectivity 29, 257

interview xvi, 11–12, 51, 107, 126, 150, 157, 167–168, 205, 219–237, 239–241, 252, 263, 326

introduction (in writing) 41, 295–296, 302–304, 315

intuition 93, 144–145, 215, 236

investment (in research) 3, 4, 8, 12, 18, 174, 253

journal (writing) 47–48, 146, 149–152, 184, 247

journalism xv, 2, 212, 223

journalist xv–xvi, 2, 136, 166, 220, 236, 239

judgment 118, 163, 229–230
    (and bias) 108, 250, 264
    (suspending) 8, 108–110, 115, 195

juxtapose 181, 193, 248

labels (for research organization) 187–188, 282–273

listening 49, 216, 221–225, 229–230, 233, 236–237, 301; *see also* self-listening

location 29, 57, 134, 139, 195–196, 208, 255

meditation 3, 109, 284

memory 49, 69, 87, 90, 94, 109, 125, 144, 151, 179

middle (position in polarized debate) 240, 272–273; *see also* third position

mindfulness 33, 60, 166, 295

moral argument 211, 268

moral 12, 17, 119, 169, 171, 264, 278

muscle (as research metaphor) 6, 8, 35, 41, 57, 83, 144, 147, 161, 288

narrative 16, 234–235, 275, 299, 325

newspaper 127–129, 131, 135–139, 148, 188, 190, 201, 204, 212, 217, 220, 223, 225, 228

noodling 11, 193, 195, 198, 203, 209

noticing (as research skill) 25, 34–35, 47–48, 70, 83, 112, 135

not-knowing 130, 159, 161–162, 164–166

notebook: *see* research notebook *and* obsession notebook

note-taking 11, 191, 290: *see also* taking notes

objectivity 12–13, 27–30, 115, 150, 253, 255–257

observation: *see* self-observation

observer effect 255

obsession 10–11, 22, 24, 48, 50, 114, 117–118, 141–144, 146–147, 149–151, 155, 158, 160, 245

obsession notebook 112–113, 143, 160

open-ended research 39–40, 49, 171, 224

open questions: *see* questions

openhearted 229–230

organizations 92 116–117, 120

outline 43, 66–67, 183, 187, 282, 289, 296

passion 2, 22, 24, 33, 49, 64, 114–115, 117, 127, 142–145, 217, 253, 272

patterns (in writing and research) 24, 29–30, 33, 43, 48, 56, 59, 92, 112, 163, 250–252, 256, 283, 296, 310

perspective (as detachment or distance) 5–6, 13, 28–30, 48, 56, 86, 147, 150, 164, 168–169, 173–175, 180, 189, 308; *see also* distance (as point of view) 1, 3, 92, 137–138, 190, 204–205, 212, 225, 229–230, 233, 237, 256, 268, 286, 305

plagiarism 12, 17–18, 80–82, 210–211, 270

polarized (debates or arguments) 79, 272, 313

procrastination 40, 58, 274, 310

process-driven 83, 196

process approach (to research) 3–5, 17

quantum physics 13, 150, 255–257

questioning 4, 139, 169, 191, 311 (as a muscle or skill) 50, 83, 97, 166 (as negative in various cultures) 83, 87, 315 (as part of research) 44, 50

questions (in research) xvi, 6, 9–13, 16–17, 25, 27–28, 39–40, 42–44, questions (in research) cont'd

48–52, 58–60, 69–83, 85–104,
109–122, 128–129, 132–139, 141,
143, 146–153, 160–176, 182–187,
205, 207–208, 216, 221, 223,
225–234, 237, 246, 248, 250, 253,
256–258, 265–266, 268, 271–278,
281, 285–290, 292, 301–302, 305,
310–316
    closed 167–168, 172, 228, 231
    net of 183
    open 120, 167–168, 229, 231
quotes (used in writing) 1, 26, 67,
139, 157, 180–181, 185, 188,
190,197, 204, 209, 223, 229,
232–237, 268, 270, 276, 283–284,
289, 292, 295; *see also* direct
quotes
reader 29, 30, 111, 117, 120–121,
128, 138, 141, 156–158, 171, 173,
175, 188–190, 204–205, 209,
211–212, 272, 275–279, 284–296,
298–299, 301–304, 306, 310–311,
330; *see also* audience
recursive 27, 176, 180
reflection xv–xvi, 2, 5, 6, 8, 14, 17,
27, 49, 57, 65, 76, 204
    (as a skill) 74, 139, 153, 160,
    176, 306
    (in Experiments) 26, 45, 77, 80,
    137, 143, 151, 182
    (in research process) 72, 82–83,
    104, 153, 184, 191
    (in writing) 210, 276, 295
reflective 33, 35, 139, 223, 316
relationship (to topic or subject) 4,
11, 132, 135, 151, 251, 254, 258,
264, 316
relationships (and knowledge
creation) 46, 64–65, 87, 107, 114,
148, 170, 227, 235

relax 7–8, 10–11, 27, 36, 38, 70–71,
73, 75, 82–83, 104, 122, 134, 139,
153, 160, 176, 191, 197, 220, 232,
249, 258
release form 227
reliable (source) 115, 118, 197, 199,
204, 206, 250, 330
reliability 150, 189, 199
research agenda 13, 30, 31, 60, 83
research notebook xvi, 14–17, 31,
36, 115, 180, 187, 195–196, 247,
249, 277, 283
research topic 17, 40–42, 48, 55, 59,
71–72, 82, 104, 118–119, 121–122,
130, 132, 153, 158, 169–170, 173,
176, 181–182, 186, 189, 195, 206,
228, 248, 272, 300, 303–304, 310
revision 4, 12, 14, 45, 236, 306–311,
314–316
roadblock 11, 48, 259, 268–270,
273, 278, 311
scene (in descriptive writing)
134–136, 187, 275, 279, 299–300,
306
search engine 159, 173, 194–197,
199, 202–209, 228, 289, 329
search terms 194, 196–198, 202–203,
209, 273
self-awareness 3–4, 11, 44, 57,
107–108; *see also* awareness
self-observation 6–7, 10
self-reflection: *see* reflection
sensory (detail or information) 49,
69, 132–134, 145, 296–297
situated 29, 181
six degrees of separation 148–149
skepticism 91–92, 189
snowball sampling 227
source (of information) 11, 15,
29–30, 44–45, 63, 66–67, 89,

source (of information) cont'd

115, 117–118, 126, 131, 137–139,
173–175, 183–191, 194, 198–199,
203–207, 209–212, 250, 268, 270,
272–274, 276–278, 281–293, 295,
297, 301–302, 313–315, 325
   (in interviews) 220, 223,
   225–225, 234–236, 240
subjective 29, 157, 204, 258
stack (as research organization) 44,
187–188, 195, 282–284, 293
story (of research) 11, 65, 225,
234–235, 239–240, 269–273,
287–295, 298, 302, 308
   (as anecdotes in research and
   writing) 186, 199, 212, 217,
   219–220, 227–228, 246,
   256–259
tagging 283
taking notes 43–44, 61, 122, 178,
180

third position 117
thought process 4, 7, 24, 33, 40, 177,
215, 281
tone 297, 303–304, 306–307
topic: see research topic
transcript 221, 226, 227, 229–230
transitions 137, 184, 301, 303
unreliable 111, 194, 199
vision 4, 240, 270, 277
visual 132, 141–142, 146, 180,
183–184, 245, 271, 276, 278, 285,
289
voice 48, 139–140, 161, 226–227,
303–305
wabi-sabi 155–156
wiki 155, 169, 193–194
writing process xv–xvi, 12, 29, 40,
64, 169, 300, 308

Author Index

Almond, Steve 141–142, 145–146, 149–150, 155–158, 325, 330
Brady, Richard 164, 330, 331
Capra, Fritjof 256, 331
Chiseri-Strater, Elizabeth 29, 39, 144, 167, 184, 222, 228–229, 310, 327, 334
Christman, Jill 246, 261–266, 325, 331
Cook, Ian 28, 331
Dickinson, Emily 33, 332
Davis, Robert 276, 330, 332
Didion, Joan 179–180, 332
Einstein, Albert 133, 255
Elbow, Peter 3, 31, 307, 332
Goleman, Daniel 7, 166, 193, 267, 332
Goulet, Jean-Guy 251, 332, 334
Hamilton, Mary 235, 332
Hart, Tobin 4, 6, 17, 29, 145, 332
Hemley, Robin 223, 239–241, 325, 332–333
Holland, Norman 32, 330, 333
Iacoboni, Marco 230, 333
Lamott, Anne 49–50, 327, 333
Loori, John Daido 281, 284–285, 327

Mackall, Joe 207, 215–218, 326, 333
Macrorie, Ken xvi, 3, 111, 270, 275, 296, 327, 333
McClintock, Barbara 251–253, 333
Mikkelson, Barbara 189
Mikkelson, David 189
Miller, Bruce Granville 251, 332, 334
Naylor, Gloria 219, 221, 333
O'Reilly, Mary Rose 222, 229, 333
Palmer, Parker 13, 28, 86, 334
Plato 4
Pouget, Alex 32
Rethman, Petra 248–249, 251, 334
Rilke, Rainer Maria 85–86, 334
Roorbach, Bill 69, 112, 125–126, 326, 327, 334
Rose, Deborah Bird 107–108, 334
Shadle, Mark 276, 330, 332
Sunstein, Bonnie 29, 39, 144, 167, 184, 222, 228–229, 310, 327, 334
Suzuki, Shunryu 164, 174, 334
Tremmel, Robert 164, 334
Vogt, Benjamin 40, 63–67, 334
Wallace, Alan 150, 256–257, 335